SOCIAL INCLUSION AND SOCIAL PROTECTION IN THE EU: INTERACTIONS BETWEEN LAW AND POLICY

SOCIAL INCLUSION AND SOCIAL PROTECTION IN THE EU: INTERACTIONS BETWEEN LAW AND POLICY

Bea Cantillon
Herwig Verschueren
Paula Ploscar
(eds.)

intersentia
Cambridge – Antwerp – Portland

Intersentia Publishing Ltd.
Trinity House | Cambridge Business Park | Cowley Road
Cambridge | CB4 0WZ | United Kingdom
Tel.: +44 1223 393 753 | Email: mail@intersentia.co.uk

Distribution for the UK:
Hart Publishing Ltd.
16C Worcester Place
Oxford OX1 2JW
UK
Tel.: +44 1865 517 530
Email: mail@hartpub.co.uk

Distribution for the USA and Canada:
International Specialized Book Services
920 NE 58th Ave. Suite 300
Portland, OR 97213
USA
Tel.: +1 800 944 6190 (toll free)
Email: info@isbs.com

Distribution for Austria:
Neuer Wissenschaftlicher Verlag
Argentinierstraße 42/6
1040 Wien
Austria
Tel.: +43 1 535 61 03 24
Email: office@nwv.at

Distribution for other countries:
Intersentia Publishing nv
Groenstraat 31
2640 Mortsel
Belgium
Tel.: +32 3 680 15 50
Email: mail@intersentia.be

Social Inclusion and Social Protection in the EU: Interactions between Law and Policy
Bea Cantillon, Herwig Verschueren and Paula Ploscar (eds.)

Cover image: The Grapes (detail), Juan Gris (1887-1927)

GPRC
Guaranteed
Peer Reviewed
Content

ISBN 978-1-78068-056-9
NUR 828

British Library Cataloguing in Publication Data. A catalogue record for this book is available from the British Library.

ACKNOWLEDGEMENTS

The chapters of this volume result from an expert seminar held at the University of Antwerp on 10–11 February 2011. The seminar was organized within the framework of a research project sponsored by the Research Foundation Flanders and was co-sponsored by the Faculty of Law of the University of Antwerp. First of all we are very grateful to the authors of the various chapters for their willingness to adapt their papers in accordance with the discussions and comments during the seminar, and also for their openness to our editorial suggestions.

We would also like to thank the other participants at the seminar for their invaluable contributions to the debate. We would like to acknowledge Malcolm Ross' (Sussex Law School) contribution to the seminar, and we appreciate the fruitful thoughts of the discussants (in alphabetical order): Rita Baeten (European Social Observatory), Gareth Davies (VU University of Amsterdam, Faculty of Law), Jo De Cock (Belgian National Institute for Health and Disability Insurance), Eric Marlier (CEPS/INSTEAD, Luxemburg), Charlotte O'Brien (York Law School), Anne-Pieter van der Mei (Maastricht University, Faculty of Law), Koen Vleminckx (Belgian Federal Ministry of Social Security) and Fritz von Nordheim (European Commission).

In addition, we are much indebted to those who in their quality of chairs of the various sessions facilitated the meaningful discussions: Willy Palm (European Observatory on Health Systems and Policies), Philippe Pochet (European Trade Union Institute) and Anne-Marie Van den Bossche (University of Antwerp, Faculty of Law). Also, we are appreciative of the participation of Dagmar Schiek (University of Leeds, School of Law) and Jérôme Vignon (European Commission) particularly for their concluding remarks.

Additional thanks go to the editors of the *Law and Cosmopolitan Values Series* and its anonymous reviewers. Finally we are very grateful to all those involved in the editing and publication of the book, in particular the publisher *Intersentia* and Tom Scheirs for their support and timely publication.

Antwerp, November 2011

Bea Cantillon, Herwig Verschueren and Paula Ploscar

CONTENTS

LIST OF ABBREVIATIONS

AG	Advocate General
Art.	Article
BEPGs	Broad Economic Policy Guidelines
CEBS	Committee of European Bank Supervision
CEE	Central Eastern European
CEIOPS	Committee of European Insurance and Occupational Pensions Supervisors
CESifo	Munich Society for the Promotion of Economic Research
CESR	Committee of European Security Regulators
Cfdt	Confédération française démocratique du travail
Cgt	Confédération générale du travail
CML Rev	Common Market Law Review
CSB	Herman Deleeck Centre for Social Policy
DG	Directorate General
DG SANCO	Directorate General for Health and Consumers
EAPN	European Anti-Poverty Network
EC	European Community
ECB	European Central Bank
ECHP	European Community Household Panel
ECJ	European Court of Justice
ECOFIN	Council of Ministers of Economic and Financial Policy
ECR	European Court Reports
ECSA	European Community Studies Association
EEA	European Economic Area
EEE	Exempt contributions, exempt investment income and capital gains, exempt benefits
EEEPB	European Economic and Employment Policy Brief
EES	European Employment Strategy
EET	Exempt contributions, exempt investment income and capital gains, tax benefits
EGTC	European Grouping for Territorial Cooperation

EHPF	EU Health Policy Forum
EIOPA	European Insurance and Occupational Pensions Authority
EJML	European Journal of Migration and Law
EJSS	European Journal of Social Security
EL Journ	European Law Journal
EL Rev	European Law Review
EMCO	Employment Committee
EMPLOY	Directorate General for Employment, Social Affairs and Inclusion
EMU	Economic and Monetary Union
EOT	Economics of Transition
EPC	Economic Policy Committee
EPSCO	Employment, Social Policy, Health and Consumer Affairs
ESAs	European Supervision Authorities
ESF	European Social Fund
ESPAnet	European Network for Social Policy Analysis
ESRB	European Systemic Risk Board
ESRC	Economic and Social Research Council
ETT	Exempt contributions, tax investment income and capital gains, tax benefits
ETUI	European Trade Union Institute
EU	European Union
EU-SILC	EU Statistics on Income and Living Conditions
EURACTIV	EU Information Website
EUROGOV	European Governance
EUROMOD	Multi-country Europe-wide tax-benefit model
Eurostat	Statistical Office of the European Union
FAQ	Frequently Asked Questions
FPS	Federal Public Service
GASPP	Globalism and Social Policy Programme
GDP	Gross Domestic Product
HiAP	Health in All Policies
HiT	Health Care Systems in Transition
HTA	Health Technology Assessment
Ibid.	Ibidem
IGC	Inter-Governmental Conference
IHS	Institute for Advanced Studies

IMC	Inter-Ministerial Conference
IMF	International Monetary Fund
INAMI/RIZIV	National Institute for Health and Disability Insurance
INTERREG	Interregional cooperation
IORP	Institutions for Occupational Retirement Provision
ISD	Investment Services Directive
ISG	Sub-Group on Indicators
JCMS	Journal of Common Market Studies
JEPP	Journal of European Public Policy
JESP	Journal of European Social Policy
MARKT	(DG) Internal Market and Services
MIFID	Markets in Financial Instruments Directive
MIPI	Minimum Income Protection Indicators
ML Rev	Modern Law Review
MPE	Monetary Policy and the Economy
n./N.	(Foot)note
NBER	National Bureau of Economic Research
NGO	Non-Governmental Organization
NHS	National Health Service
NIER	National Institute Economic Review
NSRs	National Strategic Reports
NZa	Dutch Healthcare Authority
OECD	Organization for Economic Cooperation and Development
OJ	Official Journal
OMC	Open Method of Coordination
OPOCE	Office for Official Publications of the European Communities
OREP	Oxford Review of Economic Policy
OSE	European Social Observatory
PAYGO	Pay-as-you-go
PPMI	Public Policy and Management Institute
PROGRESS	Community Programme for Employment and Social Solidarity
QMV	Qualified Majority Voting
RBSS	Revue belge de sécurité sociale
RPS	Rivista delle politiche sociali
SEA	Single European Act

SGEI	Services of General Economic Interest
SGP	Stability and Growth Pact
SNAP	Supplemental Nutrition Assistance Program
SPC	Social Protection Committee
SPSI	Social Protection and Social Inclusion
TANF	Temporary Aid for Needy Families
TEE	Tax contributions, exempt investment income and capital gains, exempt benefits
TERL	Transfer: European Review of Labour and Research
TEU	Treaty on European Union
TFEU	Treaty on the Functioning of the European Union
TILEC	Tilburg Centre of Law and Economics
TTE	Tax contributions, tax investment income and capital gains, exempt benefits
TTT	Tax contributions, tax investment income and capital gains, tax benefits
UCITS	Undertakings for Collective Investment in Transferable Securities
UNDESA	United Nations Department for Economic and Social Affairs
WEP	West European Politics
WHO	World Health Organisation
WRAMSOC	Welfare Reform and Management of Societal Change

LIST OF AUTHORS

Bea Cantillon is Professor of Social Policy and Director of the Herman Deleeck Centre for Social Policy at the University of Antwerp.

Mark Dawson is Professor of European Law and Governance at the Hertie School of Governance, Berlin.

Bruno de Witte is Professor of European Union Law at Maastricht University, and part-time Professor at the Robert Schuman Centre of the European University Institute (EUI) in Florence.

Maurizio Ferrera is Professor of Political Science at the University of Milan.

David Natali is Research Director at the European Social Observatory (OSE) and Associate Professor at the University of Bologna/Forli, Italy.

Paula Ploscar is PhD candidate at the University of Antwerp.

Wolf Sauter is Professor of Health Care Regulation at Tilburg University and competition expert at the Dutch Healthcare Authority (NZa).

Yves Stevens is Professor of Social Security and Pension Law at the University of Leuven, president of the occupational pension commission at the Financial Services and Markets Authority and member of the OPSG at the European Insurance and Occupational Pensions Authority.

Bart Vanhercke is Co-Director at the Brussels-based European Social Observatory and associate academic staff at the Centre for Sociological Research (CESO), the University of Leuven.

Natascha Van Mechelen is Post-Doctoral Researcher at the Herman Deleeck Centre for Social Policy, University of Antwerp.

Herwig Verschueren is Professor of International and European Social Law at the University of Antwerp and visiting professor at the University of Brussels.

Lena Wegener was junior researcher at the European Social Observatory and is now enrolled in the International Relations master programme at Freie Universität Berlin, Humboldt-Universität zu Berlin and University of Potsdam.

SOCIAL PROTECTION AND SOCIAL INCLUSION IN THE EU: ANY INTERACTIONS BETWEEN LAW AND POLICY?

Bea Cantillon, Herwig Verschueren and Paula Ploscar

1. SOCIAL INCLUSION AND SOCIAL PROTECTION: HIGH ON THE AGENDA OF EU LAWYERS AND POLICYMAKERS

The Treaty of Lisbon brought issues of social inclusion and social protection to the fore of political and academic discussions. First, it now regards the fight against social exclusion, the promotion of social justice and protection, as well as social cohesion as being part of the aims of the Union (Article 3 TEU). Secondly, it also requires that both at the level of design and implementation of EU policies and activities, 'requirements linked to (…) the guarantee of adequate social protection, the fight against social exclusion' shall be considered (Article 9 TFEU). In addition, the EU Charter of Fundamental Rights also contains a title on 'Solidarity' that encompasses references to rights and principles of social inclusion and social protection.

Yet, considerations of social protection are surely not completely novel to the European legal vocabulary. Social protection of migrant workers has been an issue from the early days of market integration, and the coordination mechanisms of social security systems of the Member States put in place (originally) to that end is over 50 years old. Also, the Social Protocol adopted at Maastricht acclaimed the common market to be not an aim in itself, but to lend itself to the promotion of social protection. This was consolidated in the Treaty of Amsterdam in Article 136 TEC which spoke of 'proper social protection' and the combat of social exclusion as social policy measures of both the, then Community, and the Member States. Nevertheless, these objectives were not translated into EU powers to legally intervene in matters of national social policy. Member States maintained full competences regarding their social protection systems, whereas the competences of the EU were to be limited to the economic sphere. Nonetheless, economic integration appeared to have an indirect impact on Member States' social protection systems, in particular via the rules on the free movement of services as well as the competition rules. Scholars therefore warned against the weaknesses of this formula of division of competences. Perhaps the most famous alarm signals in this regard were Scharpf's arguments of asymmetrical treatment of social and economic spheres in the EU,[1] and Liebfried and Pierson's emphasis on the fragmented structure of European social policy.[2]

Partially in response to this criticism, the EU political discourse has, since 2000, increasingly taken up issues of social inclusion and protection. The Lisbon Council held that year incorporated social inclusion as intrinsic to the overall strategy of the Union becoming 'the most competitive and dynamic knowledge-based economy in the world, capable of sustainable economic growth, with more and better jobs and greater social cohesion'. The Open Method of Coordination (OMC) for social inclusion launched then was extended to pensions and retirement systems in 2001, and three years later to the health and long-term care sector. In 2005 the three strands: pensions, health and long-term care, and social inclusion were converged into the Social Protection and Social Inclusion (SPSI) OMC.

Defining the OMC is a taunting task, yet a few things can be said about its working: It is a method of governance which functions by setting common objectives at Union level implemented through national action plans, which are then evaluated at EU level. The OMC is designed to complement the legislative and financial instruments of social policy, and lead to some degree of 'cross-fertilization' both among Member States on the one hand, and EU and national levels of governance, on the other. Therefore, the prevailing approach to social policymaking in Europe is one of 'soft coordination': common goals and indicators[3] are put forward for each Member State to strive for in national and regional policies. Yet, these goals are not binding – the model rests merely on a shared belief in the inspirational effect of 'good practices' and 'peer pressure'.

A quick glance at the latest policy major documents leaves a number of questions unanswered about the dialogue between the legal and policy dimensions of the Union in addressing issues of social inclusion and protection, the relevance of

---

1 F.W. Scharpf, *Governing in Europe: Effective and Democratic?*, Oxford University Press, Oxford 1999 and more recently F.W. Scharpf, 'The Asymmetry of European Integration, or Why the EU Cannot Be a "Social Market Economy"' (2010) 8 *Socio-Economic Review*.

2 S. Leibfried and P. Pierson, *European Social Policy: Between Fragmentation and Integration*, Brookings Institution, Washington, D.C. 1995.

3 E. Marlier, A. Atkinson, B. Cantillon and B. Nolan, *The EU and Social Inclusion: Facing the Challenges*, The Policy Press, Bristol 2007.

which is likely to increase in the (near) future. First, admitting defeat in eradicating poverty, in its Renewed Social Agenda of 2008, the Commission re-affirmed its commitments towards reinforcing the OMC.[4] The goals of the Agenda – opportunities, access, solidarity – were designed as interrelated and of equal priority. Creating opportunities roughly translates into job creation, but the document emphasizes the need of ensuring 'real equality of opportunity',[5] which cannot develop without access and solidarity. Improving access to education, health care, social protection, and other services should ensure universal access to the created opportunities. The most important target of the Renewed Social Agenda, manifesting social solidarity, be it between generations, rich and poor individuals, regions, or Member States, 'means fostering social inclusion and integration, participation and dialogue and combating poverty'.[6] Secondly, taking in some of the lessons of the economic crisis, the Commission's strategy for Europe 2020 focused on the need to have 'smart, sustainable and inclusive growth' in the EU.[7] At face value the document seems to engage in a cross-discipline dialogue by providing a vision for what the TEU calls in Article 3 the 'social market economy'.[8]

2. NEED FOR DIALOGUE BETWEEN LEGAL AND SOCIAL POLICY SCHOLARS

Both the role of the provisions on social inclusion and social protection within the legal architecture of the EU, as well as the working of the OMC have been of perennial academic concern. With a few notable exceptions,[9] studies of social inclusion and social protection take a one-dimensional disciplinary approach. Considering also the socio-economic and political environments, a thoroughly analytical collection of legal essays under the editorship of Shaw concluded in 2000 that social policy was no longer an essentially national matter.[10] This was followed by a number of juridical researches about the role of *social* rights in the Union in the context of the *economic* integration.[11] Another well explored issue is

---

4 European Commission, 'Renewed Social Agenda: Opportunities, Access and Solidarity in 21st Century Europe' (Communication) COM (2008) 412 final.

5 *Ibid.*, p. 7.

6 *Ibid.*, p. 7.

7 European Commission, 'Europe 2020: A European strategy for smart, sustainable and inclusive growth' (Communication) COM (2010) 2020.

8 See p. 10.

9 J. Shaw (ed.), *Social Law and Policy in an Evolving European Union*, Hart, Oxford 2000; K.A. Armstrong, *Governing Social Inclusion: Europeanization through Policy Coordination*, Oxford University Press, Oxford 2010.

10 *Ibid.*

11 M. Dougan and E. Spaventa (eds.), *Social Welfare and EU Law*, Hart, Oxford 2005; G. de Búrca and B. de Witte (eds.), *Social Rights in Europe*, Oxford University Press, Oxford 2005;

the Europeanization of social policy, i.e. the influence of European law upon domestic law, and national government responses.[12] In terms of social studies, the first investigations of the OMC had the task of shedding light on its mechanisms[13] and its indicators. Later publications focused on assessing its operation and function on national and sub-national levels,[14] and its effectiveness in reforming the national welfare systems.[15] Armstrong's recent monograph about social inclusion governance, which is informed by social policy, political science and law, investigates the process of 'Europeanization' of economic and social exclusion.[16]

The question as to how the legal and political areas of the EU (inter)act to achieve the goal of promoting social inclusion and protection has not been addressed, to our knowledge, by the academic literature to date. This book calls attention to the interactions between law and policy at EU level, and their potential impact upon the national one. The theme of this collection is the interaction between legal instruments and policy coordination in the field of social inclusion and social protection. The essays herein essentially inquire whether there is any interaction at all, or if the two realms of law and policy of the EU function in parallel. If there is any sort of interchange between the two, in what areas is it taking place, and what does it result into? Is there perhaps a phenomenon of formalization of policy into binding instruments? Or is the SPSI OMC yet another example of the regulatory asymmetry from which the EU has been suffering because its social ambitions are not translated into legally binding instruments?

Legal and political scholars were invited to address these questions and analyze EU's involvement in promoting social inclusion and protection. The book opens with two papers which introduce the political and legal contexts, and then focuses on the specific cases of health care, pension systems, and means of combating poverty. The choice of topics follows logically from the strands of the

---

U. Neergaard, R. Nielsen and L.M. Roseberry (eds.), *Integrating Welfare Functions into EU Law: From Rome to Lisbon*, DJØF Publishing, Copenhagen 2009; D. Schiek, U. Liebert and H. Schneider (eds.), *European Economic and Social Constitutionalism after the Treaty of Lisbon*, Cambridge University Press, Cambridge 2011.

12 Notably J. Kvist and J. Saari (eds.), *The Europeanisation of Social Protection*, The Policy Press, Bristol 2007.

13 C. de la Porte and P. Pochet, *Building Social Europe through the Open Method of Co-ordination*, P.I.E. Peter Lang, Brussels 2002.

14 J. Zeitlin, P. Pochet and L. Magnusson (eds.), *The Open Method of Coordination in Action: The European Employment and Social Inclusion Strategies*, P.I.E. Peter Lang, Brussels 2005.

15 M. Heidenreich and J. Zeitlin, *Changing European Employment and Welfare Regimes: The Influence of the Open Method of Coordination on National Reforms*, Routledge, London 2009; P. Graziano, S. Jacquot and B. Palier, *The EU and the Domestic Politics of Welfare State Reforms: Europa, Europae*, Palgrave Macmillan, Basingstoke 2011.

16 K.A. Armstrong, n. 9.

SPSI OMC, and the book takes a cross-disciplinary approach in the sense that each subject matter has been addressed in a complementary fashion through the lenses of juridical and political sciences. What we have attempted through this edited book is to confront both legal and political scholars with the above questions, and perhaps it comes as no surprise that the answers they provided often point into different directions.

3. IS THERE ANY INTERACTION BETWEEN THE LEGAL AND THE POLICY DISCOURSE ON SOCIAL INCLUSION AND SOCIAL PROTECTION?

In the following part we will present in broad lines the analyses and the conclusions of the various contributions. Needless to mention that the analytical tools employed by the authors vary in accordance with the requirements of the different disciplines: Some of the papers rely heavily on (first hand) empirical research (Vanhercke and Wegener, Cantillon and Van Mechelen), while some other ones draw more on the existing literature. The level of abstract theorizing and analytical intensity of the papers also differs.

3.1. FRAMING THE DISCUSSION: A PROMISING TREATY FRAMEWORK, BUT CAN IT DELIVER?

The first two papers provide a general framework for the discussion about social protection and social inclusion in the EU from a policy and legal perspective. Ferrera's paper, drawing on some of his previous work on the impact of the EU on welfare states,[17] notes from the beginning that the process of market Europeanization is not only a source of economic growth, but also of 'social and spatial disruptions', which can be resolved, he argues, through 'a socially-friendly institutional re-articulation' of the interactions between the national and EU levels. Thus, he pleads for a *proper* 'nesting' of nation-based welfare within the EU, meaning integrating the logic of closure which underpins nation-based social programmes and the logic of opening which drives the EU integration process. This requires that the social and the economic spaces rest on an equally strong legal basis in the Union, and thus necessitates that the EU constitutional framework defines 'the content and the boundaries of social protection as a distinct and relatively autonomous space' and prescribes the limits of free movement and competition rules in respect of the social space. The reconciliation

17 In particular M. Ferrera, *The Boundaries of Welfare: European Integration and the New Spatial Politics of Social Protection*, Oxford University Press, Oxford 2005.

between the welfare state and the EU he advocates implies mutual acknowledgement and concessions. The EU should recognize the role played by national welfare programmes for citizens' life chances, and the national welfare state must learn 'how to live with and hopefully take advantage of' European integration. Also, the welfare state must be ready to transfer some of its traditional social policies to EU forms of risk-pooling and redistribution.

His chapter argues in favour of a positive answer to the possibility of reconciling the EU and the welfare state, and discusses possible pathways towards the 'happy marriage' scenario. To that end, the Lisbon Treaty is, in his view, a promising basis for a (more) 'virtuous nesting between social welfare and economic integration'. The horizontal social clauses and the recognition of fundamental rights could potentially induce all EU institutions to find an adequate balance between economic and social objectives. They could also serve to define and implement the notion of 'social market economy'. The Europe 2020 Strategy in particular seems to have a favourable institutional potential for steering the Union's architecture towards a more virtuous nesting.

Dawson and de Witte analyse the legal resources currently offered by EU law to combat social exclusion and to promote social protection, but they are sceptical about the capacity of the EU to deliver solid social inclusion and protection policies. Evidence suggests that the SPSI OMC is secondary to other objectives, such as the economic goals pursued under the 'integrated guidelines' for jobs and growth, and in their view the new Europe 2020 Strategy does little to remediate that situation. The greatest failure of the Strategy, however, is the complete absence of interactions between governance tools and 'hard law' in the field of social inclusion. The 'missed opportunity' here is not only to provide a legal basis for action and to increase effectiveness, but also to advance the legitimacy of Union action in this regard.

When looking at the horizontal provisions in the Lisbon Treaty with regard to social inclusion and social protection, Dawson and de Witte fear them to be 'rhetorical because they are not supported elsewhere in the Treaties by new law making competences or decision making procedures'. They point out the unbalanced EU Treaty framework which, *although admitting that social inclusion and social protection are fundamental values, does not provide the EU institutions with concrete instruments to pursue them.* The same 'significant discord' between social goals and the implementing mechanisms is valid for the policy coordination. Therefore, social protection and inclusion policies in the EU are in an unusual position: they are intended to inform and influence other fields of EU policy, rather than to be free-standing values.

Dawson and de Witte highlight the potential of the EU Charter of Fundamental Rights to limit the liberalizing impact of EU law on national social protection policies. In addition, it could also contribute to formulating duties to act for the EU institutions, but its impact on day-to-day social policies remains to be seen.

At this point, the dialogue between legal and social scholars with regard to the general framework for social inclusion and social protection at EU level is rather disheartening. On the one hand, political science informs us of the perils of the existing disagreement between the inherent logics of the national and Union levels of policymaking, and places some hope in the current legal framework to appease the inconsistencies. On the other hand, jurists are alarmed about the apparent incapacity of the Lisbon Treaty to achieve a harmonious 'nesting'.

3.2. HEALTH POLICY OBJECTIVES RECENTLY LAID DOWN IN A LEGAL INSTRUMENT DRIVEN BY 'CONSUMER PROTECTIONISM'

Despite the explicit reference that health care is a national competence in Article 168 TFEU, March 2011 saw the adoption of the Directive on Patients' Rights in cross-border health care (the Directive).[18] What is more, this directive was adopted as an internal market harmonization instrument, and interestingly, it translates some of the governance tools into 'hard' law. Vanhercke with Wegener, and Sauter embark on an analysis of the interactions between law and policy in the field of health care, and the effects for social inclusion and protection.

The chapter of Vanhercke and Wegener sets out to look into the 'toolbox' of what started off as an 'incomplete institutional architecture', and its impact on national and EU policies. Their assessment of the impact of OMC Health at EU level discusses its interaction with other forms of 'soft' law, such as the Europe 2020 Strategy and the Structural Funds, as well as its impact upon the 'hard' law, i.e. the Union legislative processes and judicial adjudication. They notice that the 'OMC is increasingly seen as a template for EU health care governance', but share Dawson and de Witte's concern regarding the relation between the social (including access to health care) and economic goals in the integrated guidelines of the Europe 2020 Strategy. The authors appreciate the interaction between the European Social Fund and the OMC as a case of 'instrument hybridity', and drawing on studies of the impact of governance upon legal adjudication, they suggest the existence of OMC Health spill-overs in case law, particularly with regard to the justifications available for restrictions of the free movement of

18 Directive 2011/24/EU of the European Parliament and of the Council of 9 March 2011 on the application of patients' rights in cross-border healthcare [2011] OJ L88/45.

services. As such, the Court of Justice of the EU (ECJ) might be inspired by 'soft' law when interpreting concepts such as 'public interest', 'undue delay', or more generally resolving questions of proportionality in cases of health care. In as far as the interaction between the OMC Health and the EU legislation goes, a number of OMC-inspired forms of cooperation are identified in the above-mentioned Directive. They include cooperation and mutual assistance with regard to standards and guidelines of quality, the European reference networks, and cooperation regarding eHealth issues. This translation of 'soft' law into 'hard' law brings governance practices 'closer to a rule of law framework' and again point to the 'increasing hybridity of the instruments in the field of health care'.

Their empirical research shows that the influence of the OMC upon national policies is confined to what they call 'needles in the haystack': some self-reflective experiences creating discussion platforms, peer review participation, etc., but no 'solid evidence of substantive policy change'. They conclude that despite the limited influence of the OMC Health upon national policies, its effects at EU level cannot to be ignored. In both cases, nonetheless, the impact is procedural.

Sauter's chapter focuses on the substantive content of the Directive on the rights of patients to cross-border health care. The new Directive codifies the ECJ's case law, which applied the internal market rules to reimbursement of cross-border costs incurred within the framework of national public health systems, and establishes new patients' rights. Placing the Directive within the context of the European social policy agenda, Sauter sees these new rights, i.e. the right to transparency and accountability, as the main elements of the instrument. The common principles for health care spelled out in the Directive are another novelty: as responsibilities of the Member States of treatment, these are not based on the case law. Inferred from the national health systems, the principles are based on the Council Conclusions regarding the common values and principles in the EU. Universality, access to high-quality care, equity and solidarity are asserted as the guiding principles for the Member States of treatment, and are translated from what might have seemed mere political rhetoric into legally binding requirements. The implementation of these principles is under this Directive limited to situations of cross-border health care, but Sauter argues that in the future they could equally apply to internal situations.

Sauter discusses the translation into legally binding stipulations of types of cooperation, which used to be 'soft' governance tools. This is an addition to the EU integration logic wherein negative integration is followed by positive integration. He maintains that further harmonization could follow through the same pattern with regard to the calculation of costs of medical care. Overall, he assesses the Directive to be 'consistent with the consumer oriented approach of the EU integration as well as with the social policy agenda', and observes that, in light of the constitutional limitations, it 'signals a critical point in Union health law'.

3.3. OMC PENSIONS AND THE EU LEGAL REALM: PARALLEL WORLDS?

Responsibility for pension policy rests undoubtedly with the Member States, and yet, the expanding influence of the EU has led to what Natali calls a 'multi-tiered polity'. He takes up the trying analysis of non-legislative instruments that he holds to have 'hard' or 'soft' influence upon national pension policies. The requirements for budgetary discipline imposed by the Stability and Growth Pact (SGP) stand for 'a source of indirect (and hard) pressure on pension institutions', and the coordination of pension reforms through the OMC are a 'direct (and soft) version of integration'.

Ambivalence characterizes the impact of the SGP: on the one hand, it may lead to cuts in public spending, and thus statutory pensions, and on the other hand, macro-economic stability may favour economic growth, which in turn could contribute to better coping with challenges such as those posed by ageing societies. The European Monetary Union (EMU) has apparently contributed to reforms of pension policies without producing a 'race to the bottom'. Unsurprisingly in light of the severe pressure of the SGP, in times of economic crisis some of the Member States have gone as far as to re-nationalize funded pensions in order to reduce the public deficit and debt stemming from the process of privatization. Such national solutions raise questions regarding the appropriate treatment of the costs of pension reforms in budgetary rules.

It should be noted that the governance of pension policies is not limited to publicly funded pensions, and the specific goals of the OMC Pensions include ensuring universal pensions which can provide for the maintenance of an adequate living standard, ensuring financial stability of pension schemes, and assuring their transparency. However, this does not alter the paramount position of the macro-economic coordination in EU policy making. Natali notes, not without sharing some of the doubts presented in the academic literature, some influence upon national policies, such as capacity building through the development of common statistics, mutual learning, and consequently enhanced national capacities in policymaking.

Stevens continues the analysis of pensions as an instrument for social inclusion and social protection in the EU by asking how the substance given to pension protection at the policy level is mirrored in the legal domain. More specifically, if the EU is committed to developing 'adequate retirement pensions and ensure long term sustainability of the pensions systems', as its policy discourse purports, is this possible from a legal point of view? Highlighting the wide variety of pension types which exists in the EU Member States, from purely state funded pension, collectively financed occupational pension to private pensions schemes, his chapter goes beyond EU social law, and looks into legislation regarding financial markets, consumer protection, prudential measures and solvency.

Since the EU has no legal competence to set up pension systems, this remains a matter for the Member States, and only indirectly, via internal market law, does the EU impact on the national pensions systems. The prime example here is the EU coordination of social security systems, aimed at preventing negative effects on pensions rights of EU migrants due to mobility and the diversity of the national pension schemes. Irrespective of its importance for the (mobile) European citizens, this coordination system has no impact on the drafting and developing of the national schemes.

Stevens' paper submits that the negligible EU impact upon statutory pensions is countered in the field of the occupational, supplementary and individual retirement provision. The EU has more competences for privately funded pension schemes because of their economic nature. He presents a plethora of legal instruments regulating the activities and supervision of occupational pension funds, insolvency, portability of occupational pension rights, life assurance products, financial markets, investment funds, insolvency, tax issues relevant to pensions, and describes the new EU authority for insurance and occupational pensions.

The chapter notes that social aspects regarding this category of pensions are often seen as elements of consumer protection: some sort of social standards are created in the EU through competences concerning consumer protection. Yet, he regards these legal initiatives as not being influenced by the pensions policy objectives. Stevens uses the image of parallel worlds for policymakers and legal practitioners in the field of pensions. His legal analysis concludes that policy documents create a false impression that the EU is working on the pension schemes of its citizens.

3.4. COMBATING POVERTY: DOUBTS ABOUT THE FEASIBILITY OF BINDING EU INSTRUMENTS

Cantillon and Van Mechelen observe that over the past decades poverty rates in the EU have stagnated or even increased: the anti-poverty instruments were insufficient or ineffective. There are indications that the erosion of social benefits may be an important factor in explaining the poverty standstill, and they discuss a number of studies on poverty trends that have formulated the recommendation to define minimum income protection standards at the EU level. Legally binding common standards would serve as guidelines for national governments and might perhaps resolve the asymmetry between social and economic legal standards in the Union. Their chapter examines the desirability of and the obstacles to the introduction of binding standards with regard to minimum income in Europe.

Cantillon and Van Mechelen's contribution argues that there are good reasons to assume that the adequacy of guaranteed minimum income schemes could become the subject of the first legislative and legally binding initiative in the field of social protection: it has featured prominently in the European policy debate since the early 1990s, and most Member States already have minimum income schemes in place. However, they notice considerable politico-legal, conceptual and practical impediments to such a strategy. They point to the uncertainty regarding the appropriate definition of adequate minimum income. Moreover, in particular in the poorer EU Member States, the budgetary burden of raising social assistance benefits would be substantial, and any such measure would generate unemployment traps.

Although research suggests that an effective European anti-poverty strategy would essentially include adequate income protection, between the dream of an EU minimum income scheme and reality stand conceptual as well as technical and budgetary considerations. Any binding agreement with regard to minimum incomes, Cantillon and Van Mechelen submit, would have to be formulated flexibly and introduced gradually.

To this analysis from a social-policy perspective, Verschueren contributes an examination of whether the policy initiatives taken at EU level regarding the fight against poverty and social exclusion have been or could be translated into legally imperative provisions that would compel the Member States to introduce certain rights for citizens with regard to minimum subsistence schemes. He concludes that a big contradiction exists in this respect. On the one hand, there is a lack of political will to compel the Member States to provide for certain minimum requirements with regard to the citizens' right to minimum subsistence schemes by means of an EU legal instrument, despite the explicit references in the Treaties to the EU's objective of combating social exclusion. Furthermore, considering the limited powers the TFEU granted to the EU institutions regarding the 'combating of social exclusion', it is uncertain, in his view, that there is a legal basis in the Treaties for the EU to take such an initiative.

On the other hand, the EU legislature, supported and stimulated by the ECJ, created various legal means to *guarantee that persons using the right of free movement within the EU have the same rights as the nationals of their host country with regard to a whole range of social benefits, including minimum subsistence benefits*. This legislation and case law do not only apply to the traditional beneficiaries of the right to free movement within the internal market, i.e. economically active persons, but *this right to equal treatment has recently also been guaranteed to persons who are not, not yet or no longer economically active*. Moreover, the role of the Union in guaranteeing sufficient income for migrant persons has been confirmed by the EU social security coordination system, which guarantees that persons migrating within the EU maintain their social security rights.

Nonetheless, these instruments of 'free movement' in themselves do not impose any obligation on the Member States with regard to the conditions, extent and amount of their minimum benefit schemes. They only lay down that, in principle, Member States should offer citizens of other Member States living on their territory the same rights as their own nationals. Verschueren highlights the contrast between the lack of political will, and probably even a legal basis, to adopt EU legislation that would impose obligations on the Member States with regard to the content and amount of their minimum benefits schemes, on the one hand, and the large number of instruments to give migrating persons access to these schemes in a host Member State, on the other. This contrast seems to be a reflection of the fact that within the EU the emphasis is still on free movement in the context of an internal market, *even if this is complemented with the right to free movement for economically inactive persons*, rather than on the integration of the social policies of the Member States.

4. A WAY FORWARD FOR AN ADEQUATE 'NESTING' OF SOCIAL POLICY OBJECTIVES?

One thing is apparent from the contributions to this book: they do not amount to a neutral examination of the interactions between law and policy in the field of social inclusion and social protection. Rather, the collection favours a *better* balancing of social and economic goals, or a more 'virtuous nesting' of EU and national policy levels, as Ferrera would call it. To this end, *some noteworthy* potential does exist both in the EU constitutional context and the various Union *policy initiatives* taken in the field of social inclusion and social protection, but it has not been attained yet. Although we might speak of the insignificant impact of both the new social objectives of the Lisbon Treaty and the 'soft' policy guidelines, it would appear inaccurate to speak of *interactions* between law and policies. Rather, we should refer to the influence of policy objectives upon law making and legal adjudication. And still, not many such cases have been reported in the area of social protection and social inclusion.

Nonetheless, active interaction between social policy and law at EU level is shown in recent developments in the field of cross-border health care. It seems that some of the policy objectives are incorporated both in the case law of the ECJ and EU legislature. The result is a hybrid ('soft' and 'hard') form of governance of EU health. However, the *'consumer oriented approach of the EU integration'*, as Sauter puts it, characterizes the resulting legal instrument, and is intrinsic to the case law. Surely, this could be the consequence of the development of EU law on cross-border patients' mobility rights through the fundamental freedom of movement of services. The nature of the EU competences could be said to be another reason.

Although the field of pensions is not a case where policy considerations are taken up by law, a similar approach can also be observed here. EU legal instruments governing occupational, supplementary and individual retirement provisions largely aim at *consumer* protection, which is justifiable in light of the private nature of the pensions and their reliance on the profitability of the economic activity. This (consumer protection) can be perceived as the creation of 'social' standards of sorts, but it is questionable whether it is sufficient, or whether, in light of the socio-economic and demographic situation in Europe, the introduction of more traditional forms of *social* protection is necessary.

Analysing the social protection of EU migrants reinforces the finding that the existence of a link to European *economic* integration eases the exercise of social rights. Even though economic goals take precedence at the level of EU legislature and judiciary, Union law does contribute to the protection of social security rights of some vulnerable citizens in the so-called 'host' state and therefore to the combating of poverty of these migrants. Nevertheless, despite the SPSI OMC, the obstacles to a *social* minimum income defined at EU level are major.

It can be concluded that in the absence of a connection with EU economic integration, social inclusion and social protection policy objectives formulated through the OMC encounter more difficulties. The discrepancy between the political discourse and the legal possibilities in the field of social inclusion and social protection points to an EU still in the process of self-searching. Anticipating negative effects upon national social policies partly resulting from the compelling influence of the Union upon the public finances of the Member States, we appreciate that the pertinence and intensity of this search for a 'social identity' will increase in the years to come. In the absence of a strengthened European social space, the internal market law will impact further on the supplementary social insurance schemes, in particular on pensions and health care, as well as on the public social services sector. Therefore, there are good reasons to act at EU level towards the kind of 'nesting' advocated by Ferrera. The SPSI OMC could facilitate more than just a better entrenchment of a social EU space: provided it leads to a sufficient convergence of national law and policies, it could create the conditions for EU social legislation. The experience and knowledge that has been gained at EU level as a result of the SPSI OMC could then definitely be very useful in the preparation and adoption of legally binding measures. EU legal norms could for instance be underpinned with the data and insights regarding the Member States' social protection schemes obtained in the context of this OMC.

So, what is the possible shape and content of feasible as well as effective European initiatives aimed at achieving a somewhat better balance in the Union's 'highly asymmetrical juristic framework'?[19] What kind of policy tool would allow the EU to introduce the rationale of social cohesion and social justice more forcefully into thinking and discourse, as well as policy making? Although calls for a more social Europe have been heard for many years, those voices have usually remained rather silent when asked what precisely the objective of such a social policy alignment should be. What should European social policy look like? Considering the great political, economic and institutional differences within the Union, and given that anti-poverty policy cannot and must not be restricted to the financial dimension alone, is there any other option but that of 'soft coordination' towards common goals? Or are there opportunities for enhancing the social dimension by means of concrete policy instruments and hard law?

Whichever policy tool is deployed, though, it will undoubtedly have to be modest. In view of the considerable differences in economic development, the divergent design of the various national social protection systems, the multitude of interest groups involved and the lack of any political consensus, the approach taken will need to be incremental and it will have to rely on opportunities that are inherently present: *'one should proceed à petits pas (as Jean Monnet would have put it) and (...), tactically, one should take advantage of emerging "opportunity structures"'*.[20]

As Goodin pointed out in the past 'there was no single founder and no single set of intentions'[21] for the creation of national welfare states. The same is true for the

19 See among others F.W. Scharpf, 'The Asymmetry of European Integration or Why the EU Cannot Be a "Social Market Economy"' n.1.

20 Ph.C. Schmitter and M.W. Bauer, 'A (Modest) Proposal for Expanding Social Citizenship in the European Union' (2011) 11 *Journal of European Social Policy (JESP).*

21 R.E. Goodin, *Reasons for Welfare: The Political Theory of the Welfare State,* Princeton University Press, Princetion, NJ 1988, p. 13.

emerging Social Europe. Instead, it will be shaped incrementally just as in the past – 'with the handiwork of many successive groups with only partially overlapping members'.[22]

In this book we identified consumer protection and the right of free movement as possible 'stepping stones' in a next step towards Social Europe. With the possible exception of health care, the policy goals set through the OMC do not alter EU law considerably. However, because the political discourse necessarily precedes any legal developments, the SPSI OMC could be perceived as a form of 'brain-storming' for more binding agreements. This book only makes a modest contribution to comprehending the development and status quo of the (peculiar) input of the Union to social inclusion and protection,[23] but the expected increased search for an EU 'social identity' in the years to come invite further research. Delivering more tangible and visible results in the field of social inclusion and social protection could improve the – presently highly questioned – legitimacy of the Union.

22 *Ibid.*, p. 13.

23 E Marlier and D. Natali (eds.) with R. Van Dam, *Europe 2020: Towards a More Social EU?*, P.I.E. Peter Lang, Brussels 2010; H. Frazer, E. Marlier and I. Nicaise (eds.), *A Social Inclusion Roadmap for Europe 2020*, Garant, Antwerp 2010.

MODEST BEGINNINGS, TIMID PROGRESSES: WHAT'S NEXT FOR SOCIAL EUROPE?

Maurizio FERRERA*

1. INTRODUCTION

In 2010, the welfare state surpassed its centennial in several European Union (EU) Member States. Public protection schemes, a genuine European invention, were originally introduced to respond to the mounting 'social question' linked to industrialization. The disruption of traditional, localized systems of work-family-community relations and the diffusion of national markets – based on free movement and largely unfettered economic competition within the territorial borders of each country – profoundly altered the pre-industrial structure of risks and need. The regulation of the new national labour markets, by establishing common standards, rights and obligations (through labour laws, unemployment and more generally social insurance, national labour exchanges etc.), was one of the fundamental institutional and political responses that European states gave to the big 'social question' which confronted them.

In his ground-breaking historical analysis of modern citizenship, T.H. Marshall suggested that the evolution of the national welfare state involved a two-fold process of fusion and of separation.[1] The *fusion* was geographical and entailed the dismantling of local privileges and immunities, the harmonization of rights and obligations throughout the national territory concerned, and the establishment of a level playing field (the equal status of citizens) within state borders. The *separation* was functional and entailed the creation of new sources of nationwide authority and jurisdiction as well as new specialized institutions

* This paper is a modified and updated version of the chapter 'Mapping the Components of a Social EU: A Critical Analysis of the Current Institutional Patchwork' in E. MARLIER and D. NATALI (eds.) with R. VAN DAM, *Europe 2020. Towards a More Social EU?*, P.I.E. Peter Lang, Brussels 2010. Address for correspondence: maurizio.ferrera@unimi.it.

1 T.H. MARSHALL, *Citizenship and Social Class and Other Essays*, Cambridge University Press, Cambridge 1950.

for the implementation of that authority and that jurisdiction at a decentralized level. The development of national markets, accompanied by the creation of new 'social' entitlements and public protection schemes, triggered off – at least in liberal democracies – a phase of unprecedented economic growth and social progress, while at the same time strengthening the political loyalty of citizens and the overall legitimacy of the state.

To a large extent, the present historical phase is witnessing the emergence of a new (a 'second') social question in Europe, which is reproducing under new guises the double challenge of fusion and separation already experienced between the XIXth and the XXth centuries. Historical parallels are always slippery and can be misleading when taken too literally, yet they may serve a useful heuristic function. As was the case one hundred years ago at the domestic level, the Europeanization ('fusion') of national markets through freedom of movement and competition rules is (already has been) a tremendous trigger for growth and job creation in the EU's economy, enhancing life chances and welfare for European citizens. But it is also a source of social and spatial disruptions. Again, economic 'fusion' requires the introduction of some common social standards, rights and obligations through a socially-friendly institutional re-articulation of the novel Europeanized space of interaction.

We can think of at least three reasons which make such a socially-friendly re-articulation desirable.[2] First, the re-articulation is needed in order to secure a fairer, more equitable distribution of life chances for EU citizens, both within and between Member States. This is the 'social cohesion', or 'social justice' rationale. Unless one believes in a naive version of the trickle-down effect of growth, the pursuit of economic prosperity through efficient and open markets should be accompanied by an agenda for social progress, resting on key values (such as 'social justice and protection, equality between women and men, solidarity between generations and protection of the rights of the child' – now enshrined in Article 3 TEU) which are widely shared and deeply rooted in Europe's political cultures. While there can be no doubt that this agenda includes areas and policies which legally come under national jurisdiction, it should be equally clear that the EU can play an important role, both directly (by exercising its legal powers to sustain and complement national social justice agendas) and indirectly (by 'mainstreaming' social cohesion/ justice considerations within its entire array of policies). Second, a more social EU is desirable in order to improve the very functioning of the internal market, and thus generate more growth and

---

2 For a more expanded discussion and references see: M. Ferrera and S. Sacchi, 'A More Social EU: Issues of Where and How' in S. Micossi and G.L. Tosato (eds.), *The European Union in the 21st Century: Perspectives from the Lisbon Treaty*, Centre for European Policy Studies, Brussels 2009.

jobs (this is the 'economic efficiency' rationale). A wealth of political economy research has in fact shown that social policies can play an important role not only as redistributive instruments, but also as 'productive factors'.[3] Thirdly, and possibly most importantly, a more social EU is needed in order to secure continuing support for the integration process itself on the part of increasingly worried national electorates (this is the 'social and political legitimacy' rationale). There is indeed growing evidence that the EU is now perceived as a potentially dangerous entity by a majority of its citizens, as a threat to national labour markets and social protection systems, as a 'Trojan horse' serving the malevolent interests of globalization. As noted above, post-war social protection systems have built extraordinary bonds between citizens and their national institutions, bringing about a very robust form of allegiance, based on the institutionalized exchange of material benefits for electoral support. The EU, conversely, has been rather weak in terms of identity and allegiance building. If voters' anxieties vis-à-vis markets and competition are not alleviated, if voters are not convinced that 'the EU cares' (through direct and indirect action, or non-action), the integration process as such may be seriously de-legitimized and jeopardized by xenophobic sentiments and neo-protectionist demands voiced by those social groups that are most directly affected by economic opening – and the economic crisis has undoubtedly intensified this challenge.[4]

The institutional re-articulation which is required in order to build a stronger social EU (better: a fully fledged 'EU social model') is much more complex and difficult than the organizational separations that took place within the nation states about a hundred years ago. In late XIXth century Europe, social rights emerged on a *tabula rasa* (or at least almost *rasa*): there was not much to 'fuse' and there were wide margins for creating *ex novo* in terms of social policies. In today's EU, the institutional material to be integrated is very complex and very solid in the welfare realm, and decision making rules at the EU level are inherently biased against efforts of positive integration. But there is an even more fundamental obstacle: the institutional clash between the logic of closure, which underpins nation-based social programmes, and the logic of opening which drives the integration process. By its very nature, the welfare state presupposes the existence of a clearly demarcated and cohesive community, whose members feel that they belong to the same 'whole' and that they are linked by reciprocity ties vis-à-vis common risks and similar needs. Since the XIXth century (or even earlier in some cases) the nation-state has provided the closure conditions for the

---

3 D. Fourage, 'Costs of Non-Social Policies. Towards an Economic Framework of Quality Social Policy and the Costs of Not Having Them' (2003) Report prepared for the Employment and Social Affairs DG <www.temaasyl.se/Documents/ETG/Cost%20Of%20Non%20 Social%20Policy.pdf> accessed 12 October 2011.

4 N. Fligstein, *Euroclash: The EU, European Identity and the Future of Europe*, Oxford University Press, Oxford 2008.

development of an *ethos* of social solidarity and redistributive arrangements within its geographical territory. By contrast, EU integration is clearly guided by a logic of 'opening', aimed at fostering free movement (in the widest sense) and non-discrimination by weakening or tearing apart those spatial demarcations and closure practices that nation-states have historically built around themselves, especially in the social sphere.

Finding a well-designed and viable institutional response to the EU's 'second social question' means, essentially, addressing the clash between the logic of closure and the logic of opening. Can the Union reconcile these two logics and transform the encounter between nation-based welfare and EU-based economic unification into a 'happy marriage', i.e. into an institutional engine for further expanding and strengthening the life chances of its citizens? This paper argues in favour of a positive answer and discusses possible pathways towards the 'happy marriage' scenario. Section 2 presents the main argument by illustrating the programmatic contrast and growing tensions between the welfare state, on the one hand, and the EU, on the other. Section 3 outlines a possible strategy of institutional reconciliation. It argues that the key for a successful reconciliation lies in a more explicit and effective 'nesting' of the national welfare state within the overall spatial architecture of the EU. The subsequent two sections try to identify and discuss some possible building blocks (and even some ongoing developments) which may promote the formation and consolidation of the new architecture and thus activate a virtuous nesting scenario, in which the economic and the social spaces of Europe will be able not only to co-exist without colliding, but also to re-enforce each other. Section 6 concludes.

2. THE CHALLENGE: CLOSURE VS. OPENING

As has been shown by a large scholarship in sociology and political science,[5] welfare state formation can be seen as the last phase or step in the long-term historical development of the European system of nation-states: the step through which territorially bounded political communities came to introduce redistributive arrangements for their citizens, thus transforming themselves into self-contained and inward-looking spaces of solidarity and inaugurating novel and original models of state-mediated social sharing.

---

5 I have reconstructed and discussed this strand of scholarship in M. Ferrera, *The Boundaries of Welfare: European Integration and the New Spatial Politics of Social Protection*, Oxford University Press, Oxford 2005. See P. Flora with S. Kuhnle and D. Urwin (eds.), *State Formation, Nation Building and Mass Politics in Europe: The Theory of Stein Rokkan*, Oxford University Press, Oxford 1999 on Stein Rokkan, one of the most prominent Founding Fathers of this tradition.

While this transformation was being completed within each domestic arena, during the so-called *Trente Glorieuses*, a new institutional development took off in the inter-state or supranational arena: the process of EU integration. Even though originally meant to 'rescue the nation-state' by boosting economic growth,[6] the Rome Treaty pulled a strong brake on the long-term dynamic of nation- and state-building in Europe.

The original EU Treaties envisaged a division of labour between supranational and national levels: the European Community was to be instrumental in opening up markets and helping achieve otherwise unattainable economies of scale, so as to fully exploit Europe's (initially, the Six's) economic potential. Member States could use part of the extra surplus in the institutionalized exchange of social benefits – flowing from their national welfare institutions – for 'anchoring' support on the part of their domestic political communities. 'Keynes at home, Smith abroad', as Robert Gilpin aptly dubbed this kind of embedded liberalism arrangement.[7] This justified the weakness of the social provisions in the Rome Treaty: from equality of treatment for men and women to the coordination of social security regimes, all the social provisions and articles contained therein were instrumental in the dismantling of non-tariff barriers to trade and the creation of a higher economic order featuring unconstrained economic trade flows. However, this supranational liberal order rested upon, or rather was embedded into national welfare states that were to be equally unconstrained in terms of social regulation capabilities, and in particular would not be constrained by the supranational authorities. This division of labour implied separating jurisdiction between the supranational and national levels, thus establishing 'mutual non-interference' between market-making and market-correcting functions. EU competition law and the four freedoms (free movement of workers, capitals, goods and services) were not supposed to impinge upon Member States' sovereignty in the social sphere.[8]

This did not last. Firstly, since the 1970s international political economy conditions have changed, and the embedded liberalism compromise has floundered. Moreover, and more importantly still as regards EU integration, the Community legal order has been constitutionalized.[9] The supremacy of Community law over domestic legislation has, along with direct effect, torn the initial division of labour to pieces: if Community law trumps national law, then provisions geared to foster free movement and unconstrained competition (i.e.

6 A. Milward, *The European Rescue of the Nation State*, Routledge, London 2000.

7 R. Gilpin, *The Political Economy of International Relations*, Princeton University Press, Princeton 1987, p. 335.

8 S. Giubboni, *Social Rights and Market Freedom in the European Constitution: A Labour Law Perspective*, Cambridge University Press, Cambridge 2006.

9 J.H.H. Weiler, *The Constitution of Europe*, Cambridge University Press, Cambridge 1999.

the Treaty provisions) trump social regulation, as enshrined in national constitutions and laws, and European Court of Justice judges, contrary to national constitutional judges, will be constrained in balancing economic and social interests whenever these clash.[10] To be sure, the ECJ has not always operated as a 'market police force', and has on several occasions granted some degree of 'immunity' against EU market law to national welfare institutions and practices – or it has at least tried to embed the internal market in a wider social fabric.[11] However, in the absence of a Treaty 'hook', it has done so on the grounds of judicial doctrines that lack a stable legal anchoring and may well be overridden in other rulings or legislative acts.

The de-bounding and opening logic of EU integration has raised increasingly severe problems for the welfare state, as it has put in question two central tenets of this institution: the territoriality principle and the principle of compulsory affiliation to state-controlled insurance schemes. More specifically, through the four freedoms, competition rules and the rules of coordination of national social security systems, the EU law has launched two basic challenges to nation-based welfare:

- A challenge to its territorial closure, through the explicit prohibition of (most) cross-border restrictions regarding access to and consumption of social benefits, and to some extent also the provision of services. The nationality filter has been neutralized for admission into domestic sharing spaces and some core social rights (such as pensions) have become portable across the territory of the whole EU.
- A challenge to the very 'right to bound', i.e. the right of each national welfare state to determine autonomously who can/must share what with whom and then enforce compliance through specific organizational structures backed by coercive power (e.g. setting up a compulsory public insurance scheme for a given occupational category).

These challenges have manifested themselves gradually and incrementally over time, affecting in different ways and with different intensity the various risk-specific schemes and the various tiers and pillars of provision in different countries.[12] So far the two challenges have not caused major organizational

---

10 F. Scharpf, 'Legitimacy in the Multi-Level European Polity' (2009) 1 *European Political Science Review*.

11 J.A. Caporaso and S. Tarrow, 'Polanyi in Brussels: Supranational Institutions and the Transnational Embedding of Markets' (2009) 63 *International Organization*.

12 D.S. Martinsen, 'The Europeanization of Welfare: The Domestic Impact of Intra-European Social Security' (2005) 43 *JCMS*. D.S. Martinsen, 'Social Security Regulation in the EU: The De-Territorialization of Welfare?' in G. De Búrca (ed.), *EU Law and the Welfare State: In Search of Solidarity*, Oxford University Press, Oxford 2005. D.S. Martinsen and G. Falkner, 'Social Policy: Problem Solving Gaps, Partial Exits and Court Decision Traps' in G. Falkner

upheavals. But during the last two decades the institutional status quo has been explicitly and directly attacked on several occasions in some of its founding properties: for example the link between legal residence and the right to enjoy means-tested social assistance benefits or the public monopoly over compulsory insurance (cf. Box 1).

Box 1: Examples of effects of EU law on national social spaces

- Nationality/citizenship no longer a legitimate instrument of 'closure' in the access to social benefits → Equal treatment for all 'legal residents'
- Increasing top-down harmonization of criteria for obtaining 'legal residence'
- Compulsory membership to public social insurance schemes ('*monopoles sociaux*') legitimate only if certain conditions apply
- Patients legally residing in a EU Member State can seek medical care abroad at the expenses of national schemes
- Liberalization of 'second pillar' pension schemes
- Right to industrial action/strike and application of collective agreements challenged if clashing with freedom of movement (*Laval, Viking, Rüffert* cases)
- Closure rules in higher education challenged if clashing with freedom of movement

During the last couple of decades, Member States have been investing a lot of energy in cushioning their social protection systems against challenges stemming from EU law, e.g. by not complying with rulings, agreeing among themselves to change EU law, or even failing to introduce new social programmes that could subsequently become the object of ECJ action. This may well be one of the reasons why such issues have not yet come to the fore of public debate at EU level and remain confined to restricted insider circles: their potentially disruptive outcomes have so far been (relatively) buffered by Member States' reactions. But how long can this last? What risks are involved in terms of social and political consensus?

In recent years the new situation of social 'semi-sovereignty' (a term originally coined by Leibfried and Pierson[13]) has already prompted a growing politicization of the 'opening' issue, and in some countries more than others, of the integration process as a whole. The most evident manifestation of this politicization occurred

(ed.), *The EU's Decision Traps: Comparing Policies*, Oxford University Press, Oxford 2010. Cf. also the other chapters of this volume.

13 S. Leibfried and P. Pierson (eds.), *European Social Policy between Fragmentation and Integration*, Brookings Institution, Washington D.C 1995.

in the spring of 2005, during the campaigns for the French and Dutch referendums, which rejected the EU Constitutional Treaty (and the Irish referendum on the Lisbon Treaty held in June 2008 confirmed that popular fears about 'opening' have certainly not abated). Not surprisingly, questions regarding the social sharing dimension (who shares what, and how much? Is it appropriate for the EU to interfere in such decisions? More crucially still, is the EU undermining national welfare arrangements and labour markets?) have been playing a central role in this process of politicization, while national governments find themselves increasingly sandwiched between the growing constraints imposed by the EU on the one hand, and the national basis of their political legitimacy on the other – a legitimacy which remains highly dependent on decisions in the social protection domain.

As witnessed, again, by the referendum debates, the vast majority of ordinary citizens and a good number of policymakers think that the growing friction between the welfare state and the EU has or could have an easy solution: the two institutions should be put back on 'separate tracks', as they were in the first couple of decades after the Rome Treaty. However, anyone that has some familiarity with institutional theory knows better: macro historical trends cannot be reversed.[14] The welfare state and the EU – which can undoubtedly be regarded as the two most important achievements of the XXth century in Europe – have now encountered each other and are bound to remain on the same track of development: there is no going back to separate tracks. If, as is argued here, the logic of integration does have a high destabilizing potential with respect to national social protection, then can we think of ways to mitigate this potential and imagine a strategy of compromise and 'institutional reconciliation'?

3. A NEW 'NESTED' ARCHITECTURE

Our answer to such question is affirmative. As mentioned in the introduction, the key for a successful reconciliation lies in a more explicit and effective 'nesting'[15] of the national welfare state within the overall spatial architecture of the EU. Figure 1 shows how the nesting between the welfare state and the EU could be achieved. Let us illustrate and discuss the underlying rationale and the various elements of this figure in some detail.[16]

---

14 P. Pierson, *Politics in Time: History, Institutions and Social Analysis*, Princeton University Press, Princeton 2004.

15 I have discussed the concept of 'nesting' and its use in the social sciences in M. Ferrera, 'The JCMS Annual Lecture: National Welfare States and European Integration: In Search of a "Virtuous Nesting"' (2009) 47 *JCMS*.

16 An earlier version of this figure is included in M. Ferrera, *The Boundaries of Welfare: European Integration and the New Spatial Politics of Social Protection*, n.5. I re-propose here a

Figure 1. The nesting of nation-based welfare within the EU

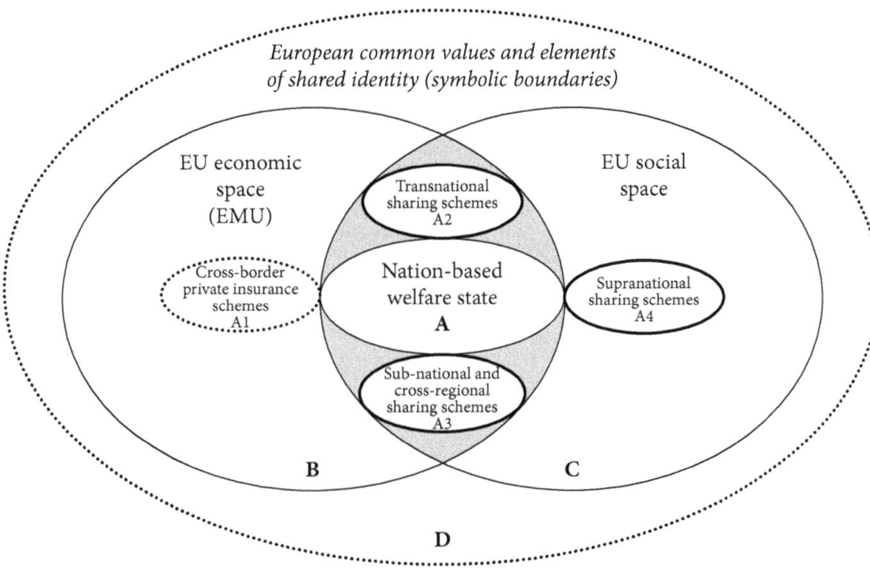

As can be seen, the national welfare state is placed at the very centre of Figure 1. For responding to the big social risks of the life cycle, the broad-based national insurance schemes remain today the most efficient and equitable institutions at our disposal. Of course these schemes must be updated and modernized in order to respond to a host of endogenous transformations (cf. below). But they must also be safeguarded as precious instruments to promote distributive equity (the 'social justice rationale'), cohesion and social consensus (the 'legitimacy rationale') and even a smooth and correct functioning of market transactions (the 'economic efficiency' rationale).

In the wake of half a century of supranational integration, the welfare state is already inserted – as shown in the previous section – within the economic spaces of the EU: space B consists of the Economic and Monetary Union (EMU), resting on free movement provisions, competition law, and, in the euro-zone, a common currency and monetary policy as well as the fiscal rules of the Stability and Growth Pact. Space B has been the very epicentre of the opening waves of the integration process. We know that such waves were well-meant, so to speak, and that they have brought unquestionable advantages from an economic point of view. The EMU project was elaborated during the 1980s and 1990s in order to

---

slightly modified version: not only do I still consider it a useful heuristic tool, but my impression is that a number of developments since 2005 have made that nesting scenario more feasible, i.e. have brought it within an easier reach.

respond to the threats of stagnation and Euro-sclerosis, with a view to revamping 'growth, competitiveness and employment': the EU Gross Domestic Product (GDP) is now significantly larger than it would have been without enhanced market integration. Liberalizations have made many goods and services more affordable to consumers (think of low-cost air fares), increasing the range of options available to them (including cross-border private insurance schemes, as shown by the Figure). In certain areas (e.g. health and safety), market integration has also brought about more consumer protection and higher labour standards. In addition, the tighter coupling between economic integration and national welfare states has prompted several countries to undertake much needed functional and distributive 'recalibrations' of their social protection systems.[17]

However, as explained in the previous section, space B has also increasingly become a source of instability for national welfare state programmes: its principles and policies are eroding the foundations of the 'nest', i.e. those closure preconditions which are necessary from an institutional and political point of view for sustaining social solidarity over time. As convincingly argued by Fritz Scharpf, this process of erosion is largely driven by decision making rules that systematically favour negative over positive integration, but is also intensified by a sort of general pro-integration bias on the side of supranational authorities (and in particular the ECJ) 'that treats any progress in mobility, non discrimination and the removal of national obstacles to integration as an unmitigated good and an end in itself'.[18] In other words, the destabilizing pressures of space B are linked to institutional and ideational dynamics that often push the logic of opening well beyond the functional and normative requirements (and overall rationale) of economic integration *per se*.

A strategy of reconciliation thus calls for the formation within the EU architecture of a second circle, which Figure 1 calls the EU 'social space' and whose main function should be to safeguard or reconstruct those institutional preconditions (the 'boundary configuration') that underpin domestic sharing arrangements. To be sure, especially after the Amsterdam and Nice Treaties (not to speak of the Lisbon Treaty: cf. below), various important steps have already been taken in this direction: in space C we now have a Charter of Fundamental Rights, hard laws on some common labour and social security standards (some of them decided upon by the social partners through social dialogue) and soft laws on employment, social inclusion, pensions as well as health care and long-

[17] M. Ferrera and A. Hemerijck, 'Recalibrating European Welfare Regimes' in J. Zeitlin and D.M. Trubeck (eds.), *Governing Work and Welfare in a New Economy*, Oxford University Press, Oxford 2003; M. Ferrera and E. Gualmini, *Rescued by Europe*, Amsterdam University Press, Amsterdam 2004.

[18] F. Scharpf, n.10, p.15.

term care. In recent years, the Spring European Councils have also agreed on a number of grand 'Pacts'[19] that have reaffirmed the EU's recognition of fundamental social objectives, its commitment to the 'caring' dimension of the Union. These are all steps in the right direction, but, as will be argued below, some key and strategic elements are poorly defined or altogether missing. Before discussing what is to be improved, let us complete the description of the nested architecture of Figure 1.

As mentioned earlier, an institutional reconciliation between the welfare state and the EU implies not only mutual acknowledgement, as it were, but also some mutual concessions. A strengthened Space C can be seen as the concession that the EU makes to the welfare state, recognizing the fundamental role played by nation-based sharing programmes in enriching and stabilizing citizens' life chances. But the national welfare state must make concessions too. First, it must learn how to live with (and hopefully take advantage of) some of the opening spurs coming from space B – a learning process that seems to be already under way, as we have seen. But the welfare state must also be ready to delegate or transfer some of its traditional social sharing functions to novel post-national forms of risk-pooling and redistribution.

More specifically, Figure 1 indicates three new possible types of sharing spaces:

1. transnational sharing spaces, centred on specific risks and occupational sectors and resting on novel functional alignments;
2. sub- and cross-regional sharing spaces, possibly addressing a plurality of risks or social needs and resting on new territorial alignments;
3. supranational sharing spaces, i.e. novel redistributive schemes directly anchored to EU institutions and based on EU citizenship (or denizenship) alone, i.e. without the filter of national institutions and politics.

In the 'virtuous nesting' scenario envisaged by the Figure, the spatial architecture of the EU must become more protective of the institutional core of the national welfare state, but at the same time it must make room and encourage innovation and experimentation on each of these three post-national fronts. What kind of institutional reforms, specifically, could be introduced in order to make progress in both directions?

---

19 European Council, 'European Youth Pact', Annex 1 of Presidency Conclusions of the European Council, 22–23 March 2005, 7619/05; European Council, 'European Pact for Gender Equality', Presidency Conclusions of the European Council, 23–24 March 2006, 7775/1/06 REV 1; European Council, 'Alliance for Families', Presidency Conclusions of the European Council, 8–9 March 2007, 7224/07.

4. A MORE SOCIAL EU: RECONFIGURING THE PATCHWORK

Let us first address the issue of how to introduce stronger protections for the core social schemes operating at the national level, enabling them to withstand the destabilizing challenges originating from space B. As is well known, such challenges rest on the strongest base that the EU constitutional framework can offer: primary law, i.e. explicit and binding Treaty clauses on free movement and competition. In order to be effective, the institutional buffers which must be provided by space C should rest on an equally strong legal basis. Identifying these buffers is far from easy and requires a delicate balancing act. However, the general goal is sufficiently clear: the EU constitutional framework (in the wide sense) ought to define the content and the boundaries of 'social protection' explicitly as a distinct and relatively autonomous space, and specify the limits of free movement and competition rules in respect of this space.

Ever since the landmark rulings of the ECJ in the 1990s (especially the *Poucet and Pistre*[20] and *Albany*[21] rulings, which had to adjudicate on some foundational questions regarding the balance between 'opening' and 'closure'),[22] we know that this goal has been on the EU agenda: not only the social agenda, but also the wider agenda of broad institutional reform, and some progress has indeed been made. A detailed reconstruction of the winding road of such progress from the Single European Act to the Lisbon Treaty would fall far beyond the scope of this chapter: let us therefore focus on the latter only.

The Treaty of Lisbon does contain a series of provisions that could significantly strengthen space C and offer a promising basis for a (more) virtuous nesting between social welfare and economic integration. A highly competitive 'social market economy', full employment and social progress have been explicitly included amongst the Union's objectives (Article 3 TEU) – while 'the protection

20 Joined cases C-159/91 and C-160/91 *Christian Poucet v. Assurances Générales de France and Caisse Mutuelle Régionale du Languedoc-Roussillon and Daniel Pistre v. Assurances Générales de France and Caisse Mutuelle Régionale du Languedoc-Roussillon* [1993] ECR I-637 (hereinafter *Poucet and Pistre).*

21 Case C-67/96 *Albany International BV v. Stichting Bedrijfspensioenfonds Textielindustrie* [1999] ECR I-5751 (hereinafter *Albany).*

22 In *Poucet and Pistre* the Court had to establish whether the state monopoly over social insurance in France was legitimate according to EU law. In its ruling the Court found that the freedom of service and competition norms could not be invoked to justify exit from mandatory public insurance schemes. In the *Albany* case the Court had to establish whether a textile company in the Netherlands was obliged to pay the contributions requested by its industrial pension fund, as envisaged by collective agreements. The Court ruled in favour of the pension fund. These cases and the political contexts under which they occurred are reconstructed in detail in M. Ferrera, n. 5.

of undistorted competition' has been omitted from the same article.[23] The coordination of Member States' economic policies and employment policies is now within the sphere of competence of the Union, which allows for the possible coordination of Member States' social policies as well. Fundamental rights have also been explicitly recognized by the Lisbon Treaty through the incorporation of a legally binding reference to the Charter of Fundamental Rights and Freedoms. The latter contains a section on solidarity, which lists a number of rights and principles directly relevant to the social field, such as the right to information and consultation within undertakings, the right to negotiate collective agreements and to take collective action, the right of access to free placement services and protection against unjustified dismissals, and the right to have access to social security and social assistance. With the new Treaty, the EU has also acceded to the European Convention for the Protection of Human Rights and Fundamental Freedoms, which shall constitute general principles of the Union's law (Article 6 TEU).

Possibly the most important innovation of the Lisbon Treaty is however the so-called 'horizontal social clause' (Article 9 TFEU), which states that:

> *'In defining and implementing its policies and activities, the Union shall take into account requirements linked to the promotion of a high level of employment, the guarantee of adequate social protection, the fight against social exclusion, and a high level of education, training and protection of human health.'*

It must be added that two other 'horizontal clauses' (Articles 8 and 10 TFEU) extend the scope of what might be called 'social mainstreaming' to the reduction of inequality and the fight against discrimination.[24] The horizontal clauses and the recognition of fundamental rights mark the appearance within the EU constitutional arena of two potentially strong anchors that can induce and support all EU institutions (including the European Court of Justice) in the task of finding an adequate (and more stable) balance between economic and social objectives. They could also serve to better define and implement the symbolically salient but institutionally ambiguous notion of 'social market economy'.[25]

---

23 This objective is restated, however, by Protocol (No. 27) on the internal market and competition, Consolidated Version of the Treaty on European Union [2010] OJ C83/309.

24 Interestingly, the horizontal social clause did not exist in the Treaty establishing the European Community (TEC), which only dealt with equality between men and women and non-discrimination. Article 9 TFEU thus represents a genuine 'social improvement' achieved during the Intergovernmental Conference, especially in the wake of effective mobilisation of the former members of the Social Europe Working Group of the European Convention (Vandenbroucke, personal communication). It also owes much to the direct efforts of civil society and in particular to EAPN's intervention with the Irish Presidency to highlight the importance of such a clause.

25 Cf. M. Dawson and B. de Witte in this volume.

There are at least two additional provisions of the Treaty which deserve to be highlighted for their 're-bounding' potential. The first is Protocol 26 on services of general interest, included as an annex to the TFEU (especially in the wake of Dutch, French and Belgian pressure). Article 2 of this Protocol explicitly says that 'the provisions of the Treaties do not affect in any way the competence of Member States to provide, commission and organize non-economic services of general interest'. As can be immediately appreciated, this is an important statement, that seems to grant to these services a sort of 'constitutional' immunity from the opening logic of the integration process and in particular from the competition regime that pervades space B. The article is very short and its wording is not very precise. But it introduces for the first time in primary law the notion of 'non-economic services of general interests', presumably of a social nature. As argued by Dawson and de Witte in another chapter of this volume, the 'non-affectation' goal as stated by Article 2 seems wholly unviable (think of non-discrimination provisions: could they be suspended in this sphere? Obviously not.). However, Article 2 can set the stage for the identification of a specific class of 'social services' in respect of which a balancing of competences and objectives must be sought by EU authorities, *in primis* the ECJ: in a number of pre-Lisbon documents[26] the Commission has already suggested that non-economic services of general interest should include, precisely, 'social services', which in turn comprise the institutional core (and also some of the periphery) of national welfare programmes, namely: 1) health care; 2) statutory and complementary social security schemes covering the main risks of life; and 3) personal social services (such as social assistance, employment and training services, social housing, childcare and long term care services).

The second provision of the Lisbon Treaty that deserves to be highlighted is Article 48 TFEU.[27] This article (which in 'euro-treaty' parlance is known as the 'social security emergency brake', a term apparently coined by UK negotiators) recognizes to each Member State the right to suspend the adoption of a legislative proposal related to the social entitlements of migrant persons if its implications are considered to negatively affect 'important aspects of its social security system, including cost, scope, financial balance or structure'. If a Member State requests the suspension, the matter is referred to the European Council where the proposal can be blocked.[28] Under the pre-Lisbon status quo, Member States did

---

26 See in particular European Commission, 'Biennial Report on Social Services of General Interest' SEC (2008) 2179/2.

27 For an in-depth discussion, cf. H. Verschueren, 'The EU Social Security Coordination System: A Close Interplay Between the EU Legislature and Judiciary', in Ph. Syrpis (ed.), *The Judiciary, the Legislature and the EU Internal Market*, Cambridge University Press, Cambridge 2012.

28 The European Council has four months for either referring back the draft legislative proposal to the Council (in which case the ordinary legislative procedure will continue) or requesting

have the possibility of ultimately blocking a proposal in this delicate sphere: the co-decision procedure that regulates legislation on the social security rights of migrants envisaged unanimity for Council decisions. But a blockage that can be exerted (or threatened) at the very beginning of a legislative process – as in the new Article 48 TFEU procedure – is likely to be much more effective than a blockage that is attempted at its very end, possibly after a lengthy and controversial conciliation process between Parliament and Council. Article 48 TFEU is, in other words, a second important innovation of the Lisbon Treaty that puts back into the hands of the nation-state some 'gating' powers in respect of its own sharing spaces and thus strengthens its capacity to respond to the destabilising potential linked – in this case – to free movement provisions.

The new provisions of the Lisbon Treaty will obviously require time, intellectual and political mobilization, litigation and jurisprudence in order to become effective as re-balancing tools. But if we compare the current climate with that which prevailed at the time of the Single European Act (SEA) there are some reasons for moderate optimism about the 'virtuous nesting' scenario outlined in Figure 1. Could more have been achieved with the new Treaty? Certainly, yes: various interesting proposals did in fact emerge during the work of the Convention and the Treaty negotiations (from the constitutionalization of the Open Method of Coordination (OMC) to the introduction of qualified majority voting for the social issues on which the EU has legislative powers). Without entering into the merit of such proposals, it can be generally said that the goal of reaching a full (or at least quasi-full) symmetry between Economic and Social Europe still remains to be attained.[29] For the time being, the best strategy is that of a full exploitation of the existing building blocks for a better balancing. There are three more obvious critical priorities for moving in this direction. The first and possibly top priority has to do with the new 'horizontal social clause' of the Lisbon Treaty, which needs to be clarified in its meaning and scope and made operative as soon as possible, especially by linking it with the already existing

---

the Commission to submit a new proposal (in which case the act originally proposed will be considered as non adopted). There is also a simpler solution for the European Council: 'taking no action', which means that the proposed act falls without the need for further initiatives. This simpler option was not envisaged by the Constitutional Treaty and has been inserted. during the Lisbon negotiations. A declaration agreed by all Member States specifies that the European Council shall decide 'by consensus' in the procedure envisaged by Article 48 TFEU.

29 On the persistent conditions of asymmetry and bold proposals (through political action by the European Council) for breaking the negative integration bias of the EU and in particular the ECJ, see F. Scharpf, n.10. The European Trade Unions have proposed further amending the Lisbon Treaty with a 'Social Progress Protocol' clearly stating that 'Nothing in the Treaties and in particular neither economic freedoms nor competition rules shall have priority over fundamental rights (...). In case of conflict fundamental social rights shall take precedence'. See A. Bückert and W. Warneck, *Viking-Laval-Rüffert: Consequences and Policy Perspectives*, European Trade Union Institute, Brussels 2010, pp. 143–145.

procedural framework for the impact assessment of EU policies (see Box 2). The clause can serve as a leverage for systematically and transversally identifying and, if possible, quantifying, the social impact of all EU policies, thus encouraging (or even making possible) a better balancing.[30]

Box 2: Impact assessment in the EU and the horizontal social clause

2002: The European Commission establishes a new system of integrated Impact Assessment (IA) to consider the effects of policy proposals in their economic, social and environmental dimension
2005: Better Regulation Action Plan, European Strategy for Sustainable Employment and Lisbon Strategy adopt IA
2009: External evaluation of IA → revision of the guidelines and extension of IA to all legislative initiatives
2009: Lisbon Treaty enters into force: horizontal social clause
2010: European Court of Auditors presents own evaluation of IA and recommends enhancement and more publicity
2010: The Belgian Presidency (2nd semester 2010) launches a debate on strengthening the social dimension within the IA in the wake of the new horizontal social clause (→ generating evidence-based knowledge for its systematic implementation)[31]

The second priority is that of working on Article 2 of the Social Protocol and transforming its general principles into more detailed and operational regulations, taking into account all the pertinent articles of the Treaty.[32] The third priority is finally the introduction/strengthening of what might be called the 'social complements' of the internal market,[33] i.e. positive measures that are capable of offsetting the specific negative social implications of free movement and cross-border competition as they clearly manifest themselves (as, for

30 M. Kühnemund, 'Social Impact Assessment as a Tool for Mainstreaming Social Protection and Inclusion Concerns in Public Policy' in E. Marlier and D. Natali (eds.) with R. Van Dam, *Europe 2020. Towards a More Social EU?*, P.I.E. Peter Lang, Brussels 2010.

31 Under the spur of the Belgian Presidency, the EPSCO Council has already started a reflection on strengthening social mainstreaming in the follow up of the Horizontal Social Clause <www.eutrio.be/pressrelease/informal-meeting-epsco-council-social-security-and-social-inclusion> accessed 12 October 2011.

32 See M. Dawson and B. de Witte in this volume for some elaboration on this point. The Social Protection Committee has started to work in this direction as well. See Social Protection Committee, 'A Voluntary European Quality Framework for Social Services' 2010/10/8/ final. In December 2011 the Commission has adopted a communication presenting a Quality Framework for Services of General Interest in Europe. See European Commission 'A Quality framework for Services of General Interest in Europe' (Communication) COM (2011) 900 final.

33 M. Ferrera and S. Sacchi, n.2.

example, in the case of the *Laval*,[34] *Viking*[35] and *Rüffert*[36] rulings of the ECJ, which seem to have challenged three fundamental rights of the modern EU institutional order, i.e. freedom of association, freedom to strike and freedom to establish and enforce collective agreements).[37] Interesting proposals on this front have been recently advanced by Mario Monti's Report on the re-launching of the internal market,[38] especially as regards the posted workers regime and the right to strike (cf. Box 3).[39] It is to be noted that the Monti Report also calls for a strengthening of social evaluation within the European Commission's impact assessment exercises. The Single Market Act adopted by the Commission in April 2011 does contain commitments to move in both directions.[40]

Box 3: Workers' rights in the internal market: Key recommendations of the Monti Report

- Clarify the implementation of the Posting of Workers Directive and strengthen dissemination of information on the rights and obligations of workers and companies, administrative cooperation and sanctions in the framework of free movement of persons and cross-border provision of services.
- If measures are adopted to clarify the interpretation and application of the Posting of Workers Directive, introduce a provision to guarantee the right to strike modelled on Article 2 of Council Regulation (EC) No. 2679/98 and a mechanism for the informal solutions of labour disputes concerning the application of the directive.

34 Case C-341/05 *Laval un Partneri Ltd. V. Svenska Byggnadsarbetareförbundet, Svenska Byggnadsarbetareförbundets avdelning 1, Byggettan and Svenska Elektrikerförbundet* [2007] ECR I-11767 (hereinafter *Laval*).

35 Case C-438/05 *International Transport Workers' Federation and Finnish Seamen's Union v. Viking Line ABP and OÜ Viking Line Eesti* [2007] ECR I-10779 (hereinafter *Viking*).

36 Case C-346/06 *Dirk Rüffert v. Land Niedersachsen* [2008] ECR I-1989 (hereinafter *Rüffert*).

37 See: A. Bückert and W. Warneck, n.29; M. Höpner and A. Schäfer, 'Polanyi in Brussels? Embeddedness and the Three Dimensions of European Economic Integration' (2010) MPIfG Discussion Paper 10/8, Max Planck Institute for the Study of Societies, Cologne <www.mpifg.de/pu/mpifg_dp/dp10-8.pdf> accessed 12 October 2011.

38 M. Monti, 'A New Strategy for the Single Market' (2010) <http://ec.europa.eu/bepa/pdf/monti_report_final_10_05_2010_en.pdf> accessed 12 October 2011.

39 Directive 96/71/EC of the European Parliament and of the Council of 16 December 1996 concerning the posting of workers in the framework of the provision of services [1997] OJ L18/1.; Council Regulation (EC) 2679/98 of 7 December 1998 on the functioning of the internal market in relation to the free movement of goods among the Member States [1998] OJ L337/8.

40 European Commission, 'Single Market Act. Twelve levers to boost growth and strenghten confidence. "Working together to create new growth"' (Communication) COM (2011) 206 final.

But what about the other element of this scenario, i.e. the formation of post-national sharing spaces? On at least two of these fronts some signs of innovation and experimentation are already clearly visible.

As far as transnational sharing spaces are concerned (space A2 in Figure 1), the most significant development is the formation of the so-called 'cross-border institutions for occupational retirement provision' (IORPs).[41] An EU directive adopted in 2003 has laid down the legal framework for the establishment of occupational pension funds covering workers of different Member States.[42] Closely linked, as they are, to contributions, second pillar pension schemes incorporate limited amounts of redistribution and solidarity; nevertheless, they still are, recognizable sharing spaces, with the potential for activating a modicum of 'bonding' among their affiliates. As mentioned, the Commission's doctrine already counts second pillar pension schemes among 'social services of general interest'.[43] A number of cross-border schemes were already operating prior to the 2003 directive, mostly based in the UK. However, the directive has given a significant spur to new establishments of this kind. In the years since the implementation of the directive (which entered into force in 2005), the number of cross-border pension schemes has increased from 9 to 61.[44]

These are very new developments on which reliable data are lacking and empirical research is urgently needed. It would thus be imprudent and unwarranted to make bold evaluative statements. For the time being and for the purposes of this chapter, it is sufficient to conclude that the institutional landscape is in flux, that a new phase of transnational experiments in the field of social protection has clearly dawned and that the EU seems to be providing at least some of the correct incentives and support.

The same holds true for the other front, that of cross-regional experiments providing jointly some types of services (space A3 in the Figure). Here, especially in the wake of the INTERREG initiatives of the European Commission, a growing number of interesting experiences have been taking place during the last fifteen years, in the context of a wider process of sub-nationalization of welfare provision within the domestic arenas and the activation of what has been

---

41 See the chapter of Y. Stevens in this volume.

42 Directive 2003/41/EC of the European Parliament and the Council of 3 June 2003 on the activities and supervision of institutions for occupational retirement provision [2003] OJ L235/10.

43 European Commission, 'Biennial Report on Social Services of General Interest', n. 26.

44 I. Guardiancich, *Report on Cross-Border IORPs: The Implications for the Creation of Pan-European Pension Plans of Directive 2003/41/EC of the European Parliament and of the Council of 3 June 2003 on the Activities and Supervision of Institutions for Occupational Retirement Provision (IORP Directive)*, Department of Labour and Welfare Studies, University of Milan, Mimeo 2009.

called 'competitive region building'.[45] Virtually all these experiences include a social policy component, typically in the field of health, employment or care services and all of them have set up permanent institutional structures for the managing and monitoring of cooperation.[46] Full use should be made of the potential of the European Grouping for Territorial Cooperation (EGTC), a promising instrument aimed at facilitating economic and social cohesion through cross-border, transnational or interregional initiatives.[47] A host of public and non-public actors are allowed to join forces and establish the EGTC through direct agreements, within a general legal framework set up by the EU – a framework which recognizes the legal personality of the 'grouping'. Though not exclusively centred on social sharing objectives, this instrument is likely to encourage the coming together of sub-national territories belonging to different Member States and thus open up channels and opportunities for spatial reconfigurations above and beyond the established boundaries of nation-states – including their social boundaries.[48] The Barca Report on the reform of cohesion policies contains several insights and proposals for 'place-based' measures and incentives that may facilitate this process, with a view to 'socializing' the territorial agenda of the EU as well as 'territorializing' the social agenda.[49] The place based approach may also play an important role for promoting and underpinning sub-national policies and social agendas. The Europe 2020 Strategy should be improved in this respect, as suggested by the Committee of the Regions.[50]

Finally, what about innovation and experimentation on the third front of post-national solidarities (space A4 in the Figure), i.e. supranational sharing schemes

---

45 M. Keating, *The New Regionalism in Western Europe: Territorial Restructuring and Political Change*, Edward Elgar, Cheltenham 1998; N. Mcewen and L. Moreno (eds.), *The Territorial Politics of Welfare*, Routledge, London 2005.

46 F. Pancaldi, 'The Spaces Between. Interregional Cooperation in the EU: Evidence on Cross-border Social Policies' (2010) WP 1/2010 Graduate School of Social, Economic and Political Studies, Milan <www.graduateschool.unimi.it//files/gsseps_wpseries_1_2010_pancaldi_pols.pdf> accessed 12 October 2011.

47 Regulation (EC) No. 1082/2006 of the European Parliament and of the Council of 5 July 2006 on a European grouping of territorial cooperation (EGTC) [2006] OJ L210/19.

48 G. Spinaci and G. Vara-Arribas, 'The European Grouping of Territorial Cooperation (EGTC): New Spaces and Contact for European Integration?' (2009) Eipascope 2009/2, Maastricht <www.eipa.eu/files/repository/eipascope/20100114121643_Eipascope_2009_2_Article1.pdf> accessed 12 October 2011.

49 F. Barca, 'An Agenda for a Reformed Cohesion Policy: A Place-Based Approach to Meeting European Union Challenges and Expectations: Independent Report Prepared at the Request of Danuta Hübner, Commissioner for Regional Policy' (2009) European Commission <http://ec.europa.eu/regional_policy/policy/future/pdf/report_barca_v0306.pdf> accessed 12 October 2011.

50 Committee of the Regions, 'Consultation: Your Voice on Europe 2020: Final Report' (2010) <http://portal.cor.europa.eu/europe2020/news/Documents/Your%20Voice%20on%20Europe%202020%20Final%20Report.pdf> accessed 12 October 2011.

directly anchored to the EU? The last two decades have indeed witnessed an increasingly richer and imaginative debate on possible institutional 'pioneers', such as a pan-European minimum income scheme for the needy (dubbed as Euro-stipendium by Schmitter and Bauer),[51] a child or birth grant payable to all (or needy) newly born Europeans,[52] an 'EU minimum income for children',[53] or the establishment of a supranational social insurance scheme for migrant workers (a proposal originally put forward in the 1970s under the name of '13th state scheme' and recently resurrected by the French debate).[54]

As is known, a number of redistributive funds are already operative at the supranational level for broad social cohesion purposes. None of these funds and programmes qualifies, however, as a genuine pioneer for supranational social sharing. The fault line that needs to be crossed is that which separates forms of territorial or inter-level redistribution from inter-personal redistribution. Even the last addition to the long list of EU 'social policy' funds, the Globalisation Adjustment Fund, has not made this quantum leap, as the Fund does not grant benefits to individual workers, but limits itself to transferring funds to the local-level collective actors that have applied for assistance.[55] Crossing this critical fault line will not be easy from a political and institutional point of view, as witnessed by the experience of all historical federations in the XXth century.[56]

51 P.C. Schmitter and M.W. Bauer, 'A (Modest) Proposal for Expanding Social Citizenship in the European Union' (2001) 1 *Journal of European Social Policy (JESP).*

52 The proposal to establish an EU Capital Grant for Youth was presented by Julian Le Grand at a seminar of the Group of Social Policy Advisors to the European Commission, held in Brussels on 8 September 2006. See L. Barrington-Leach, M. Canoy, A. Hubert and F. Lerais, 'Investing in Youth: An Empowerment Strategy' (2007) European Commission, Bureau of European Policy Advisers <http://ec.europa.eu/dgs/policy_advisers/publications/docs/Investing_in_Youth_25_April_fin.pdf> accessed 12 October 2011.

53 A.B. Atkinson, and E. Marlier, 'Income and Living Conditions in Europe' in A.B. Atkinson and E. Marlier (eds.), *Income and Living Conditions in Europe*, Office for Official Publications of the European Communities (OPOCE), Luxembourg 2010.

54 On the French debate see A. Lamassoure, *Le Citoyen et l'application du droit communautaire*, La Documentation Française, Paris 2008. The Monti report discusses this proposal in respect of occupational pensions and health insurance schemes: 'The Commission should prioritise the issue of obstacles to transnational labour mobility in its forthcoming consultation on the pensions systems in Europe. In this context, an option to explore would be to develop a 28th regime for supplementary pension rights. This would be a regime entirely set by EU rules but existing in parallel to national rules, and thus optional for companies and workers. A worker opting for this regime would be subject to the same rules for its non-statutory benefits wherever it goes in Europe. To make things easier, a sub-option would be to limit the possibility to opt in this regime only to workers taking up their first work contract. This would serve as an incentive for the mobility of certain young workers, who are the keenest on international mobility.', M. Monti, n.38, p. 57.

55 K. Novaczek, 'The European Globalization Adjustment Fund: A Social Pilot Project between Political and Economic Realms' (2007) 1 *European Governance*, pp. 21–24 <www.urge.it/files/socialeuropeissues1.pdf> accessed 12 October 2011.

56 H. Obinger, S. Leibfried and F. Castles (eds.), *Federalism and the Welfare State: New World and European Experiences*, Cambridge University Press, Cambridge 2005.

A more realistic medium-term target for the consolidation of the EU's social space could be the strengthening of binding regulatory standards and possibly the establishment of some 'social snakes' (to use the jargon of the 1970s and 1980s)[57] forcing the Member States to loosely align themselves to a European 'norm' regarding certain areas of social protection – social inclusion in particular.[58] The setting of precise and measurable targets within the Social OMCs (a goal that has already been on the agenda for some time)[59] could be the first concrete step in this direction, in the wider framework of the newly launched Europe 2020 Strategy.

5. EUROPE 2020 AND ITS INSTITUTIONAL POTENTIAL

Europe 2020 must certainly be appreciated as a promising governance tool for the strategy of institutional reconciliation discussed in the previous section. A number of critics at both national and supranational level have already started to dismiss it as 'cheap talk', taking it for granted that it is doomed to the same destiny of (alleged) failure of its soft and wet predecessor, the Lisbon Strategy.[60] As noted by a number of authors,[61] such sweeping negative judgements are largely unwarranted: programmatic pessimism is itself 'cheap'. To begin with, significant empirical evidence signals that the Lisbon Strategy has not been a failure, even acknowledging its many shortcomings and limitations, especially in respect of its over-ambitious original goals. The impact of Lisbon is clearly also detectable with regard to employment and social objectives.[62] More importantly, Europe 2020 does contain some significant improvements compared to Lisbon on the specific front which interests us, namely the relationship between Economic and Social EU.

First, there is improvement at the ideational level (which is anything but 'cheap' in political matters). As it clearly emerges from all the 'soft' and 'hard' acts that have launched the new strategy, its overall blueprint for a 'smart, sustainable and inclusive growth' offers a wealth of normative and functional justifications for

---

57 F. Pennings, *Introduction to European Social Security Law*, Kluwer, The Hague 2001.

58 H. Verschueren, n. 27.

59 See Commission Recommendation 2008/867/EC of 3 October 2008 on the active inclusion of people excluded from the labour market [2008] OJ L307/11.

60 A good source for the Europe 2020 debate is Euroarchiv <www.euractiv.com> accessed 12 October 2011.

61 D. Natali, 'The Lisbon Strategy, Europe 2020 and the Crisis in Between' in E. Marlier and D. Natali (eds.) with R. Van Dam, n.30.

62 J. Zeitlin, and M. Heidenreich (eds.), *Changing European Employment and Welfare Regimes: The Influence of the Open Method of Coordination on National Reforms*, Routledge, London 2009.

both the protection ('nesting', in our language) and the ameliorative recalibration of the nation-based welfare state. In line with a vast literature, we have noted above that welfare programmes are in urgent need of modernization and updating in the wake of the changed structure of risks and needs (in particular demographic ageing). Three out of the seven so-called flagship initiatives ('Youth on the move', an 'Agenda for skill and jobs', and in particular the 'European platform against poverty') of Europe 2020 are geared towards this task and, if correctly developed and articulated, can provide precious ideational resources for national 'puzzling' around welfare reform. A significant step forward in respect of Lisbon is that the Europe 2020 Integrated Guidelines for the annual cycles of the strategy will integrate the economic policy and the employment policy dimensions and – via the latter – the social policy dimension as well. Guideline 10 is entirely devoted to 'promoting social inclusion and combating poverty', with the headline target that will consist of 'promoting social inclusion, in particular through the reduction of poverty by aiming to lift at least 20 million people out of the risk of poverty and exclusion' (based on three indicators: poverty risk, severe material deprivation and very low work attachment).[63] Needless to say, the ideational component of Europe 2020 will be able to make a difference only if accompanied by a deliberate strategy of both 'communicative' and 'coordinative' discourses on the part of EU institutions, the Commission in particular.[64] The proposal of launching a Social Investment Pact, through which Member States would take credible commitments to implement the social dimension of the strategy – within the budgetary constrains of the Growth and Stability Pact – goes precisely in this direction.[65]

Second, there is improvement at the practical, operational level. The addition of 'thematic coordination' to the overall governance of the strategy (i.e. focused monitoring on growth enhancing reforms, including welfare state modernization, with the possibility of issuing recommendations based on Article 148 TFEU not only on employment but also 'other selected thematic issues', presumably including social policies), the launch of the European Semester, the institutional re-location and procedural refinement of the Social OMC: these are all promising

63 The significance of this guideline is discussed in M. Daly, 'Assessing the EU Approach to Combating Poverty and Social Exclusion in the Last Decade' and H. Frazer, E. Malier, 'Strengthening Social Inclusion in the Europe 2020 Strategy by Learning from the Past' in E. Marlier and D. Natali (eds.) with R. Van Dam, n. 30; on the issues raised by targets, see also R. Walker, 'The Potential of Eurotargets: Reflecting on French Experience', in *Ibid.*

64 According to Vivien Schmidt, discourse is the interactive process of conveying ideas throughout a political system. It comes in two forms: the coordinative discourse among policy actors and the communicative discourse between political actors and the public. See: V. Schmidt, *Democracy in Europe*, Oxford University Press, Oxford 2006.

65 A. Hemerijck, B. Palier and F. Vandenbroucke, 'The EU Needs a Social Investment Pact' (2011) Observatoire Social Europeen, Opinion papers no. 5 <www.ose.be/files/OpinionPaper5_Vandenbroucke-Hemerijk-Palier_2011.pdf> accessed 12 October 2011.

innovations that can contribute to a more effective 'nested' delivery of the strategy's array of policies. It is to be noted that the horizontal social clause has already played a role in fostering and underpinning the operational definition of Europe 2020, especially as regards the enhancement of horizontal coordination and mainstreaming of the Lisbon common social objectives – which will be hopefully firmed up and articulated through pertinent indicators.

Referring back to Figure 1: Europe 2020 does seem to have a promising institutional potential for steering the Union's architecture towards a more virtuous nesting, both between nation-based welfare and its wider supranational spaces and between space B (Economic Europe) and space C (Social Europe). Acknowledging the potential of Europe 2020 does not mean, of course, that the strategy has no weaknesses – both substantive and procedural – that ought to be addressed (as recommended by the various chapters of this volume). With appropriate 'institutional gardening' in the years to come, coupled with some political ambition, imagination, and consensus-building, Europe 2020's social agenda could be used to lay the conditions not only for creating a somewhat stringent social snake binding Member States to remain within certain quantitative 'bands' after reaching the headline targets (e.g. in terms of social inclusion levels) but also for establishing a fully fledged 'EU system of social protection' consisting of coordinated and correctly nested national, sub-national and post-national sharing spaces.

6. CONCLUSION

The national welfare state and the EU are probably the most salient and distinctive institutional legacies that the XXth century has bequeathed to our continent: two institutions that have given an invaluable contribution to enriching and expanding the life chances of millions of ordinary people, in a context of economic growth, social security, cohesion and peace. However, the XXIst century has opened with some turbulence and tension regarding, precisely, the mutual relationship between these two institutions. As argued in this chapter, this tension ought to (and can) be contained. The search for a strategy of institutional reconciliation must become a top priority for the political agenda and the most promising point of departure should be a rapid definitional and procedural 'operationalization' of the horizontal social clause, in parallel with a cleared definition of the scope and legal implications of Article 2 of the Protocol on services of general interest. The challenge ahead of us is that of imagining and then engaging in the actual construction of a recognizable EU social model: not just and generically 'European', but a distinctive 'EU' social model, resting on a well-designed and protective nesting of social sharing goals and practices (including nation-based practices) within the overall legal framework of the Union and the symbolic framework of the 'social market economy'. The prime institutional rationale behind this new model should be that of promoting a virtuous and dynamic balance between the logic of opening and the logic of closure, in order to effectively underpin the self-sustaining production of both individual opportunities and social 'bonds', i.e. the two sides of life chances European style.

THE EU LEGAL FRAMEWORK OF SOCIAL INCLUSION AND SOCIAL PROTECTION: BETWEEN THE LISBON STRATEGY AND THE LISBON TREATY

Mark DAWSON and Bruno DE WITTE

1. INTRODUCTION

The European Union decided to designate 2010 as the 'European Year for Combating Poverty and Social Exclusion',[1] which indicates, at the very least, that combating poverty and social exclusion is seen as a common European endeavour, and that the European Union has a meaningful role to play in that context. Yet, it is far from clear whether the European Union possesses the legal resources needed to promote social inclusion and guarantee social protection in its Member States. For many critical observers, EU law has an incurable social deficit, and only a complete renegotiation of the EU Treaties could genuinely allow for the development of a Social Europe, or at least for the protection of the national welfare systems from the onslaught of European market fundamentalism.[2] At the other end of the ideological spectrum, it is thought that EU law tends to impose on the Member States an avalanche of costly bureaucratic obligations in the social sphere, which should be resisted by all available means – for example by the negotiation of a treaty protocol seeking to exclude the domestic enforcement of the social rights chapter of the EU Charter of Fundamental Rights in the United Kingdom.

In this paper, we propose to discuss the legal resources currently offered by EU law to combat social exclusion and to offer social protection (using the broad definitions of those concepts proposed by the organizers of the conference preceding this book). We believe the current EU Treaty framework to be

1 Decision No. 1098/2008 of the European Parliament and of the Council of 22 October 2008 on the European Year for Combating Poverty and Social Exclusion (2010) [2008] OJ L298/20.

2 This criticism of the European Union, and of EU law, is particularly widespread in France. See, for an elaborate argument in this sense, F. DENORD and A. SCHWARTZ, *L'Europe sociale n'aura pas lieu*, Raisons d'agir, Paris 2009.

unbalanced: it now recognizes (particularly after the enactment of the Lisbon Treaty) that social inclusion and social protection are fundamental values, and that their preservation and development is a matter of common concern; but it does not provide the EU institutions with the concrete tools to pursue that common concern effectively. Partly because of this, the political and judicial institutions of the European Union tend to give secondary importance, or sometimes mere lip-service, to those social objectives.

We are not the first to note that, when examining the EU legal framework of social inclusion and social protection, one is likely to move 'from Lisbon to Lisbon'.[3] On the one side, the Lisbon Strategy, inaugurated in 2000 and recently revamped, has made national policies for social inclusion and social protection a matter of quasi-legal European coordination by means of the Open Method of Coordination (section 2 of this paper). On the other side, the Lisbon Treaty, which entered into force in December 2009, but has its origins in the early years of the decade, introduces a new language of social inclusion and protection in the founding Treaties which may have an impact on the role of the European Union institutions in these fields (section 3).

In this chapter we do not propose to examine the important indirect ways in which EU law impinges on national systems of social protection and social exclusion: namely, by requiring the equal treatment of EU citizens or, to some extent, by giving long-residing third-country nationals access to social security and social assistance in various forms; or by prohibiting discrimination on grounds of race and ethnic origin in social protection systems. The impact of EU law, in both cases, is not on the substance of social protection regimes, but on the range of its beneficiaries.[4] While this phenomenon has been studied by a rich literature on the implications of free movement principles for the welfare state,[5] it will not be our central concern in this chapter. Nor shall we examine the Union's competence to pursue social inclusion policies under the heading of

---

3 See K. Armstrong, *Governing Social Inclusion: Europeanization through Policy Coordination,* Oxford University Press, Oxford 2010, title of Chapter 7: 'From Lisbon to Lisbon: Europeanization through Constitutionalism'.

4 Admittedly, a major extension of the range of beneficiaries may, in some cases, put the social protection scheme under pressure and therefore indirectly lead to substantive changes of that regime.

5 See, among many other contributions: M. Dougan, 'The Spatial Restructuring of National Welfare States within the European Union: The Contribution of Union Citizenship and the Relevance of the Treaty of Lisbon' in U. Neergaard, R. Nielsen and L. Roseberry (eds.), *Integrating Welfare Functions into EU Law: From Rome to Lisbon,* DJØF Publishing, Copenhagen 2009; L. Roseberry, 'The Integration of Welfare Functions into EU Law through the Principle of Non-Discrimination and the Consequences for Third-Country Nationals' in *Ibid.*; H. Verschueren, 'European (Internal) Migration Law as an Instrument for Defining the Boundaries of National Solidarity Systems' (2007) 9 *European Journal of Migration and Law (EJML).*

'action to combat discrimination' in the sense of Article 19 TFEU, for example with regard to Roma communities.

Instead, the aim of this chapter is to explore and compare the innovations for EU law and policy brought about by the evolution of the overarching frameworks created by the Lisbon Strategy and the Lisbon Treaty respectively. Our hope is that by questioning both the goals for social protection and inclusion created by these twin frameworks, and the underlying mechanisms and instruments available to achieve them, we can shed light on the future place and role of social protection and inclusion policy in the EU from a legal perspective. As the chapter will finally conclude (section 4), while the Strategy on the one hand, and the Treaty on the other, have often been seen as distinct and separate structures, they share at least one thing in common – a significant discord between the social goals they set out, and the mechanisms they put in place to realize those goals practically. This leaves social protection and inclusion policy in the EU in an unusual position when compared to the EU's other objectives – it often operates not as a free-standing set of values, but instead as a set of considerations intended to inform and influence *other* fields of EU policy.

2. SOCIAL INCLUSION AND SOCIAL PROTECTION UNDER THE LISBON STRATEGY

2.1. SOCIAL EUROPE UNDER THE LISBON STRATEGY

While the language of social inclusion is by now included within the Treaties themselves, it is really the 'other' Lisbon – the strategy announced by the Lisbon European Council in March 2000 – that has done the most to place social inclusion issues at the heart of the EU's policy agenda. The Spring Council of that year was dominated by the launching of the Lisbon Strategy – a central 'blueprint' for EU policymaking in the next decade. The strategy had three central goals – to construct a knowledge-based economy in Europe; to close the Union's growth gap towards its main economic competitors; and finally – and for our purposes most importantly – to 'modernize the European Social Model, investing in people and combating social exclusion.'[6]

The Lisbon Council's fame emerges not just from these substantive goals but from the specific machinery put in place to deliver them. As social inclusion issues were primarily a national – or even regional competence – EU action was to be guided by a multilateral 'Open Method of Coordination', in which Member

[6] European Council, 'Presidency Conclusions', 23–24 March 2000, <http://www.europarl.europa.eu/summits/lis1_en.htm> accessed 25 August 2011, at [5].

States were to report on social reforms undertaken at the national level.[7] The role of the EU – in the context of complex welfare policies – was not to create a legislative framework for social inclusion from the top down, but an environment for mutual learning (through EU committees) and a set of incentives (via funding for transnational NGOs and networks) through which common social inclusion and social protection objectives could be elaborated. The promise of the OMC itself – as an instrument designed to provide a 'social dimension' to the EU's activities where legislative harmonization was impossible – led many to conclude that Lisbon was a social 'leap forward' for the Union. Was this, as one influential commentator put it, Europe's 'Maastricht for welfare'?[8]

Scepticism about the depth of Lisbon's social commitments, however, was significant.[9] It has only increased as the strategy has undertaken further reform. The first main concern regarding the strategy's ability to advance social inclusion goals has centred on the relationship between social inclusion and the strategy's other main objectives. During its mid-term review in 2004 by the Dutch Premier, Wim Kok, the strategy was heavily criticized for being about 'everything and thus nothing'.[10] The solution, Kok argued, was to 're-focus' the strategy along a central guiding arc. This would be delivered through joining the EU's fiscal and employment strategies into a singular 'strategy for jobs and growth'. Alongside this central strategy, separate coordination processes in health, pensions and social inclusion were also to be consolidated into an overarching OMC for social inclusion and social protection (OMC SPSI). The down-sizing of social inclusion – from a separate multi-lateral process, to a smaller part of an ancillary strategy – was seen by many as a betrayal of Lisbon's original design.[11] Social inclusion

---

7 *Ibid.* at [37].

8 M. Rhodes, 'Lisbon: Europe's Maastricht for Welfare?' (2000) 13 *ECSA (European Community Studies Association) Review* <http://aei.pitt.edu/7485/1/2000_V13_3.pdf> accessed 25 August 2011.

9 See e.g. M. Daly, 'Whither EU Social Policy? An Account and Assessment of Developments in the Lisbon Social Inclusion Process' (2007) 37 *Journal of Social Policy*; D. Chalmers and M. Lodge, 'The Open Method of Coordination and the European Welfare State' (2003) *Economic and Social Research Centre (ESRC) for Risk and Regulation Studies Discussion Papers* 11 <http://eprints.lse.ac.uk/35993/1/Disspaper11.pdf> accessed 25 August 2011.

10 'Facing the Challenge: The Lisbon Strategy for Growth and Employment', Report from the High Level Group Chaired by Wim Kok, November 2004, p. 16, <http://ec.europa.eu/research/evaluations/pdf/archive/fp6-evidence-base/evaluation_studies_and_reports/evaluation_studies_and_reports_2004/the_lisbon_strategy_for_growth_and_employment__report_from_the_high_level_group.pdf> accessed 25 August 2011.

11 See e.g. the EMCO/SPC Joint Opinion on the Kok report as a contribution to the mid-term review of the Lisbon Strategy <http://ec.europa.eu/social/keyDocuments.jsp?pager.offset=10&langId=en&mode=advancedSubmit&policyArea=0&subCategory=0&year=0&country=0&type=46> accessed 25 August 2011; EAPN, 'The Kok report ignores the commitment to eradicate poverty and exclusion' <www.eapn.eu/index.php?option=com_content&view=article&id=521%3Apress-release-lisbon-strategy-the-kok-report-ignores-the-commitment-to-eradicate-poverty-and-exclusion&catid=7%3Apress-releases&Itemid=100002&lang=en> accessed 25 August 2011.

was no longer part of three mutually supporting pillars but potentially subordinated to a new master narrative, focused on 'growth and jobs alone'.

The second main concern regarding the strategy from a social perspective was not the sidelining of social inclusion issues, but the decision to focus on 'soft law' as the primary mechanism to deliver them. Whereas previous EU efforts to provide the Union with a social dimension – such as its doomed 'Social Action Programme' in the 1970s – envisaged binding social commitments for the Member States, the OMC offered only soft 'recommendations' and mutual learning. What about those states that refused to 'learn'?[12] Rather than create a better balance between the EU's social and economic dimensions, the weakness of the OMC in the face of the 'hard' rules of the internal market would always, sceptics insisted, lead to a priority for the latter over the former.[13] The message was re-enforced by the Kok report itself, which lambasted the OMC for contributing to the strategy's significant 'implementation gap'. Even if Lisbon still carried forward social inclusion and protection objectives through the OMC SPSI, what did this mean when states were not obliged to follow them?

2.2. THE OMC FOR SOCIAL INCLUSION AND SOCIAL PROTECTION – EMPIRICAL STRENGTHS AND WEAKNESSES

This scepticism over the use of the OMC to deliver robust social inclusion and protection policies has been re-enforced by empirical work; work which also points to many of the advantages for social inclusion and protection policies that the creation of the OMC has borne.[14] On the positive side of the coin, the experience of the OMC SPSI seems to suggest some concrete benefits for EU

---

12 C. Offe, 'The European Model of "Social" Capitalism: Can It Survive European Integration?' (2003) 11 *European Journal of Political Philosophy*, pp. 462–466.

13 On this 'paper tiger' objection to OMC methods, see A. Heritier, 'New Modes of Governance in Europe: Policy-Making without Legislating?' in A. Heritier (ed.), *Common Goods: Reinventing European and International Governance*, Rowman and Littlefield, Lanham 2002; F. Scharpf, 'The European Social Model: Coping with the Challenges of Diversity' (2002) 40 *JCMS*.

14 The observations below are based on the PhD thesis of one of the co-authors: see M. Dawson, *New Governance and the Transformation of European Law: Coordinating EU Social Law and Policy*, Cambridge University Press, Cambridge 2011. Its conclusions should be understood, however, in light of other empirical work, see e.g. A. Heritier and M. Rhodes (eds.), *New Modes of Governance in Europe: Governing in the Shadow of Hierarchy*, Palgrave, Basingstoke 2010; J. Zeitlin and P. Pochet (eds.), *The Open Method of Coordination in Action: The European Employment and Social Inclusion Strategies*, P.I.E. Peter Lang, Brussels 2005. See also, the essays in S. Kröger (ed.), 'What We Have Learnt: Advances, Pitfalls and Remaining Questions in OMC Research' (2009) 13 *European Integration online Papers (EIoP)*, Special Issue 1 <http://eiop.or.at/eiop/index.php/eiop/issue/view/21> accessed 25 August 2011.

social inclusion policy in its development. In many countries, for example, social inclusion issues have been placed on the national agenda for the first time.[15] In others, states have shifted towards a common 'multi-dimensional' view of the *causes and nature* of social exclusion, with poverty seen not only in monetary terms, but as requiring a broad societal response, incorporating proactive health, housing, employment and social assistance policies.[16] Finally, the OMC SPSI has given many social actors, such as NGOs, a right of 'structural entry' into national discussions previously closed off to them, or allowed them – through EU programmes such as the PROGRESS fund – to form into pan-European networks able to lobby for policy changes at EU and national levels.[17]

For all these benefits, however, the OMC's operation in the social inclusion domain thus far also points to important deficits. Firstly, while the ability of EU targets and objectives to influence national policy depends on governments willing to take EU norms seriously, there is evidence to suggest that national reports under the OMC have often served merely a 'dissemination' function, listing national reforms, but rarely serving as an engine of change for the domestic policy agenda.[18] The problem may be exacerbated by the OMC's participative shortcomings. While anti-poverty policy is primarily a regional or local competence in many Member States, national reporting has most often been conducted at a federal level, with regional authorities shut out.[19] The exclusion of the very authorities with the power and authority to *implement* the Lisbon Strategy's most important social objectives has brought into question the ability of EU coordination to provide a 'common frame of reference' for national social inclusion and protection policies.

---

15 See e.g. M. Dawson, n. 14, pp. 184–185; M. Büchs and D. Friedrich, 'Surface Integration: The National Action Plans for Employment and Social Inclusion in Germany' in J. Zeitlin and P. Pochet (eds.), n. 14, p. 267.

16 See e.g. M. Dawson, n. 14, pp. 181–184; S. Bernhard, 'The European Paradigm of Social Exclusion' (2006) 2 *Journal of Contemporary European Research*.

17 See e.g. M. Dawson, n. 14, pp. 197–201; J. Zeitlin, 'The Open Method of Coordination in Action: Theoretical Promise, Empirical Realities, Reform Strategy' in J. Zeitlin and P. Pochet (eds.), n. 14, pp. 468–470; K. Armstrong, 'The Europeanization of Social Exclusion: British Adaptation to EU Co-ordination' (2006) 8 *British Journal of Politics and International Relation*, pp. 90–91.

18 See as an example, the assessment of the Lisbon 2020 evaluation document – 'while the OMC can be used as a source of peer pressure and a forum for sharing good practice, evidence suggests that in fact most Member States have used OMCs as a reporting device rather than one of policy development'. European Commission, 'Lisbon Strategy evaluation document' (Staff Working Document) SEC (2010) 114 final, p. 21. See also, M. Dawson, n. 14, pp. 230–233; M. Bűchs and D. Friedrich, n.15, pp. 258–259.

19 S. Krőger, 'When Learning Hits Politics or: Social Policy Coordination Left to the Administrations and the NGOs?' (2006) 10 *EIoP* <http://eiop.or.at/eiop/index.php/eiop/article/view/2006_003a/17> accessed 25 August 2011, pp. 6–9; M. Dawson, 'EU Law "Transformed"? Evaluating Accountability and Subsidiarity in a "Streamlined" OMC for Social Inclusion and Social Protection' in S. Krőger (ed.), n. 14.

Finally, there is evidence to suggest that the OMC SPSI has been placed in a secondary position when compared to other objectives, such as the economic goals pursued under the 'integrated guidelines' for jobs and growth. While these guidelines, for example, are supposed to 'feed into' and reflect upon social inclusion objectives there is scant evidence of them doing so.[20] As noted by one key EU-level anti-poverty organization, EAPN:

> *'While it is clear that the economic and employment processes, whether "wrapped" in the national reform programme or not, dominate and constrain the social processes (feeding in)(...) there is little evidence of poverty proofing of strategies or measures in other dimensions of the Lisbon process (feeding out).'*[21]

This final deficit has led to a common perception among social actors that Lisbon is primarily about growth, with social protection systems considered relevant only in so far as they can be re-calibrated to support further growth in the future.[22] These empirical findings suggest that while concrete benefits have been derived from the OMC's emergence in the social inclusion and protection domains, its impact has been ambiguous. Many of the early criticisms of the Lisbon Strategy – that its instruments were either too weak to effectuate meaningful policy change, or left social inclusion too closely tied to broader economic objectives – seem to have been re-enforced as the strategy has developed.

2.3. SOCIAL INCLUSION AND SOCIAL PROTECTION UNDER THE RENEWED 'LISBON 2020' STRATEGY

These are the challenges which faced the EU institutions when considering what shape a 'renewed' strategy for 2010 to 2020 should take. As recognized by its evaluation document, the new 2020 strategy faced two important quandaries.[23] Firstly, how could Lisbon 2020 address the criticism that the original strategy had failed to achieve its core objectives because of a strong 'implementation' deficit, in which its main coordination instruments were simply too weak (e.g. to encourage national governments to take EU objectives seriously)? Secondly, while the original strategy, as seen above, had been criticized by social actors for

---

20 See Social Protection Committee, 'The Mutual Interaction between the Common Social Objectives and the Integrated Guidelines for Jobs and Growth' (2007) (Report) <http://ec.europa.eu/employment social/spsi/docs/social protection commitee/2007/spc en.pdf> accessed 25 August 2011. See also, M. Dawson, 'The Ambiguity of Social Europe in the Open Method of Coordination' (2009) 34 *European Law Review (EL Rev).*

21 EAPN, 'The 2006–2008 National Reports on Strategies for Social Protection and Social Inclusion: What Do They Deliver for People in Poverty?' (2006), p. 23.

22 See e.g. EAPN, 'Making Lisbon Deliver for People Experiencing Poverty: EAPN Response to 2006 Implementation Reports on the National Reform Programs' (2007), p. 3; C. Offe, n. 12.

23 See European Commission, n. 18, p. 3.

containing a liberal or pro-growth bias, the economic crisis also prompted a wave of concerns among national governments for ballooning public deficits (which could prompt speculation over the future of the euro).[24] The crucial question arose of how the strategy could be substantively 're-balanced' to take account of social and environmental concerns.

Along both dimensions, the new strategy agreed in June 2010 was cautious in its outlook.[25] The most daring suggestions – for example, the idea of the Spanish Prime Minister that financial sanctions could be applied to those states that failed to meet common targets, or even that well-performing states could take a bigger slice of cohesion or structural funding – were quickly rejected.[26] The main instruments used to deliver the strategy would remain open coordination mechanisms – in particular, the 'national reform programmes', where national governments annually report on domestic efforts to meet EU targets. While coercive penalties for breach of the stability and growth pact were beefed-up, the most that under-performing states could expect to receive from the EU-level for failing to meet their 2020 poverty or other targets was a 'policy warning'. One wonders what the consequences, in practical terms, of a failure to heed such a warning will be (presumably yet another warning!).

The main reform in the 2020 proposals was a shift in the actors responsible for monitoring the strategy's delivery. While in the early stages of the EU's governance debate, the Commission was keen to retain full ownership of Lisbon, the Commission used the strategy's 2020 review to insist that 'the European Council will have full ownership, and be the focal point, of the new strategy'.[27] Faced with criticisms under the first strategy that the Commission had made itself responsible for the achievement of targets that could only be delivered at the national level, the Commission used the 2020 revision to loosen the chain of responsibility for policy delivery hanging from its own neck.

As part of this, the new strategy supplements EU-wide targets with specific national targets. Overall EU targets were to be broken down into national goals, ensuring that each Member State took its own share of responsibility for the performance of the whole. While this move may seem sensible – given the

---

24 European Council, 'Presidency Conclusions', 17 June 2010, EUCO 13/10.

25 For a more in-depth examination of the new strategy, see M. Dawson, 'Learning from Past Failures? New Governance in the European Union from Lisbon 2000 to Lisbon 2020' (2010) 17 *Maastricht Journal of European and Comparative Law*.

26 Prime Minister Jose Luis Zapatero had argued that a robust strategy 'must include, in my opinion, incentive measures and, if advisable, introduce corrective measures (…) we need to make sure each Member State has a binding incentive'. Quoted at <www.europeanvoice.com/article/imported/2020-vision/66873.aspx> accessed 25 August 2011.

27 European Commission, 'Europe 2020: A Strategy for Smart, Sustainable and Inclusive Growth' (Communication) COM (2010) 2020 (hereinafter Lisbon 2020), p. 4.

strategy's deep penetration into areas of national competence – when the European Council met to discuss the Commission's proposal, the Member States insisted that they should set their own targets 'according to their national decision-making procedures'.[28] If one of the primary goals of the target setting proposal was to increase the accountability of national policy – creating independent and ambitious goals for each Member State to achieve – the clear ability of the Member States to define their own targets may be a cause for significant scepticism. To what extent can states create meaningful and accountable targets *for themselves*; targets ambitious enough to help the strategy overcome the implementation gap of its predecessor?

A similarly cautious approach applied to the second area of change – the substantive orientation of the new strategy. On the face of it, Lisbon 2020's reforms along its 'social dimension' are much more ambitious. On top of the original strategy's commitment to raising the overall employment rate, the 2020 strategy included for the first time an explicit EU-wide poverty target – to lift 20 million individuals across the EU out of poverty by 2020.[29] The new strategy also addressed the concern that Lisbon had become too growth centric by re-establishing the strategy's original 3-pillar structure. The new strategy has three guiding arcs – of inclusive, sustainable and smart growth – supplanting the old strategy's focus on 'growth and jobs' with an emphasis on making economic growth sustainable in economic and environmental terms. This includes – within the 'inclusive growth' pillar – a specific 'flagship programme on poverty', which is to include allocating EU structural and cohesion funding to better target the least advantaged, as well as assessments of the adequacy of pension and social security systems for the socially excluded.[30]

For all this initial promise, however, there remain good reasons to be sceptical towards the ability of Lisbon 2020 to transform the standing of social inclusion and anti-poverty policies in the EU. The 20 million target was only agreed after significant disagreement between the Member States over the suitability of a target in a field controlled largely by the Member States forced the issue to be decided at a later Council meeting. The 20 million goal eventually agreed to was in fact lower than the target originally proposed by the Commission, which involved cutting by 25% the number of Europeans 'at risk of Poverty' by 2020 (a significantly more ambitious objective).[31]

---

28 European Council, 'Presidency Conclusions', 25 March 2010, EUCO 7/10 at [5].

29 European Council, 'Presidency Conclusions', 17 June 2010, EUCO 13/10 at [12].

30 See on this, the specific measures proposed in the European Commission, 'The European Platform Against Poverty and Social Exclusion: A European framework for social and territorial cohesion' (Communication) SEC (2010) 1564 final.

31 This standard measurement used in the context of the OMC SPSI measures the number of households holding an income below 60% of the national median. See the Social Protection

More seriously, the strategy did little to address the myriad shortcomings of the instruments used to deliver Lisbon's objectives, particularly its open coordination mechanisms. The ties between the fiscal and employment coordination strategies and the OMC SPSI – criticized, as noted above, as subordinating social policies by many social NGOs – were re-enforced in the new strategy with the Commission calling for an integrated national response, in which budgetary, economic and social policies were closely aligned, and reported upon simultaneously.[32] Furthermore, the Commission and European Council have little to offer as regards addressing the participative shortcomings of the OMC. In its Communication on Lisbon 2020, the Commission simply stated that 'all national, regional and local authorities should *implement* the [Lisbon] partnership, closely associating parliaments, as well as social partners and representatives of civil society'.[33] This token gesture mirrors a concern long held by local actors in the OMC SPSI – they are seen as useful instruments in *implementing* the strategy's goals, but at the same time, have no real say in how the overall *objectives* or substantive orientation of the strategy are framed. To this extent, the substantive reforms made by the new strategy – including in areas directly related to social inclusion – can too easily be read as empty gestures; there are both few changes in the governance structures through which social inclusion is to be monitored in the EU and a distinct lack of detail over how the weaknesses of the old Lisbon Strategy are to be addressed in the future.

2.4. LISBON AND THE LAW – AN OPPORTUNITY MISSED?

For a paper that is ostensibly about the legal framework for social inclusion and protection policies in the EU, the account above gives very little indication of the legal dimension to EU social policy under the Lisbon Strategy. This lack of attention to the law is unwarranted for at least two reasons. Firstly, the Lisbon 2020 framework – unlike its predecessor – goes to some lengths to resuscitate a strong 'legal dimension' to its policymaking framework. Much of the Commission's discussion in its 2020 communication is on the single market, where the full toolbox of traditional legal instruments applies.[34] Law – even in its most harmonizing and hierarchical forms – is seen as a crucial element to making the new strategy deliver. Secondly, this renewed respect for the law

---

Committee, 'Portfolio of Over-arching Indicators in the Streamlined Social Inclusion, Pensions and Health Portfolios' (Report) D(2006), p. 17. On the original target, see European Commission, n. 27, p. 3.

32 One positive development here may be the specific inclusion of a new 'integrated guideline' (no. 10) on 'promoting social inclusion and combating poverty'. On the integration of the OMC SPSI within the Lisbon framework, see European Commission, n. 30, p. 18.

33 European Commission, n. 27, p. 27 (authors' emphasis added). A similar rather non-descript commitment to civil society is given by the European Council, n. 29, at [6].

34 European Commission, n. 27, pp. 18–19.

should be seen in the context of an increasing recognition among academics and policymakers that even 'soft' or non-binding OMC mechanisms often rely upon a surrounding infrastructure of 'hard' legal rules in order to be effective.[35] A prime example of this is employment, where the multiple references in the strategy – and in the central 'integrated guidelines for jobs and growth' – to anti-discrimination goals is also legally enforced through horizontal directives outlawing discrimination on a number of enumerated grounds.[36] The level of interaction between Lisbon's policymaking instruments and conventional forms of 'hard law' illustrates how the strategy also operates within an established legal framework.

Interestingly, however, the area in which this interaction seems *least* evident is precisely the social inclusion and protection example that is the focus of this chapter. While the 2020 strategy contains plenty of discussion about legal instruments in the context of the single market, legal discussions were entirely absent in the context of social inclusion and protection objectives, with the 'flagship' poverty programme including little by way of binding legislative commitments. The only exceptions to this are proposed recommendations on adequacy in pension provision, child poverty, and early school leavers, which will anyway take the form of non-binding Council recommendations.[37] While the integrated guidelines for jobs and growth display numerous examples of 'interaction' with directives on anti-discrimination and safety and work, it is much more difficult to pin-point interaction between EU legislation and the OMC SPSI.[38] To this extent, if there is a field of EU policy which is operated exclusively through experimental forms of 'soft' governance alone, social inclusion and protection policy is a prime candidate.

While – in the context of the restrictive legal bases for social inclusion legislation provided by the Lisbon Treaty – this may seem understandable, the 2020

35 See e.g. D. Trubek, P. Cottrell and M. Nance, 'Soft Law, Hard Law and EU Integration' and G. de Búrca, 'EU Race Discrimination Law: A Hybrid Model?' both in G. de Búrca and J. Scott (eds.), *Law and New Governance in the EU and the US*, Hart Publishing, Oxford 2006.

36 See Directive 2000/43 implementing the principle of equal treatment between persons irrespective of racial or ethnic origin [2000] OJ L180/22; Directive 2000/78 establishing a general framework for equal treatment in employment and occupation [2000] OJ L303/16; Directive 2004/113 implementing the principle of equal treatment between men and women in the access to and supply of goods and services [2004] OJ L373/37.

37 See European Commission, n. 30, pp. 7–9. See also, the lack of legislative commitments in the European Commission, 'Renewed Social Agenda: Opportunities, Access and Solidarity in a 21st Century Europe' SEC (2008) 2156.

38 Another candidate may be the new directive on patient's rights in cross-border health care. On the use of this directive as a hybrid instrument combining 'hard' and 'soft' elements, see T. Hervey and L. Trubek, 'Freedom to Provide Health Services in the EU: An Opportunity for a Transformative Directive' (2007) 13 *Columbia Journal of European Law*.

strategy's failure to consider the legal dimension to Lisbon's social inclusion objectives may be yet another missed opportunity. In simple terms, there is much more to law's role than simply to provide a 'strong' legal basis to act. Law – and Courts – can also play a crucial role in improving the legitimacy and effectiveness of new governance instruments themselves, either – as in the anti-discrimination example above – providing a broad framework of overall rights and duties for citizens which governments may then elaborate on, or by demanding the thresholds of participation and transparency necessary to make these processes legitimate.[39]

This use of law – not to make policymaking under the Lisbon Strategy 'harder' or more binding, but to improve its effectiveness and legitimacy – seems to be as applicable in the social inclusion domain as in any other. Yet there is no conscious effort within the 2020 strategy to seek to harness EU law as a mechanism to improve the framework within which EU social inclusion policies are delivered. This seems a major opportunity missed. As we will go on to explore, many of the same lessons – of a strong language of social inclusion and protection, combined with a lack of reflection over the instruments and mechanisms that can be used to achieve social inclusion goals – are replicated in the case of the other great project of the era – the Lisbon Treaty.

3. THE LISBON TREATY: NEW LEGAL TOOLS FOR EUROPEAN SOCIAL INCLUSION AND PROTECTION?

3.1. THE 'OTHER LISBON'

In the second part of this chapter, we argued that the role of law in the Lisbon Strategy was very limited. The OMC SPSI is certainly part of the overall EU legal order, in that all the actors of the coordination framework must act within the limits of the powers attributed to them by the Treaties, but the instruments used to develop the OMC process are of an exclusively soft law nature. Here, the term 'soft law' is really a euphemism for a policy framework that was deliberately established in a manner that avoids the binding features commonly associated with the notion of 'law'. The follow-up Lisbon 2020 strategy, again, does not propose to make use of hard law instruments, at least not in respect of its social pillar.

---

39 On this process enhancing role for law in the context of new governance processes, see S. Sturm and J. Scott, 'Courts as Catalysts: Re-Thinking the Judicial Role in New Governance' (2007) 13 *Columbia Journal of European Law*; M. Dawson, '3 Waves of New Governance in the European Union' (2011) 36 *EL Rev.*

At the time the Lisbon 2020 strategy was being prepared, the Treaty of Lisbon entered into force. It inserted into primary EU law new language in relation to social protection and social inclusion. In the following pages, we will discuss this new wording and reflect on whether the new Treaty and Charter provisions are merely, or primarily, of symbolic importance – indicating the will, from the side of the Member State governments, to give the European Union a friendlier, more social face – or whether on the contrary they renovate the existing legal framework and herald a new role for European law in shaping social protection and social inclusion policies.[40]

The Lisbon Treaty, it must be remembered, is a stratified document. It consists of legal rules that were agreed at different stages of the very long process of deliberation and negotiation that preceded the entry into force of the Treaty in December 2009. This phenomenon is particularly visible in the field that is of our concern in this chapter. Indeed, part of the relevant content of the Lisbon Treaty was agreed already in 2000, namely the 'solidarity' rights of the Charter of Fundamental Rights. As is well known, the substantive content of the Charter was not modified at any of the later stages, in contrast with some of its institutional provisions and its overall legal status which were modified at various points in time after December 2000. The main reforms agreed at the 2002–4 stage of the drafting of the Constitutional Treaty were the introduction of new 'social language' in the introductory articles of the Treaty and, on the other hand, a rewriting of Article 16 EC (now Article 14 TFEU) which included a new legislative competence to deal with services of general economic interest. At the final stage of the Treaty reform process, namely the drafting of the IGC mandate of June 2007 and the subsequent Lisbon Treaty, the most obvious novelty – again, for our purposes – was the enactment of a new Protocol on services of general interest. This was, in fact, one of the few substantive additions which were made to the Constitutional Treaty by the IGC of 2007, whose general aim was to reshuffle the provisions of the Constitutional Treaty so as to modify its appearance beyond recognition, rather than to add new substantive rules. Therefore, many of the Lisbon Treaty's changes to primary EU law are a 'warmed up' version of reformist legal language that emerged in earlier years of the past decade, in particular during the Convention on the Future of the Union that drafted the Constitutional Treaty.

---

40 This part of our paper borrows elements from a previous article: D. Damjanovic and B. de Witte, 'Welfare Integration through EU Law: The Overall Picture in the Light of the Lisbon Treaty' in U. Neergaard, R. Nielsen and L. Roseberry (eds.), *Integrating Welfare Functions into EU Law: From Rome to Lisbon*, DJØF Publishing, Copenhagen 2009.

3.2. NEW TREATY OBJECTIVES – BUT WITHOUT NEW POLICY COMPETENCES

The Lisbon Treaty has considerably rewritten and expanded the formulation of the basic values and objectives of the European Union. The relevant Treaty articles include wording that rebalances, rhetorically at least, the weight of market and non-market values in the foundational provisions of the European Union. Solidarity is included among the values, listed in Article 2 TEU, on which the Union is based. Article 3 TEU, which lists the Union's main objectives, starts with the ringing sentence that '[T]he Union's aim is to promote peace, its values and the well-being of its people', and then mentions, among the other main objectives, 'a highly competitive social market economy' and 'social progress'. The Union is, furthermore, directed to 'combat social exclusion' and 'promote social justice and protection'. In this way, the central values and principles that underlie national welfare systems are recognized and incorporated at the European level.

At first sight, these amendments may seem to be purely rhetorical because they are not fleshed out, elsewhere in the Treaties, by new law making competences and decision making procedures (apart from, as we will see, a new law making competence relating to services of general interest). In this respect, social inclusion and social protection stand apart from most of the other policy objectives listed in Article 3 TEU, which can be effectively pursued by means of binding EU acts or binding international treaties of the EU. For social inclusion and social protection, the competence situation remains what it was prior to the Lisbon Treaty. Article 153 TFEU maintains a strict distinction between the available means of EU action: whereas the social protection of workers may form the object of minimum harmonization by the EU, the 'combating of social exclusion' and the 'modernization of social protection' may form the object only of measures 'designed to encourage cooperation between Member States', which is a reference to the OMC process described in the previous section of this paper.[41]

The disjunction thus created between lofty Treaty proclamation and lack of law-making instruments was not an oversight of the drafters of the Constitutional Treaty and the Lisbon Treaty, but rather the result of a power struggle. Through this struggle, a consensus was reached on including the rather innocuously sounding statements of principles, while excluding – as a result of resistance by a number of country delegations and centre-right politicians in the Convention – the extension of the Union's law making competences.[42] The effect of the

---

41 See, for this distinction, points (a) and (b) of Article 153.2 TFEU.

42 O. Treib, 'Der EU-Verfassungsvertrag und die Zukunft des Wohlfahrtsstaates in Europa' (2004) IHS Working Paper Political Science Series 99 <www.ihs.ac.at/publications/pol/

disjunction can be illustrated by a recent own-initiative resolution of the European Parliament, in which it pleaded for the introduction of guaranteed minimum income schemes in all EU Member States, and gave detailed guidelines on how those schemes should be shaped.[43] The resolution made some intriguing references to a possible 'Commission initiative' or to 'a legislative proposal it [i.e. the Commission] may submit',[44] but it did not specify what kind of legal basis the Commission could use for a legislative initiative in this field – understandably so, since no Treaty basis for EU legislation seems to be available under the present Lisbon Treaty.

This does not mean that the new language contained in Articles 2 and 3 TEU is entirely useless or even misleading. That language may come to play another, indirect, role by prompting the EU institutions, including the Court of Justice, to give more consideration to social inclusion and protection implications when applying and interpreting other rules of EU law, for example the internal market or competition rules. In fact, Article 9 TFEU contains a new mainstreaming clause that aims precisely at achieving this. It states that, in defining and implementing all its policies and activities,

> *'the Union shall take into account requirements linked to the promotion of a high level of employment, the guarantee of adequate social protection, the fight against social exclusion, and a high level of education, training and protection of human health.'*

This provision originally emerged from the 'Social Europe' working group of the European Convention that drafted the EU Constitution, but it was not adopted by the main Convention organs and it did not figure in the draft Constitutional Treaty. However, an amended version of the clause was inserted in the Treaty text by the subsequent IGC of 2003–4, on an initiative of the Belgian government, and remained there all the way until the entry into force of the Lisbon Treaty.[45] The horizontal clause does not transfer any new competences to the EU. Thus, it cannot be used as a legal base for the establishment of a pro-active and comprehensive EU social policy, covering all the domains mentioned in the text of the article. Compared with earlier Treaty revisions (in particular the Maastricht Treaty), this time almost no new competences and/or legal instruments were added by the Lisbon Treaty,[46] through which the European Union could actively try to achieve the goals defined in Article 9 TFEU.

---

pw_99.pdf> accessed 25 August 2011, pp. 26–27. Treib lists, as the reluctant national governments, those of Ireland, the UK, Spain, Estonia and the Czech Republic.

43 European Parliament, 'Resolution of 20 October 2010 on the role of minimum income in combating poverty and promoting an inclusive society in Europe', 2010/2039(INI).

44 See, respectively, points 36 and 21 of the Resolution.

45 O. Treib, n. 42, pp. 25–26.

46 The only changes with regard to social protection consist in a) declaring 'common safety concerns in public health matters' a shared power of the Union (Article 4.2 (k) TEU), which is

What then could the practical legal significance of Article 9 TFEU be? By mainstreaming social policy into all EU policy fields, Article 9 TFEU affirms that social objectives are equivalent to economic objectives within EU primary law. Thereby it requires all EU actors to find a proper balance between economic, social and other aims in all fields of public policymaking and implementation in which the EU is engaged. The fields that are particularly relevant in this context are, most likely, competition law, internal market law and external trade law – the latter two being policy areas in which the European Parliament possesses full co-decision and/or consent powers. 'To find a proper balance' concretely means – one might argue – that social considerations shall play a greater role than they have done so far in EU policies outside the strict domain of social policy. Only such an understanding of the clause could make a difference compared to the pre-Lisbon situation and could thereby adequately mirror the increased recognition given to the idea of a Social Europe by the text of the Treaties in their post-Lisbon version.

In any case, the clause makes the question of achieving a proper balance a subject for discussion within the Council and of course the Parliament, whenever a proposed piece of EU legislation is likely to have an impact on national social policies and welfare systems (and, indeed, whenever a proposed EU agreement might impact on social protection and inclusion in a third country). Arguably, this mainstreaming clause should also be taken into account by the European Court of Justice, when interpreting the Treaties and secondary legislation, in particular in relation to the internal market. Although the mainstreaming clause is not directly addressed to the Court, it certainly expresses a value judgment which the Court cannot ignore.

One way of putting the social mainstreaming clause to good use would be to redefine the market rules (in competition law, state aid law and internal market law) in the sense that their aim should not merely be that of establishing and safeguarding a free competitive market but, more broadly, that of improving the functioning of a 'social market economy' (as mentioned in Article 3 TEU). The aims listed in the social clause should become part and parcel of the objectives of internal market and competition policies. Whereas such social mainstreaming is strongly resisted by most competition law experts, including the Commission's

---

primarily a change at the formal level, as it just provides a clearer presentation of the previously existing delimitation of powers between the Union and the Member States in this area; and b) modifying the legislative procedure for social security measures connected to the free movement of workers from unanimity to QMV (Article 48 TFEU). Despite the shift to QMV, social security coordination measures will, however, still be subject to a veto power of the single Member States, so that, in reality, the unanimity requirement is maintained.

Competition DG,[47] it does already happen occasionally in internal market legislation. Indeed, internal market legislation never consists in harmonization for its own sake but always entails the explicit or implicit formulation of policy objectives which often comprise non-market objectives such as the protection of health, the environment, the protection of workers, of culture or animal welfare.[48] The 'level-playing field' which internal market laws seek to achieve, is not necessarily a deregulated field; rather, the appropriate regulatory mix is, in each case, decided by the EU legislator in the framework of the co-decision procedure; there is, thus, every opportunity for the European Parliament to push for the incorporation of social protection objectives in internal market rules or, at least, to make sure that internal market directives will not affect social protection regimes.[49]

3.3. A NEW TREATY REGIME FOR SOCIAL SERVICES?

The one new legislative competence introduced by the Lisbon Treaty is to be found in Article 14 TFEU, which is based on the former Article 16 EC, but has modified that article significantly. The main novelty consists in the creation of a *new legislative competence for the European Union in respect of services of general economic interest (SGEIs)*, which – due to a quite complicated drafting process[50] – is laid down in an ambiguous way.[51] The second part of the sentence ('without prejudice to the competence of Member States') was added in a second stage of the drafting process, during the IGC that followed the Convention, and seems

47 See the discussion of this question in C. Semmelmann, *Social Policy Goals in the Interpretation of Article 81 EC*, Nomos, Baden-Baden 2008.

48 See B. de Witte, 'Non-Market Values in Internal Market Legislation' in N. Nic Shuibhne (ed.), *Regulating the Internal Market*, Edward Elgar, Cheltenham 2006. The Posted Workers Directive is a prominent pre-Lisbon example of this approach, in that it seeks to combine an improved functioning of the internal market for services with a basic level of worker protection.

49 The latter happened in the general services directive, in which social services were expressly excluded from consideration.

50 For more details on this drafting process, see A. Winterstein, 'The Internal Market and Services of General Interest' in G. Amato, H. Bribosia and B. de Witte (eds.) *Genesis and Destiny of the European Constitution*, Bruylant, Bruylant 2007.

51 The text of the article is as follows: '*Without prejudice to Article 4 of the Treaty on European Union or to Articles 93, 106 and 107 of this Treaty, and given the place occupied by services of general economic interest in the shared values of the Union as well as their role in promoting social and territorial cohesion, the Union and the Member States, each within their respective powers and within the scope of application of the Treaties, shall take care that such services operate on the basis of principles and conditions, particularly economic and financial conditions, which enable them to fulfil their missions. The European Parliament and the Council, acting by means of regulations in accordance with the ordinary legislative procedure, shall establish these principles and set these conditions without prejudice to the competence of Member States, in compliance with the Treaties, to provide, to commission and to fund such services.*'

intended to restrict the scope of the competence given in the first part of the sentence. It is not clear, however, to what extent it does so. There is some tension between the statement that the EU will now have the power to lay down the main principles and conditions for the operation of the SGEIs, and the statement that the Member States preserve their power to provide, organize and finance these services. The new legal base for the SGEIs is therefore open to widely different interpretations as to its potential scope and impact.[52]

This new legislative competence was added to the draft Constitutional Treaty quite late in the life of the Convention and in a kind of a surprise move. Although this choice was not reversed in the preparation of the Lisbon Treaty, the European Commission has seemed less than keen to take the initiative for a wholesale 'horizontal' regulation dealing with services of general economic interest in Europe, preferring, if at all, more specific legislation dealing with a particular service, as had been done before, on the basis of other Treaty articles, such as ex-Article 95 EC (now Article 114 TFEU).[53] On the other hand, in 2006 the socialist group in the European Parliament already elaborated a draft text of horizontal legislation on public services,[54] which it prepared on the basis of the (very shaky) internal market competence given by Article 95 EC, but which could now more firmly be justified, in legal terms, by Article 14 TFEU. In a resolution of 2009, the European Parliament as a whole called on the Commission to 'consider' the elaboration of a legislative instrument on social services.[55]

The importance of this new Treaty article, as far as the subject of this paper is concerned, depends on whether the notion of 'services of general economic interest' to which the article refers, also comprises social services. At first sight, one would think not. But in fact, this is a question which is hotly debated in the literature, and the Commission, from its side, has consistently taken the view that many social services are sufficiently 'economic', in the way they are delivered, so as to be covered by the SGEI concept and, therefore, by the rules on state aid, public procurement, and the internal market generally.

---

52 See, for discussion of some of the puzzles posed by this new EU competence M. Krajewski, 'Providing Legal Clarity and Securing Policy Space for Public Services through a Legal Framework for Services of General Economic Interest: Squaring the Circle' (2008) *European Public Law*; S. Rodrigues, 'Les services d'intérêt (économique) général et le Traité de Lisbonne. Ou comment assumer pour l'Union européenne et les Etats membres une responsabilité commune à l'égard des consommateurs' (2010) *Revue européenne de droit de la consommation*.

53 This Treaty article (now renumbered as Article 114 TFEU) has served as the legal basis for directives dealing with telecommunication, gas and electricity services, as well as for the draft directive on the mobility of patients.

54 Socialist Group in the European Parliament, 'Proposal for a Framework Directive on Services of General Economic Interest', November 2006.

55 European Parliament, 'Resolution of 6 May 2009 on the active inclusion of people excluded from the labour market' 2008/2335(INI), point 50.

Apart from this reformulation of the former Article 16 EC Treaty, the Lisbon Treaty includes another new legal instrument pertaining to the same field, namely Protocol No. 26 on services of general interest.[56] This Protocol emerged from the IGC that modified the Constitutional Treaty, or rather, from the secret negotiations which led to the detailed IGC mandate that was adopted by the European Council of June 2007 and then inexorably led to the Treaty of Lisbon. Indeed, the exact text of what became the Protocol was already contained in a footnote of the IGC mandate.[57] It is difficult, in view of the total lack of transparency of that IGC, to understand why this Protocol was deemed necessary, and what its political and legal significance is. We know that the initiative for the Protocol came from the Netherlands, whose government had included it in the list of modifications to the Constitutional Treaty which it declared to be indispensable in order to ratify the Treaty without recourse to a second referendum. However, this particular Dutch request, unlike the others, was not inspired by the will to dismantle the constitutional language of the Treaty. Rather, its origins are more coincidental; they seem to be linked to a controversy caused by a Commission investigation, in 2005, into the existence and legitimacy of state aid to the public housing sector in the Netherlands, a traditionally important part of the social welfare sector in that country.[58]

Article 1 of the Protocol aims to lay down an authoritative interpretation of Article 14 TFEU, but actually just spells out (in a grammatically and systematically quite clumsy way) the shared values referred to in Article 14 TFEU. It gives a flavour of the subject matter of a potential future regulation based on Article 14 TFEU, but it does not help us to understand how the division of competences between the Union and the Member States should operate and, thus, does not clarify the scope of the legal basis for EU action which Article 14 TFEU has created.

Article 2 of the Protocol is more innovative. It states that 'the provisions of the Treaties do not affect in any way the competence of the Member States to provide, commission and organise non-economic services of general interest.' We see here, for the first time in primary EU law, the notion of 'non-economic services of general interest', which, of course, are opposed to the services of general economic interest that are covered by Article 1 of the Protocol and Article 14 TFEU, and are also subject – through Article 106 TFEU (ex-Article 86 EC) – to the internal market and competition rules. It can be seen as an attempt to 'grant

56 As is well known, protocols have the same legal value as the treaty to which they are attached, so Protocol No. 26 is now also part of primary EU law.

57 European Council, 'Presidency Conclusions', 21–22 June 2007, 11177/1/07 REV 1, Annex 1 Draft IGC Mandate, p. 21, footnote 12.

58 See D. Charles Le Bihan, 'Services d'intérêt économique général et valeurs communes' (2008) *Revue du Marché commun et de l'Union européenne*, pp. 356–360.

to these services a sort of constitutional immunity from the opening logic of the integration process and in particular from the competition regime'.[59]

It is difficult, though, to take the wording of Article 2 at face value. If the Treaties are not to 'affect in any way' the non-economic public services, then, for example, the Court's jurisprudence on equal access of non-national EU citizens to public service employment and on the mobility rights of EU students would have been overruled by this Protocol. This can hardly have been the intention of its authors. Rather, the 'non-affectation clause' must probably be read in the same way in which the Court of Justice uses similar formulas in many of its judgments, when stating that EU law does not detract from a particular exclusive Member State competence when it imposes certain obligations (for example, in respect of non-discrimination) on the exercise of that national competence.[60] However, the Court has used this formula also in the context of internal market law, in particular in its health care cases,[61] without stopping to consider whether the health services at issue in those cases were 'economic' or 'non-economic'.[62] The new question raised by the Lisbon Treaty, and in particular by this Article 2 of the Protocol, is whether the Court of Justice should more rigorously examine whether a particular service is economic or not, before applying to it the rules of the internal market, public procurement or state aid. We would argue that the significance of the Protocol is that the Court (and the Commission) should indeed be more rigorous, not assuming too quickly that social services are economic and therefore within the shared responsibility of the Member States and the European Union, and therefore subject to Article 14 TFEU, Article 1 of the Protocol, and Article 106 TFEU.

Finally, it is interesting to observe that the European Commission, in its November 2007 communication on services of general interest, gave pride of place to the Protocol even before it had entered into force. It used it, 'somewhat

---

59 M. Ferrera, 'National Welfare States and European Integration: In Search of a Virtuous Nesting' (2009) *JCMS*, p. 227.

60 See, for example, Case C-267/06 *Tadeo Maruko v. Versorgungsanstalt der deutschen Bühnen* [2008] ECR I-01757, para. 59.

61 Case C-372/04 *The Queen, on the application of Yvonne Watts v. Bedford Primary Care Trust and Secretary of State for Health* [2007] ECR I-03185, para. 92, and Case C-444/05 *Aikaterini Stamatelaki v. NPDD Organismos Asfaliseos Eleftheron Epangelmation (OAEE)* [2007] ECR I-03185, para. 23.

62 More broadly speaking, the Court of Justice has readily assumed that social services have an economic dimension that made them subject to the rules of economic EU law; see discussion of this question by G. Davies, 'Welfare as a Service' (2002) 29 *Legal Issues of Economic Integration*; J. Baquero Cruz, 'Beyond Competition: Services of General Interest and European Community Law' in G. de Búrca (ed.), *EU Law and the Welfare State – In Search of Solidarity*, Oxford University Press, Oxford 2005, and several contributions in M. Krajewski, U. Neergaard, J. van de Gronden (eds.), *The Changing Legal Framework for Services of General Interest in Europe*, T.M.C. Asser Press, The Hague 2009.

cynically',[63] as an argument against the enactment of European legislation on social services since, in the Commission's view, the Protocol created sufficient clarity on the EU legal framework which could, therefore, continue to be implemented through Commission action in the field of competition, and through occasional service-specific legislation. The cynical element in the Commission's position lies in the fact that both the new competence in Article 14 TFEU and the new Protocol were promoted by political actors who are concerned with the impact of negative integration on social services, but whereas Article 14 TFEU provides for a re-regulatory competence of the EU (to compensate for the effects of negative integration), the Protocol adopts a 'hands-off' approach, instructing the EU institutions to respect the policy autonomy of the Member States. The advocates of the existing negative integration approach, including the Commission, are playing out the wording of the Protocol against the second sentence of Article 14 but without revising their existing approach to negative integration. A Commission staff working document on social services of general interest of 22 October 2010 (that is, post-Lisbon) is revealing in this respect. It notes the Lisbon Treaty novelties but does not draw any consequences from them as regards its existing broad view of the submission of social services to the economic rules of EU law.[64]

If, however, sufficient political support could be mustered for acting upon the new legislative competence given by Article 14 TFEU – and assuming that both social protection and social inclusion are covered by it – what could be the object of such action? Adopting horizontal European standards, applicable to all SGEIs, might run the risk that concepts developed for the traditional SGEIs (the public utilities such as gas, electricity and telecoms) are automatically carried over to social services. This would be undesirable from a social perspective, as welfare services differ substantially from public utilities, both in their mode of operation and in the objectives they pursue. Indeed, the core policy aim for welfare services is not so much to ensure *universal provision* (the provision of certain services to everybody at affordable prices), but, above all, *social provision* (i.e. the provision of certain services to those who are in need of them at no, or substantially reduced, cost).

A more specific purpose for an Article 14 TFEU-based Regulation could be to define, from a European perspective, the respective role of market and non-market values in the delivery of social services. It could deal separately with the impact of the various single market rules (competition, free movement, state aid

63 W. Sauter, 'Services of General Economic Interest and Universal Service in EU Law' (2008) 33 *EL Rev*, p. 173; see also, in the same sense, D. Charles Le Bihan, n. 58, p. 359.

64 European Commission, 'Second Biennial Report on social services of general interest' (Staff Working Document) SEC (2010) 1284, pp. 71–77.

and public procurement) and with the different categories of social services (health care, public education, social assistance and social security). The Frequently Asked Questions (FAQ) documents of the Commission on the application of the state aid rules to social services of general interest[65] or on the application of the public procurement rules to those social services[66] could serve as prototypes for such legislative measures, but the Parliament could also use its role as co-legislator to strengthen the place given to non-market values. As case law on these issues has not yet developed on such a large scale when compared to public utilities, such legislative measures could do more than just clarify and consolidate existing case law, but instead give an important new direction to EU law in this field.

In addition, Article 14 TFEU could also serve as a basis for the development of *common* social standards within the EU, to which the horizontal clause of Article 9 TFEU refers. Such a 'positive integration' measure would be more problematic, not only because it would run against well-established differences in the organization of social protection in the various Member States, but also, from a more specifically legal perspective, because it would undermine the provisions, elsewhere in the Treaty (Article 153 TFEU), that make social inclusion and social protection the object of merely *non-legislative* action by the EU.

3.4. THE SOCIAL PROTECTION RIGHTS IN THE EU CHARTER OF FUNDAMENTAL RIGHTS

The final novelty of the Lisbon Treaty to be considered in this chapter is the fact that it gave the EU Charter of Fundamental Rights the 'same legal value' as the Treaties themselves even though the Charter remains a separate text which is not incorporated in the Treaties (see Article 6 TEU).

When the European Council of Cologne launched, in June 1999, the process of drafting the Charter of Fundamental Rights, it specified that 'account should furthermore be taken of economic and social rights as contained in the European Social Charter and the Community Charter of the Fundamental Social Rights of Workers, insofar as they do not merely establish objectives for action by the Union.' The distinction, alluded to by the European Council, between two types of social rights (those that merely contain objectives for action and those that are legally more incisive) was not closely followed by the Charter Convention; it decided to include a number of 'rights' that were formulated as very general

65 European Commission, (Staff Working Document) SEC (2007) 1516 final <http://ec.europa.eu/competition/state_aid/legislation/faq_sieg_en.pdf> accessed 25 August 2011.

66 European Commission, (Staff Working Document) SEC (2007) 1514 final <http://ec.europa.eu/services_general_interest/docs/sec_2007_1514_en.pdf> accessed 25 August 2011.

policy objectives. This was particularly the case in Title IV of the Charter entitled 'Solidarity' which contained the three provisions that are most directly relevant to the theme of this paper, namely Article 34 on social security and social assistance, Article 35 on health care and Article 36 on access to services of general economic interest.

The Convention got away with this broad brush approach because it was understood that the Charter would not become legally binding, at least not immediately. The 'justiciability issue' came back with a vengeance during the Convention on the Future of the Union, when some delegates (particularly the UK government representative) made it clear that their agreement to incorporate the Charter in the EU Constitution, and thus make it legally binding, would be conditional on emphasizing more clearly the distinction between 'rights' and 'principles'. This eventually led to the addition of a fifth paragraph to Article 52 of the Charter which limits the justiciability of provisions containing principles: they shall be 'judicially cognizable' only in the interpretation of implementing measures taken by the EU institutions or by the Member States, and in ruling on their legality. The distinction that, in the view of the Cologne European Council in 1999, should have been the criterion for inclusion in the Charter has thus become an internal fault line within the text of the Charter. It is by no means clear how this fault line will operate in practice, now that the Charter has acquired binding legal force. Indeed, the Charter does not label its provisions as being either rights or principles (or rather, the use of those labels for denoting single norms in the Charter is quite inconsistent with the nature of the overall distinction made in Article 52). The rights/principles distinction is therefore bound to become a major source of confusion and controversy, which was already indicated in 2004 by the French Conseil constitutionnel in its decision reviewing the European Constitutional Treaty. When referring to the distinction between rights and principles, it affirmed without any qualification and without any further argument that the right to work and the entitlement to social security benefits and social assistance are examples of principles rather than rights.[67]

When trying to apply the rights/principles dichotomy to fundamental social rights, it would certainly be too simple to consider that entire chapters of the Charter (say, the title on 'Solidarity', including the three 'social welfare' provisions mentioned above) contain only marginally justiciable principles rather than fully justiciable rights. It is necessary, rather, to proceed on a case-by-case basis. Good arguments can be made for ranging most of the Charter's fundamental social rights among the category 'rights' rather than among the

67 Conseil Constitutionnel, Decision no. 2004-505 DC of 19 November 2004, *Traité établissant une Constitution pour l'Europe*, para. 15.

category of 'principles'. On this point, the interpretative practice of the European Committee of Social Rights could prove useful.[68]

This being said, it should be acknowledged that the principal role of the Charter, in the domain of our concern, is not to impose limits on the action of the EU institutions. The role of the Charter's social rights may be more promising in two other respects: that of limiting the liberalizing impact of EU law on national social protection policies, and that of formulating duties to act for the EU institutions.

As regards the first of these functions, much will depend on whether the Court of Justice will persist in its *Viking-and-Laval*[69] approach after the entry into force of the Lisbon Treaty. Although those judgments did not relate to social protection and inclusion, but to labour law, the approach taken there by the Court of Justice does not augur well for an active judicial use of Charter social protection rights to counterbalance the deregulatory impact of the common market freedoms. In those judgments, the Court – as is well known – declared its desire to reconcile fundamental social rights with the common market freedoms, but according to many commentators, 'the technique of reconciliation used does not match up to the ideal which is announced.'[70] The Court seems to have confirmed that pro-market approach in two post-Lisbon judgments, *Commission v. Germany* and *Santos Palhota*.[71] In the former case, the Court imposed far-reaching limitations on the right of collective bargaining, in the interest of promoting cross-border competition in public procurement, and in the latter case it struck down a national control system of the posting of foreign workers for being overly restrictive of the freedom to provide services. In both cases, the Advocate General had called for a 'new' post-Lisbon interpretation,

---

68 For example, the right to social security, contained in Article 12 of the Revised European Social Charter, was interpreted by the Committee as involving an obligation for states to maintain an effective and inclusive public system of social security, and a corresponding limit to its privatization; see G. Katrougalos, 'Constitutional Limitations of Social Security Privatisation: A Human Rights Approach' (2010) *European Journal of Social Security (EJSS)*, pp. 32–34.

69 See Case C-438/05 *International Transport Workers' Federation and Finnish Seamen's Union v. Viking Line ABP and OÜ Viking Line Eesti* [2007] ECR I-10779 and Case C-341/05 *Laval un Partneri Ltd v. Svenska Byggnadsarbetareförbundet, Svenska Byggnadsarbetareförbundets avdelning 1, Byggettan and Svenska Elektrikerförbundet* [2007] ECR I-11767.

70 L. Azoulai, 'The Court of Justice and the Social Market Economy: The Emergence of an Ideal and the Conditions for its Realization' (2008) 45 *Common Market Law Review (CML Rev)*, p. 1353.

71 Case C-271/08 *European Commission v. Federal Republic of Germany* [2010] ECR I-*not yet reported* (and the comment, on this part of the judgment, by F. Kessler, 'Le droit fondamental à la négociation collective n'existe, en Europe, que sous condition' (2010) 12 *Droit social*); and Case C-515/08 *Criminal proceedings against Vítor Manuel dos Santos Palhota and Others* [2010] ECR-*not yet reported*.

taking into account the binding status of the EU Charter's social rights, but the Court did not budge. So, the 'social turn' of the Lisbon Treaty has not yet left traces in the way the Court 'balances' the common market freedoms with fundamental social rights.

As regards the second function of the Charter mentioned above, namely the creation of duties to act for the political institutions, one must take into account Article 51.2 of the Charter, which provides that the Charter does not establish any new power or task for the Union. The intention of the drafters of the Charter was clearly to avoid that the mere enumeration of a fundamental right would create a competence for the European institutions to act for the protection of that right. The scope of the rights follows existing EU competences rather than the other way round. However, even though this intention is clear, the actual wording of the clause is misleading by its use of the word 'tasks'. Indeed, the very purpose of adopting a Charter of Fundamental Rights was to make it a task for the European institutions to use the Charter rights in their various activities. In fact, the first paragraph of the same Article 51 of the Charter imposes an obligation on the Member States and the European Union to 'promote the application' of the rights contained within it. Many Charter rights (including of course the welfare rights) require positive action for 'the progressive achievement of their full realization' (to use the words of the UN Social Covenant), so that the right only becomes meaningful when seen in conjunction with the measures taken for its effective enjoyment.

However, it is by no means evident what follows from this reasoning in practical terms. In addition to the cases of clear correspondence between a Charter right and an EU competence (for example, as regards the right to education), fundamental social rights might play a 'transversal' role in other competence domains that are less directly linked to a particular social right. This can occur with the Union's internal market competences, which are precisely not defined in sector-specific but in functional terms. One recent illustration was the Commission's draft directive of 2 July 2008 on patients' rights in cross-border health care. This is an internal market directive; but recital 3 of the draft's preamble referred to Article 35 of the Charter dealing with the right to health.[72] Another, not too dissimilar, example is provided by European legislation protecting the equal access to welfare benefits of foreign (non-EU) residents. The preamble of the Directive of 2003 on the status of third-country nationals who

72 However, the accompanying explanatory memorandum of the Commission did not explain in what way the draft directive would advance the Charter right to health, and one could possibly argue instead that promoting cross-border access to health care may lead to a *reduction* of overall health standards in Europe, or at least in some countries. Note that the reference to the Charter's right to health has disappeared from the final text of the Directive as adopted on 9 March 2011 [2011] OJ L88/45.

are long-term residents[73] refers to the Charter of Fundamental Rights, and its Article 12 guarantees equal treatment for long-term resident foreigners in, among other things, 'education and vocational training, including study grants', and 'social protection, including social security and health care' – which are social rights recognized by the Charter. In this manner, the European Union's competence to define the legal status of third-country nationals in their country of residence was interpreted by the EU institutions as calling for the adoption of measures to promote the exercise of Charter rights by those third-country nationals. Consider also Council Regulation 859/2003 of 14 May 2003, by which the social security exportability scheme that existed for the benefit of migrant EU nationals (Regulation 1408/71) was extended to third-country nationals migrating between two EU countries.[74] The Preamble of this Regulation refers to the right to social security and social assistance of the Charter of Fundamental Rights, but without stating in so many words that the adoption of the Regulation was mandated by the Charter text.

What happens in such cases is the legislative mainstreaming of social rights, in particular their non-discrimination element. But, as we saw before, this duty of social mainstreaming is already laid down elsewhere in primary EU law, namely in Article 9 TFEU, so that, in this respect at least, the Charter of Fundamental Rights does not add anything to the social mainstreaming clause, except perhaps a greater sense of political urgency.

Despite the fact that the Charter of Rights gave pride of place to social protection and social inclusion, its practical contribution to the lives of European citizens, in this domain, remains to be seen. The practice of the EU institutions, so far, does not show a genuine 'turn to the social'. Until now, the Charter of Fundamental Rights remains a rhetorical flourish with little or no impact on day-to-day social policies.

4. FROM LISBON TO LISBON: A STRATEGY AND A TREATY COMPARED

The last two years have seen the culmination of two vital projects for the EU's future – the first the project of Treaty reform which culminated with the entry into force of the Lisbon Treaty on the 1st of December 2009, and the second, the end of the first ten year cycle of the EU's overarching Lisbon Strategy. While both of these projects established a distinct language and set of objectives for social

73 Council Directive 2003/109 of 25 November 2003 concerning the status of third-country nationals who are long-term residents [2004] OJ L16/44.

74 [2003] OJ L124/1.

inclusion and protection policy, they can easily be seen as distinct and unrelated projects. In the first case, the Lisbon Treaty establishes a general legal architecture for the EU, creating defined legal powers for the Union; in the second, the Lisbon Strategy takes as its primary object not legal, but political goals, creating a policymaking framework delivered through soft guidelines, indicators and objectives, rather than 'hard' legal rules. It is no wonder then that the founding documents of both projects – the Lisbon Treaty itself, and the Council and Commission documents establishing the skeleton of the new 2020 Lisbon Strategy – make so few references to each other; we are dealing here with two distinct normative spheres.

In spite of these obvious differences, however, when viewed through the lenses of social inclusion and social protection, it is remarkable how much the two projects have in common. They in fact share both a common promise and a common limitation vis-à-vis the role and place of social inclusion and protection policy within the Union. Much of this paper has focused on the limitation. This concerns the disjuncture between the social objectives which each framework proclaims, and the instruments used to deliver those objectives. At first sight, both the Lisbon Treaty and the renewed 2020 strategy respond to the criticism that their previous frameworks lacked a proper balance between social and economic dimensions by including a more balanced political language. In the case of the Lisbon Treaty, this is done through the new objectives for the Union listed in Article 3 TEU, such as combating social inclusion and promoting social justice and protection. In the case of the Lisbon Strategy it is achieved through the return of Lisbon 2020 to three new mutually re-enforcing pillars of smart, sustainable and inclusive growth, with social, environmental and economic policies all given supposedly equal weight.

The legacy of both projects, however, may be an inability to translate this new 'balance' into instruments able to achieve and implement these objectives. In both cases, the re-evaluation of guiding principles has not been matched by a similar reflection on the instruments and mechanisms able to make a more equal relationship in the Union between economic and social inclusion and protection objectives a reality. In the case of the Lisbon Treaty, the reference to social rights among the objectives of the Union, and among the rights enumerated in the Charter, leaves no additional competences for the Union – bar the uncertain role of the new Article 14 TFEU – nor does it make decision making in those fields where competences do exist much easier.

In the case of the Lisbon Strategy, the new social 'pillar' of Lisbon 2020 has not led to changes in the instruments by which employment, fiscal and social protection and inclusion policy in the EU are monitored. These instruments have neither become more prescriptive nor have they been significantly modified to address the concerns of some sceptics that such 'integrated guidelines' see social and environmental policy as ancillary to economic growth. While this does not mean that the re-balancing of overall objectives and priorities via each project is of no value, that value does not seem to come from making 'social inclusion and protection' a core particle of the everyday practice of EU law and policy.

There is, however, a promise too. Even if the mechanisms to deliver social inclusion and protection objectives in the EU have not been strengthened, there may yet be an important role for those objectives, not as a free-standing set of goals of themselves, but rather as a set of values which must be mainstreamed and reflected in other fields of EU action. This again may be a point of overlap between both projects. In the case of the Lisbon Treaty, the mainstreaming approach is epitomized by the new Article 9 TFEU, which urges the Union to take into account 'the fight against social exclusion in defining and implementing its policies and activities'. While the use of this article remains to be seen, it could be used both by the Commission when considering and assessing legislative proposals, and the Court, when balancing internal market and social goals, to more carefully weigh the impact of EU laws and policies on poverty and social protection in the Member States.

This approach is, however, apparent in the other Lisbon too. Both before and after the 2020 reforms, the Lisbon Strategy has encouraged national participants to see open coordination processes in social protection and inclusion not simply as free-standing but deeply linked to other EU objectives, such as ensuring balanced and sustainable budgetary and employment policies. Thus, in defining social priorities, Member States reporting under the OMC SPSI must ensure that their policies 'feed-in' and 'feed-out' to other policies developed under the 'integrated guidelines for jobs and growth'. Social inclusion policy, and fiscal and employment policies, are not seen as isolated fields but policies that must be integrated and reconciled. In this sense, again social inclusion is not a primary and singular concern, but rather a value that must feed into and inform other policies e.g. fiscal and monetary union, the activation of the labour market and so on.

The use of this 'mainstreaming' approach asks as many questions as it answers. An important question in particular is the attitude of the Court. The approach taken in the *Viking-and-Laval* line of cases for example – as indicated in section 3 – poses serious doubts as to whether the Court will use the language of social rights to 'balance' conflicting economic goals, or rather instead, simply to extend the reach of internal market law into areas of life – such as collective bargaining – relatively insulated from economic rules. Question marks also arise regarding the use of 'feeding in and out' in the context of the Lisbon Strategy. As pointed out in section 2, this has often not been a reciprocal process, but created perceptions among social NGOs that social protection and inclusion policies are seen as an ancillary by-product of fiscal and economic coordination. We will have to wait and see whether the 2020 reforms, the new flagship programme for poverty – or, in the context of the Lisbon Treaty, the Treaty reforms on services of general economic interest – can do anything to temper that scepticism.

THE OMC AND BEYOND: 'SOFT-TO-HARD-TO-SOFT' GOVERNANCE OF HEALTH CARE IN THE EU

Bart VANHERCKE and Lena WEGENER

1. INTRODUCTION[1]

Since its launch during the Lisbon European Council of 2000 as a 'new' policy instrument that would allow to make progress in sensitive policy areas such as social protection and social inclusion, the Open Method of Coordination, has received a great (some would argue: excessive) deal of attention, both from scholars and policy makers. The OMC has indeed been widely debated in the research community.[2] Note that once the initial praise for the OMC (both by politicians and scientists) started to wane, the process was subjected to intense scrutiny and found wanting in mainstream academic literature.[3] In particular the 'social inclusion' and 'pensions' OMC[4] have been studied rather well, both in terms of emergence and impact. However, we are still flying blind with regard

---

1 The authors are grateful to the participants of the expert seminar on 'Social Protection and Social Inclusion in the EU: Interactions between Law and Policy', February 10th -11th, 2011 (Antwerp University) for their comments. Special thanks go to Jo DE COCK, DAVID NATALI and the editors of this volume for their lucid suggestions for revision. We are particularly grateful to RITA BAETEN for the exchange of ideas about the 'soft-to-hard-to-soft' governance perspective. The usual disclaimer applies. Address of correspondence: vanhercke@ose.be.

2 For recent overviews, see S. KRÖGER (ed.), 'What We Have Learnt: Advances, Pitfalls and Remaining Questions of OMC Research' (2009) 13 *(EIoP)*, Special Issue 1 <http://eiop.or.at/eiop/index.php/eiop/issue/view/21> accessed 4 November 2011; E. MARLIER and D. NATALI (eds.) with R. VAN DAM, *Europe 2020. Towards a More Social EU?*, P.I.E. Peter Lang, Brussels 2010; and M. HEIDENREICH and J. ZEITLIN (eds.), *Changing European Employment and Welfare Regimes: The Influence of the Open Method of Coordination on National Labour Market and Social Welfare Reforms*, Routledge, London 2008.

3 For a more detailed discussion, see M.P. HAMEL and B. VANHERCKE, 'Politique nationale et coopération européenne: la méthode de la coordination ouverte est-elle devenue plus contraignante?' (2008) 1 *Revue Belge de Sécurité Sociale (RBSS).*

4 To be more precise: 'social inclusion', 'pensions' and 'health and long-term care' constitute the three strands of the 'streamlined' Social Protection and Social Inclusion OMC.

to the most recent strand of the Social OMC, which is concerned with health and long-term care and received only limited scholarly attention. This stands in contrast to the impact of European legislation in the field of health, which has been extensively covered,[5] but is (for obvious reasons) largely disconnected from the research focussing on 'new governance'[6] in health.

This chapter has a twin ambition. First of all, it aims at understanding the significance of 'soft' EU cooperation in health policy through this particular strand of the Social OMC. Secondly, it wants to understand whether and how interaction is developing between EU law and policy in the area of health care. The argument is made that in this area of social protection we are moving from mere 'interaction' to a 'hybridization' of governance tools. Indeed, in between EU policy (new governance) and EU legislation, hybrid instruments are emerging that combine elements from 'hard' and 'soft' law. In this view, we begin by briefly describing the emergence of the OMC in health care, the main features of its toolbox (objectives, reporting obligations, indicators, peer reviews), and the policy learning that is intended (section two). Based on recent empirical research in Belgium, section three then raises the question whether this OMC strand has had any 'impact' (effects 'on the ground') at all on policies and policy making-processes at the domestic level. The debate about the relevance of soft governance in health care is then broadened to the impact of the OMC at EU level as well as to new governance processes other than the OMC (section four). Within this section, particular attention is paid to the OMC's interaction with other EU instruments such as the legal framework underpinning the European Social Fund (ESF). Section five then tries to provide an explanation for the limited tangible effects of this OMC, by referring to intense actor rivalry and the lack of stakeholder involvement in the EU health care arena. The final section draws tentative conclusions as regards the 'soft-to-hard-to-soft' governance of health care in the EU.

---

5 See E. Mossialos, G. Permanand, R. Baeten and T.K. Hervey (eds.), *Health Systems Governance in Europe: The Role of European Union Law and Policy*, Cambridge University Press, Cambridge 2010.

6 New governance has been defined as a 'range of processes and practices that have a normative or regulatory dimension, but do not operate primarily or at all through the conventional mechanisms of command-and-control-type legal institutions' (G. de Búrca and J. Scott, 'Introduction: New Governance, Law and Constitutionalism' in G. de Búrca and J. Scott (eds.), *Law and New Governance in the EU and the US*, Hart, Oxford 2006, p. 2).

2. THE OPEN METHOD OF COORDINATION IN HEALTH CARE: EMERGENCE AND KEY FEATURES

2.1. EMERGENCE: THE COMMISSION'S PURPOSIVE OPTIMISM VERSUS FOOT-DRAGGING MEMBER STATES

The story of the emergence of the health care OMC has been told elsewhere,[7] but the essence is the following: the European Commission has been pushing the Member States, from the beginning of the 1990s, to start some kind of EU cooperation on health care, while many Member States were dragging their feet, afraid as they were that this would imply losing grip over this important policy area. As a result, attempts to start an OMC in health care failed in 2002 and again in 2004.[8] Amazing as it may seem – given the increasing awareness that Europe was entering national health care systems by the back door of the internal market – until 2004, national governments continued to be strongly averse to formalizing the debate about health care at the EU level (submitting their consent to launch a 'soft' form of cooperation to a number of rather strict conditions).[9] In the end, the idea of having an OMC in this field became attractive to Member States when they realized that the alternative was health policy made by the European Court of Justice, Directorate General (DG) MARKT of the European Commission and possibly the Economic and Financial Affairs (ECOFIN) Council formation.

Hesitations loomed large even after the formal start of the process (and they are still present today). At every step of the institutionalization of this process the importance of 'respecting the subsidiarity principle' and 'taking into account national differences' was recalled: both of them key principles without which EU cooperation in health was a no-go. In other words: the establishment of a new governance mechanism in this area has been intensely 'political': it has been shaped *both* by deliberative norms and through hard-boiled power games between national and EU actors (and within DGs of the European Commission). Even after the health care OMC was finally launched in 2004, it was only equipped with an *incomplete institutional architecture*: the health care OMC

7 For a detailed account, see T.K. Hervey and B. Vanhercke, 'Health Care and the EU: The Law and Policy Patchwork' in E. Mossialos, G. Permanand, R. Baeten and T.K. Hervey (eds.), n. 5.

8 See S. Greer and B. Vanhercke, 'Governing Health Care through EU Soft Law' in *Ibid.*

9 European Council, Council Press Release Doc. No. 12400/04 (Council Meeting on Employment, Social Policy, Health and Consumer Affairs), 4 October 2004, p. 9: OMC in health care should not impose an excessive administrative burden; health ministries should be directly involved in the OMC process; overlaps with the follow-up of the high level reflection on patient mobility should be avoided; coherence of views should be ensured within the single EU Council formation of ministers of health and social policy; the joint working with the Economic Policy Committee should continue.

started off with provisional common objectives, no common set of indicators, 'preliminary reports' (instead of full-blown 'Action Plans') etc. It was not until 2006, when the European Commission creatively managed to include the issue of 'health care and long term care' in the new 'streamlined' Social OMC that this strand became really operational.

2.2. THE DEFINING FEATURES OF AN INCOMPLETE METHOD

What does this process look like, then? During the past decade, the Social OMC has in practice been managed by the Social Protection Committee (SPC), a group of high-level officials that was established in 2000, as well as by its Sub-Group on Indicators (ISG) (created in February 2001). The SPC is an advisory body to the Employment, Social Policy, Health and Consumer Affairs (EPSCO) Council of the EU and is composed of two delegates from each Member State and the Commission. The latter provides the secretariat, and thereby has a key role. Together these actors put in place an OMC toolbox containing: the common objectives (which constitute the political mandate and thus the framework), a reporting system (through national strategic reports and joint reports), (preliminary) indicators and peer reviews. We will discuss how these tools were made operational between the launch of the Social OMC and its 'reinvigoration' in 2011; the implications of the latter go beyond the scope of this chapter.

2.2.1. Common objectives: ambiguous words

Being aware that they all – at least to some extent – face similar problems with respect to health and long-term care policies, the Member States first of all committed themselves to a number of ***common objectives*** (i.e. political priorities). In fact, they subscribed to *two* sets of priorities (see the full list of objectives in Box 1 below):

- three 'overarching objectives', which apply to the three strands of the streamlined Social OMC. For example, with the third overarching objective, Member States commit themselves to promote 'good governance, transparency and the involvement of stakeholders in the design, implementation and monitoring' of their social inclusion, pensions, *and health care and long-term care policies*;
- three objectives that refer specifically to the area of health and long-term care and which combine high quality and financial sustainability of health systems with access for all.

The common objectives have often been criticized for their openness and ambiguity. Thus, Büchs notes that the Social OMC's objectives and guidelines contain different and sometimes conflicting elements, some of which are more likely to be interpreted in ways that promote the strengthening of the welfare state whilst others are more likely to support retrenchment.[10] Greer and Vanhercke point out that the 'ambiguous words' of these common objectives in the health care strand are in fact useful when there is no fundamental agreement on health care policies in the EU: as they are broad enough to be accepted by all Member States, they allow to expand the EU policy agenda, more particularly by providing legitimacy and new discourses. There would have been even more efforts to block the common objectives (in health) if it had been absolutely clear what they were supposed to do.[11] And yet the 'normative' orientation of these health care objectives is quite evident for Flear: they not only extend market rationality and facilitate governing at a distance by inducements to self-management, they also promote moves away from equity and solidarity.[12] Writing about the same OMC strand, Hervey strongly rejects the claim that the health care OMC would be promoting neoliberal policies,[13] while others finds strong confirmation of pertinence of overarching objectives of the health care strand of the OMC.[14]

Box 1. Common objectives in the Social OMC (re-affirmed by the Council of the EU in May 2011)

A. Overarching objectives covering the three strands of the open method of coordination for social protection and social inclusion (*including* health)

Promote:

(a) social cohesion, equality between men and women and equal opportunities for all through adequate, accessible, financially sustainable, adaptable and efficient social protection systems and social inclusion policies;

10 M. Büchs, 'The Open Method of Coordination – Effectively Preventing Welfare State Retrenchment?' in S. Kröger (ed.), n. 2 <http://eiop.or.at/eiop/texte/2009-011a.htm> accessed 4 November 2011.

11 S. Greer and B. Vanhercke, n. 8.

12 See M. Flear, 'The Open Method of Coordination on Health Care after the Lisbon Strategy II: Towards a Neoliberal Framing?' in S. Kröger (ed.), n. 2 <http://eiop.or.at/eiop/index.php/eiop/article/view/2009_012a/111> accessed 4 November 2011.

13 T.K. Hervey, 'The European Union's Governance of Health Care and the Welfare Modernization Agenda' (2008) 2 *Regulation & Governance*.

14 European Commission, 'Quality in and Equality of Access to Healthcare Services' (2008) (Report produced by European Health Management Association, EuroHealthNet and the European Centre for Social Welfare Policy and Research) <www.euro.centre.org/data/1237457784_41597.pdf> accessed 4 November 2011.

(b) effective and mutual interaction between the Europe 2020 objectives of smart, sustainable and inclusive growth, taking full account of the relevant social provisions of the Lisbon Treaty; and
(c) good governance, transparency and the involvement of stakeholders in the design, implementation and monitoring of policy.

B. Common objectives with regard to health care and long-term care

Member States should provide accessible, high-quality and sustainable health care and long-term care by ensuring:

(a) access for all to adequate health and long-term care; that the need for care does not lead to poverty and financial dependency; and that inequities in access to care and in health outcomes are addressed;
(b) quality in health and long-term care, and the adaptation of care, including developing preventive care, to the changing needs and preferences of society and individuals, notably by developing quality standards reflecting best international practice and by strengthening the responsibility of health professionals and of patients and care recipients; and
(c) that adequate and high-quality health and long-term care remains affordable and financially sustainable by promoting a rational use of resources, notably through appropriate incentives for users and providers, good governance and coordination between care systems and public and private institutions. Long-term sustainability and quality require the promotion of healthy and active life styles and good human resources for the care sector.

Source: European Council (EPSCO), 'Endorsement of the Opinion of the SPC on reinvigorating the Social OMC in the context of the Europe 2020 Strategy' (2011) 10405/11 SOC 418.

2.2.2. Reports to Brussels and (not so) soft recommendations

Every two to three years, Member States explain the progress made towards these common objectives. They do this in so-called ***national strategic reports***[15] (NSRs) which contain a section on health and long-term care. Once the Commission (DG Social Affairs) has received all the national strategic reports (which present in many countries a 'container of measures taken' or a 'report to Brussels', rather than being a forward-looking or strategic document), it analyzes and assesses Member States' progress towards the common objectives with the help of

15 Formally speaking 'National report on strategies for social protection and social inclusion'.

national and European indicators. The assessment is then published in a joint report on social protection and social inclusion, which is adopted by the Commission and the Council and submitted, every year, to the (Spring) European Council.

It is worth noting that an agreement on this joint report can normally only be reached after hard negotiations, and ultimately political compromises, between Member States and the Commission. Particularly controversial points are, for instance, the relationship between the state and the market as health care provider, and the adequate level of resources 'necessary' for health care funding. This again illustrates how Member States resist EU involvement in 'their' health care systems, while also demonstrating that governance is taken seriously (as opposed to being regarded as irrelevant) by Member States. In their analysis of health care policies in the context of the Lisbon Agenda, de Ruijter and Hervey similarly find that 'governments of the Member States do not necessarily view the OMC-social in health care policy as a "soft" mechanism, posing little challenge to national competence (…) On the contrary, the wording of OMC-social documentation is often politically contested, as if it were a "hard" legally binding text.'[16]

Interestingly, the European Commission provides, as part of the joint report, a soft kind of 'recommendations' to the Member States through so-called 'country fiches'. These documents address the most important 'challenges' in (social inclusion, pensions and) health care for every country, as the following examples illustrate:

- Commenting on the 2009 German national strategic report (health section), the Commission concluded with regard to quality in long-term care that '[E]ven though quality has been steadily increased during the last years, quality controls show clearly that there is still a lot of scope for improvement'.[17]
- Regarding the quality of health care in Austria, the European Commission suggested that the system should take into account the point of view of the patient (and not the institution), that it should allow for more flexible transfer between different types of provision (inpatient/ambulant/long-term care, etc.) and that 'patients' rights had to be strengthened through clear standards'.[18]

---

16 See A. de Ruijter and T.K. Hervey, 'Healthcare and the Lisbon Agenda' in P. Copeland and D. Papadimitriou (eds.), *Evaluating the EU's Lisbon Agenda*, Palgrave *forthcoming 2012*.

17 European Commission, 'Deutschland – Gemeinsamer Bericht über Sozialschutz und soziale Eingliederung 2009' <http://ec.europa.eu/social/main.jsp?catId=757&langId=en> accessed 4 November 2011, p. 12 (authors' translation).

18 *Ibid.*, 'Österreich – Gemeinsamer Bericht über Sozialschutz und soziale Eingliederung 2009' <http://ec.europa.eu/social/main.jsp?catId=757&langId=en> accessed 4 November 2011, p. 9 (authors' translation).

- Drawing on the French NSR, the Commission found that access to health care is increasingly problematic, both from a financial and geographical point of view. The Commission also noted the absence of coercive regulation in France with regard to the control on evidence-based medicine as well as the need to prioritize ambulatory care (including with a view to avoiding unjustified use of hospitals).[19]
- Finally, the United Kingdom was asked to 'look at ways of improving integration of health and long-term care services and addressing discretion in the assessment of needs and eligibility rules' (in the UK, local authorities determine eligibility and access to care), as 'co-payments and additional user charges that are not covered for persons above the means-tested threshold can act as barriers to accessibility'.[20]

Even though these messages may come across as rather 'light' for the outside observer, they are highly contested and inevitably give rise to extensive bilateral negotiations between the Commission and the Member States, which will firmly attempt to 'control the damage'. At least some of these messages were not appreciated by German, Austrian, French or UK civil servants and politicians. In our interviews it became clear that they were not felt as 'soft' messages (at all) and in some case led to strong interrogations about continuing the Social OMC overall.

2.2.3. *Indicators: a growing but preliminary portfolio*

As far as ***indicators*** are concerned, work within the health care strand has lagged behind for a long time as compared to the areas of pensions and (especially) social inclusion, for which there is an agreement on a full battery of commonly agreed *EU* indicators (i.e., harmonized at EU level).[21] For health, a 'preliminary portfolio' of commonly agreed *national* health care indicators (with commonly agreed definitions and assumptions) was adopted in June 2006.[22] At a second stage, the SPC adopted a new list of indicators for the monitoring of the health care and long-term care objectives of the Social OMC, as well as two new health related indicators to be included in the overarching portfolio in 2008. The list as it stands now is made up of 18 primary indicators, 12 secondary indicators and 4 context indicators regrouped according to the common objective they refer

---

19 *Ibid.*, 'France – Rapport conjoint sur la protection sociale et l'inclusion sociale 2009' <http://ec.europa.eu/social/main.jsp?catId=757&langId=en> accessed 4 November 2011, pp. 7 and 9.

20 *Ibid.*, 'United Kingdom – Joint Report on Social Protection and Social Inclusion 2009' <http://ec.europa.eu/social/main.jsp?catId=757&langId=en> accessed 4 November 2011, p. 9.

21 See T. Atkinson and E. Marlier, 'Analysing and Measuring Social Inclusion in a Global Context' (Report for UNDESA) United Nations, New York 2010.

22 European Commission, 'Portfolio of overarching indicators and streamlined social inclusion, pensions, and health portfolios' D(2006), pp. 7–13, 40–50.

to.[23] Even if the new list is comprehensive, it is still 'preliminary' and 'incomplete': the full list of indicators and their meaning have not been agreed upon; review is scheduled as new data become available. Work is being continued regarding long-term care (this dimension is not fully reflected in the existing list[24]) under the new Europe 2020 Strategy, and the ISG is considering developing other indicators covering dimensions such as care utilization, out-of-pocket payments and asthma care.

In general, difficulties in data collection and handling, as well as political risks, have all slowed down the work on indicators and therefore the health care OMC as a whole. The fear of Member States to lose control over this important policy field (see section 2.1) is constantly present throughout the process and becomes particularly obvious when it comes to the development of indicators. Germany, for instance, was one of the countries that largely opposed the interference of the European level in health care policies and as a result refused the introduction of any further indicators in this area (see also Box 2 for a UK example).

Box 2. Indicators in the health care OMC: a sensitive issue

Consider, by way of illustration, the fact that the European Scrutiny Committee of the House of Commons in the United Kingdom in 2004 refused to scrutinize the Commission's Communication through which it proposed to extend the OMC to health care.[25] The Committee in fact wondered 'why such exchanges of views as are required could not be achieved by other, less intrusive, means (the Minister refers, for example, to the existing or proposed Commission and Council groups on health services and medical care)'.[26] In his response to the Committee, the Minister said that he detected no wish by Member States to use the OMC as a means to devise 'new legislation or new targets or new EU indicators' and that 'we are not having (new) targets foisted upon us by anyone'.[27] Apparently, this convinced the Committee: in March 2005, the Committee explained that it had assuaged

23 European Commission, 'Portfolio of Indicators for the Monitoring of the European Strategy for Social Protection and Social Inclusion: 2009 Update' <http://ec.europa.eu/social/main.jsp?catId=756&langId=en> accessed 4 November 2011.

24 Critical OMC scholars such as Flear argue that even indicators for access and quality of care ultimately seek to *optimize* performance, by providing the means to assess whether objectives are met, and thereby ensure that equity and solidarity are subordinated in a neoliberal frame. See M. Flear, n. 12.

25 European Commission, 'A concerted strategy for modernising social protection' COM (99) 347 final.

26 See UK Parliament (House of Commons, European Scrutiny Committee), 'Health Care and Long-Term Care', 32nd Report, 9 DOH (25576), 2004, para. 9.9.

27 See *Ibid.*, '11th Report of Session 2004–05', para. 9.12.

its concerns when the Minister 'told us repeatedly that the application of the method would not lead to the imposition on the United Kingdom of new targets and indicators'.[28] And yet it warned the government: the Committee looks 'forward to receiving the progress reports the Minister has offered to provide. We shall scrutinize them, in particular, to see if they include any targets or indicators for Member States'.[29]

In other words, the OMC might look 'soft' but, in some cases, it feels quite hard to those who are touched by it.

In view of Member States' resistance highlighted above, it may not come as a surprise that so far no ***targets*** (quantified objectives) have been set in the context of the health care OMC. This stands in contrast to the Social Inclusion OMC, which now has a 'headline target' in the newly adopted Europe 2020 Strategy.[30] But it is worth noting that the European Commission is building up pressure on Member States that provide long-term care in a devolved context to set *national targets* – as is shown by the following claim in the 2008 joint report: '[n]ational guidelines and targets can ensure uniform provision across the wide spectrum of service providers and the different levels of government involved in the management and financing of long-term care services'.[31] There is no *a priori* reason why such targets could not be extended later on to drug prescriptions for general practitioners for instance, or other health related issues. The operation of other soft law mechanisms (economic policies, employment, social inclusion) has made it very clear that once target setting has become an accepted instrument of a given OMC, the pressure to establish national or even EU-wide targets is hard to ignore for any Member State.

2.2.4. *Policy learning through peer reviews*

A final instrument of the health care OMC's toolbox is the **peer review programme**, which is at the heart of the OMC's learning objective. Each year

28 *Ibid.*, para. 9.14.
29 *Ibid.*, para. 9.15.
30 The poverty target is one of 5 'headline targets' within the EU's new strategy for smart, sustainable and inclusive growth. Its aim is to promote social inclusion, in particular through the reduction of poverty, by aiming to lift at least 20 million people out of the risk of poverty and exclusion. The target will consist in reducing the number of people in the EU (120 million) who are at risk of poverty and/or materially deprived and/or living in jobless households by one sixth (European Commission, 'Europe 2020. A Strategy for smart, sustainable and inclusive growth' COM (2010) 2020).
31 European Commission, 'Joint report on social protection and social inclusion 2008: Social inclusion, pensions, healthcare and long-term care', Office for Official Publications of the European Communities, Luxembourg 2008, p. 90.

between eight and ten peer reviews about issues relevant for social protection and social inclusion are organized in the Member States (host countries) and funded by the PROGRESS programme.[32] Many Member States, stakeholders and experts are indeed interested in sharing experiences during either of the two modalities of PROGRESS peer reviews: 'good practice' peer reviews, during which a Member State suggests a policy that has produced (exceptionally) good results; or 'policy problem' peer reviews, where an ineffective policy is studied and remedies are suggested. As a senior civil servant in the Commission explained: after 'all this hesitation, the Member States now "discovered" the OMC. If we were to follow all the issues they proposed (as topics for mutual learning), it would completely flood the Social Protection agenda for years to come'.[33]

As can be seen in Table 1 below, Member States participated in a total of 50 Peer Reviews (2005–2010) – organized through the PROGRESS programme[34] – on topics related to social inclusion, pensions as well as health and long-term care. Eleven out of those 50 peer reviews dealt with the issue of health and long-term care, which is quite significant in view of the fact that peer reviews cover no less than 10 key issues in total.[35] As can be obtained from Table 1 below – with the exception of Denmark and Slovakia – all 27 Member States have at some point participated in a peer review on health care. It is also striking that no differences can be observed when comparing the *participation* of 'old' and 'new' Member States, since both are equally present in each of the columns. This balanced picture differs when it comes to the *organization* of peer reviews: up to now, eight mostly 'old' Member States have hosted peer reviews, while Hungary is the only new Member State in the list of organizing countries. One could draw the tentative conclusion that even though the new Member States are equally interested in learning from other countries, they still seem to be afraid of (or at least uncertain about) organizing peer reviews and actively sharing their own models as examples for mutual learning.

The topics that have been discussed range from 'social integration for people with mental health problems' and 'freedom of choice and dignity for the elderly' to 'cost containment in the pharmaceutical sector', 'ensuring a functioning

32 Decision No. 284/2010/EU of the European Parliament and of the Council of 25 March 2010 amending Decision No. 1672/2006/EC establishing a Community Programme for Employment and Social Solidarity – Progress [2010] OJ L87/6.

33 Interview with Former SPC Secretary, European Commission (Brussels, Belgium, September 2007).

34 For more information on the European Commission's programme on 'Peer Review in Social Protection and Social Inclusion and Assessment in Social Inclusion', see <www.peer-review-social-inclusion.net/> accessed 4 November 2011.

35 In addition, the first peer review covering health care in particular was not held before 2006.

health care system in regions with declining and ageing populations' to 'coping with behavioural disorders in the patient's home' in the case of Alzheimer's. A recent peer review in this area, held in October 2010 in Germany, assessed 'achieving quality long-term care in residential facilities'. Interestingly, the latter peer review was organized a year after the Commission's rather straightforward comments on this issue in the 2009 Joint Report on Social Protection and Social Inclusion. Moreover, Germany hosted three peer reviews in the area of health and participated twice in peer reviews organized by other Member States, thereby outing itself as one of the keenest participants amongst the Member States (only France and Poland have participated even more intensively). This fact is quite remarkable for a Member State which has been among the most resilient to get the OMC in this area on tracks in the first place.

Table 1. Participation in peer reviews on health and long-term care topics (2005–2010)

Attended peer reviews (as host or participant)					
Number	7–8	5–6	3–4	1–2	0
	France Poland	**Germany** Finland Luxembourg Czech Republic the Netherlands United Kingdom Slovenia Sweden	Estonia Malta Romania Ireland Austria Portugal Greece	Belgium Italy Lithuania Hungary Spain Bulgaria Latvia Cyprus (Norway)	Denmark Slovakia
Total	2	10	7	9	2

Source: Peer review in social protection and social inclusion website[36]

The critical reader may argue that 'participating in peer reviews' does not necessarily equal 'policy learning'. In fact, Greer and Vanhercke pointed out that learning in the health care OMC runs the risk of being of a limited kind as often the wrong people will do the learning (i.e. representatives of the international units participate, and not the line officials).[37] The problem here is that new governance matters in particular when it successfully escapes international units and strengthens transversal specialist networks that share worldviews or policy goals (political scientists have many names for these: epistemic communities and policy advocacy coalitions are the two most common).[38] Our own research

36 <www.peer-review-social-inclusion.eu/peer-reviews> accessed 4 November 2011.

37 See S. Greer and B. Vanhercke, n.8.

38 See P.M. Haas, 'Introduction: Epistemic Communities and International Policy Coordination' (1992) 46 *International Organization*; C. Jenkins-Smith and P. Sabatier, 'Evaluating the Advocacy Coalition Framework' (1994) 14 *Journal of Public Policy*.

confirms the concern that the peer reviews in the area of health care are mainly an exercise for a select group of civil servants and experts.[39]

This brief overview of the overall architecture of the health care OMC suggests that it has most of the formal features of a 'textbook OMC': common objectives, national strategic reports, joint reports, indicators and peer reviews. The next section will look at whether this toolbox has so far delivered concrete results.

3. LOOKING FOR A NEEDLE IN A HAYSTACK: THE IMPACT OF THE HEALTH CARE OMC AT THE DOMESTIC LEVEL

Our assessment of the effectiveness and impact of the Social OMC uses Belgium as its main case study, while referring to evidence from other Member States when this is available. The assessment is first of all based on two waves of interviews with European, national, and sub-national civil servants, politicians and stakeholders (social partners and NGO representatives) working in the areas of poverty and social exclusion, pensions and health care. A first wave of 32 interviews was conducted during the second half of 2007, mainly providing information about the preparation of the 2006–2008 national strategic report, and the impact of the OMC until that moment. A second round of 20 interviews was conducted in December 2010, providing insights in the 2008–2010 reporting exercise. The 2010 round of interviews was complemented by an on-line survey which contained some 40 closed questions and was completed – between November and December 2010 – by 59 experts working in the three policy fields. Twenty respondents indicated to have their primary expertise in health care. We corroborated all the claims made by our respondents by confronting them, first, with the views of other interviewees and, second, with as many primary and secondary sources as possible.

To OMC critics, it will not come as a great surprise that by and large, Belgian health care experts who answered our 2010 on-line survey do not seem to think that the NSR process stimulated a genuine policy debate among the participants in the OMC process, or among a wider public (45% of them 'strongly disagree' with this suggestion, while 20% agree). Similarly, only a small minority of health care respondents thinks that ideas associated with the Social OMC are discussed in the key social policy discussion forums in Belgium. Unsurprisingly, then, merely 10% of health care experts in our on-line survey would agree with the

39 B. Vanhercke, 'Assessing the Effectiveness and the Impact of the Social OMC in Preparation for the New Cycle. Country study Belgium' (2011) (Report on behalf of the European Commission).

statement that the ideas associated with the Social OMC are being reflected in the policy decisions in Belgium. A recent assessment coordinated by the Public Policy and Management Institute (PPMI) came to very similar findings. Drawing on in-depth country studies in 11 Member States,[40] the impact of this strand of the Social OMC was indeed found to be weak across these countries when compared to the significant impact of the social inclusion and pensions strands.[41]

Does this mean that actors do not see a genuine added value in pursuing this strand of the OMC? The results of our research indicate that this would be jumping to conclusions. In the following we present four different mechanisms through which the health care OMC could exert some impact, and conclude with some (admittedly modest) examples of potential substantive impact.

3.1. PRUDENT MIRROR EFFECTS

A first element we call '*prudent mirror effects*'. First of all, several of our health care interviewees explained that for them the real added value of the NSR process is that it creates a *platform for discussion* between levels of government, as well as a domestic network which can be activated for other purposes (e.g. exchange of information). Thus, in Belgium, the NSR's health care chapter results from consultation between several administrations: the Federal Public Service for Social Security (which is in charge of the overall coordination), the International Department of the 'Federal Public Service for Health, Food Chain Safety and Environment', the administrations of the three Communities and (more sporadically) the National Institute for Health and Disability Insurance (INAMI/RIZIV). The document that is being produced through this consultation process (i.e. the health care section of the NSR) is considered to be the only document in Belgium that provides an encompassing overview (in Dutch and French) of the health care policies of all levels of government.[42] This makes it a rather unique document in the Belgian institutional setting. Regrettably, in view of the human resources invested in this document, it would seem that only its authors are aware of its existence.

40 Belgium, Denmark, France, Germany, Italy, Lithuania, Poland, Portugal, Romania, Spain, and the UK.

41 'Evaluation of the effectiveness and impact of the Social OMC since 2006' (Deliverable 7) (2011) and 'Suggestions for improvement and strengthening of the effectiveness and impact of the Social OMC' (Deliverable 8) (2011), both reports produced by experts led by the Public Policy and Management Institute, on behalf of the European Commission.

42 But see the Health Care Systems in Transition (HiT) country profiles (analytical description of a health care system and of reform initiatives) produced by the European Observatory on Health Systems and Policies. For more information <www.euro.who.int/en/home/projects/observatory/publications/health-system-profiles-hits> accessed 4 November 2011.

Note that a similar (self-)reflection or mirroring experience has been identified in Germany: in 2007, a report was published on behalf of the federal Ministry of Health, in which data were collected on all health and long-term care indicators.[43] According to the Minister for Health this report was the *first attempt* to systematically compare and contrast the German health care system with the other EU Member States (using indicators selected/developed at EU level), not only at the national level, but also with regard to all sixteen of Germany's Länder.[44] The OMC was identified as the main reason to conduct this study. Perhaps even more interestingly, the report includes a clear ranking of Member States (highlighting the three best performing countries within the tables). This rather open and explicit assessment of policy performance is a quite surprising step, especially coming from a Member State that put up some heroic fights against such 'rankings' at EU level.

3.2. SPREADING OF PEER REVIEWS AS A DOMESTIC GOVERNANCE TOOL

Above we explained that physical participation in PROGRESS peer reviews is restricted to a rather small group of OMC insiders. This does not, however, mean that these events do not reach a wider audience. Most respondents in the pensions (79%) and social inclusion (66%) strands claim (in our on-line survey) to have read, at some point, a document, statement or study produced by peer reviews. With regard to the health care OMC, this is the case for 50% of the experts. As important is that those (civil servants, social partners, academics) who have participated in a peer review are almost invariably satisfied (and mostly quite enthusiastic) about the information provided and the issues discussed, and would very much like to be involved more frequently (that is, if the peer review is directly relevant for their work, which normally means that it is as practical and detailed as possible).[45]

Perhaps this high satisfaction rate is one of the reasons why in Belgium the practice of organizing peer reviews has been spreading from the EU to the federal (e.g. on child poverty, active ageing, communication in pension systems), regional (e.g. on integrated services for target groups, access to housing and

---

43 See M. Schneider, U. Hofmann, A. Köse, P. Biene and T. Krauss, *Indikatoren der OMK im Gesundheitswesen und der Langzeitpflege. Gutachten für das Bundesministerium für Gesundheit*, BASYS, Augsburg 2007.

44 *Ibid.*

45 Interview with Health Attaché, Permanent Representation of Belgium to the EU (Brussels, Belgium, 10 December 2010); Interview with Director of the Social Department, Public Centre for Social Welfare of Leuven (Leuven, Belgium, 30 November 2010); Interview with Senior Advisor, Federation of Belgian Enterprises (Brussels, Belgium, 30 November 2010).

inclusive education)[46] and local level (including, again, on child poverty). Several interviewees suggest that the group of people who participate in the European peer reviews should be enlarged (e.g. including the local level). Finally, note that 'learning' is not restricted to peer reviews: several of our interviewees referred to their participation in EU Presidency events on social issues (80% of health care experts in the on-line survey have participated in such events). Taken together these people constitute an increasingly large 'OMC Community'.

3.3. NATIONAL STEERING CAPACITY

A third element that is raised quite regularly by actors in our case study has to do with the Social OMC's (alleged) contribution to national steering capacity (e.g. *use of data and indicators).* The enhanced capability for more systematic *comparison with other countries* is cited by most of the actors as one of the most important contributions of the Social OMC.

Our interviews (in Belgium and other Member States) confirm that the OMC has increased (institutionalized) awareness of policies, practices, and performances in other countries, by non-state actors as well as by governmental actors. As one key observer explained: 'With Europe, it is more in the national culture to look for what the neighbours are doing.'[47] In fact, the replies to our on-line survey with regard to this question are quite striking: in all three strands a majority of respondents believe that the NSR process indeed improved national steering capacities. Given the difficulties in the development of health care indicators described in section 2.2.3, it may come as a surprise then that 65% of Belgian health care experts confirm the impact on national steering capacities in our on-line survey.

Note that the consultation between several health care administrations described in section 3.1 would provide an excellent opportunity to further improve the national steering capacity in this area: according to our interviewees this inter-institutional coordination improved between the two rounds of NSRs (2006–2008 and 2008–2010 respectively), and it is even considered to be quite unique in the sense that there is no other platform in Belgium where all (federal and Community) administrations consult with one another. This is why the Federal Public Service (FPS) Social Security intended to institutionalize this newly created structure with a view to organizing the follow-up of the health care

46 See Flemish Parliament, 'Armoede uitsluiten, armen insluiten: Beleidsbrief Armoedebestrijding 2011', p. 11.

47 Interview with Head of Unit, Social Protection and Social Services, DG V, European Commission (Brussels, Belgium, 24 July 2007).

section of the NSR, but this plan was postponed due to the overloaded agenda of the 2010 Belgian Presidency of the EU.[48]

3.4. THE NEEDLE IN THE HAYSTACK: HEALTH INEQUALITIES

While all previously mentioned examples of 'mechanisms' through which the health care OMC could work (mirror effects, spreading of peer reviews and the contribution of this strand of the Social OMC to national steering capacities) are *governance* related, there is no solid evidence confirming any *substantive* policy change – i.e. influence of the OMC on policy framing, agendas and legislative outcomes – as a result of this.

Nevertheless, the developments regarding the issue of health inequalities should be further considered, as they may point to a more substantive impact of the OMC. Thus, some of our interviewees claimed that the Commission's insistence on the topic of 'health inequalities' – through the joint reports, indicator development, an SPC Opinion as well as through PROGRESS funding in support of innovative action in this field, etc. – led to increased awareness about this topic, which was also reflected in the 2010 EPSCO Council Conclusions. The Council indeed adopted the SPC Opinion about 'Solidarity in Health: Reducing health inequalities in the EU' that pays considerable attention to the links between social inclusion and health equality, thereby referring extensively to the Social OMC.[49] For de Ruijter and Hervey 'the equality agenda, articulated in terms of social cohesion (rather than individual rights / non-discrimination), seems to be the most likely way forward' if the health care strand is to become a success in the future.[50]

Apart from the topic of health inequalities, German interviewees claimed that the EU's focus on quality management in long-term care somewhat changed perceptions about this topic (see discussion about peer reviews and country fiches in section two). Note that in the aforementioned Social OMC assessment, Lithuanian interviewees explained that the concept of integrated long-term care was first institutionalized in their country in response to the OMC process.[51] Similarly, the OMC would have contributed to the initiation of discussions about

48 Interview with Former Advisor, Federal Public Service for Social Security (Brussels, Belgium, 2 December 2010).

49 Social Protection Committee, 'Solidarity in Health: Reducing Health Inequalities within the EU' (Opinion) SPC/2010/5/4 final.

50 A. de Ruijter and T.K. Hervey, n. 16.

51 PPMI, 'Assessing the Effectiveness and the Impact of the Social OMC in Preparation for the New Cycle. Country study Lithuania. Report on behalf of the European Commission', p. 116.

the topic of long-term care in Poland.[52] But so far these claims have not been clearly confirmed by 'triangulation' (a combination of different sources) and so they cannot be taken for granted.

4. TRACING EU SIGNIFICANCE: A PATCHWORK OF SOFT GOVERNANCE AND INSTRUMENT HYBRIDITY

While the previous sections of this chapter looked at the *domestic* impact of the health care OMC, this section discusses whether the health care OMC has any significance at the *EU level*. The key questions are: is there any empirical evidence to substantiate such 'EU impact' claims; and, as important, is there evidence of any kind of interaction between policy and law at the EU level?

4.1. OMC AS A 'TEMPLATE' FOR EU SOFT LAW MECHANISMS

A first indication that an assessment of the significance of the OMC should not discard the EU level, is the fact that the Barroso Commission, not known for being a special advocate of new governance in the social field, 'has continued to propose new OMC processes when faced with the perceived need for joint action in politically sensitive institutionally diverse policy fields'.[53] And in spite of all the scepticism (especially from academics), many (if not all) of 'other' Commission-led new governance processes on health care – which include the European Health Policy Forum, the High Level Committee on Health and the High Level Process of Reflection on Patient Mobility – sooner or later refer to the OMC as a 'goal to attain'.[54] Thus, it seems that the OMC has become a 'template' for EU soft law mechanisms in health.

52 PPMI, 'Assessing the Effectiveness and the Impact of the Social OMC in Preparation for the New Cycle. Country study Poland. Report on behalf of the European Commission', p. 21.

53 See C.F. Sabel and J. Zeitlin, 'Learning from Difference: The New Architecture of Experimentalist Governance in the European Union' (2007) European Governance Papers (EUROGOV) No. C-07-02.

54 EU Health Policy Forum (EHPF), 'Recommendations on EU Social Policy' (2003), p. 7; European Commission, 'The Internal Market and Health Services' (2001) (Report of the High Level Committee on Health), p. 26; European Commission, 'Minutes of the meeting of the high level process on patient mobility and healthcare developments in the European Union' HLPR/2003/2 REV 1, 3 February 2003, p. 5; M. Kyprianou, 'The New European Healthcare Agenda', Speech at the European Voice Conference 'Healthcare: Is Europe Getting Better?', Brussels 20 January 2005, p. 6.

This finding is confirmed by the fact that, even within the limited field of health care, new proposals for launching OMC processes arise on a regular basis: the European Commission has been thinking out loud about starting new applications of OMC-type processes to areas such as organ donation and transplantation[55] as well as nanosciences and nanotechnologies.[56] Others would like to see the method to be applied to obesity and cancer screening, or to e-health.[57]

4.2. INTERACTION WITH OTHER (HARDER) EU INSTRUMENTS: 'SOFT-TO-HARD-TO-SOFT' GOVERNANCE

A crucial finding is that the substantive messages coming from the Social OMC have been used to – selectively – influence 'harder' forms of EU soft governance, including the new Integrated Guidelines for implementing the Europe 2020 Strategy. The Council adopted (in October 2010) six broad guidelines relating to the economic policies of the Member States and the EU, and four guidelines concerning the employment (and in fact also social) policies of the Member States.[58] *Integrated Guideline 10* (see Annex 1) deals with 'promoting social inclusion and combating poverty' and underlines the role of pensions, *health care*, and public services in maintaining social cohesion. Note that the common social objectives for health care enter into Guideline 10 primarily insofar as they contribute to 'social exclusion' goals. Indeed, the latter refers to the need for modernization of social protection systems (including access to health care) so that they can provide adequate income support and services 'while remaining financially sustainable and encouraging participation in society and in the labour market'. In sum, at least on paper, the Europe 2020 Strategy welcomes some key social dimensions, including (access to) health care, back to its heart (through the Integrated Guideline 10), after these issues had been removed from the Lisbon Strategy during its 2005 revision.

---

55 European Commission, 'Organ donation and transplantation: Policy actions at EU level' COM (2007) 275 final, p. 10. Work on 'a common set of indicators to monitor organ policy' in the context of 'National Priority Actions' is currently being pursued in Organ Donation and Transplantation Experts Meetings chaired by the European Commission. <http://ec.europa.eu/health/ph_threats/human_substance/oc_organs/docs/ev_20090311_mi_en.pdf> accessed 4 November 2011.

56 *Ibid.*, 'Nanosciences and nanotechnologies: An action plan for Europe 2005–2009' COM (2005) 243 final, p. 4.

57 *Ibid.*, 'Making healthcare better for European citizens: An action plan for a European e-health area' COM (2004) 356 final, p. 16. Interview with Deputy Head, Health Strategy Unit, DG SANCO, European Commission (Brussels, Belgium, 8 October 2007).

58 Their aim is to provide guidance to Member States on defining their 'National Reform Programmes' and implementing reforms, in line with the Stability and Growth Pact.

And yet, this new situation entails some serious risks, most importantly that the 'social dimension' (including health care) becomes subsumed into the growth objectives of the new strategy (see the reference to 'financially sustainable' and 'labour market' in the aforementioned Guideline 10), especially in light of the recent strengthening of the Stability and Growth Pact. This is why one author claims that in 'a decade from now linguists may use the phrase "Social dimension of Europe 2020" as an example of an oxymoron'.[59] And yet, many of our interviewees refer to the fact that without the Social OMC, the economic discourse regarding (the financial sustainability) of health care systems would regain its earlier monopoly. To put it differently, the Social OMC is also about occupying the health care territory vis-à-vis the economic players (especially the ECOFIN Council and its Economic Policy Committee) – in other words, to support the 'social' agenda of DG Social Affairs and its network over the alternative 'economic' frameworks and networks.

The OMC has also started to interact with the EU's financial instruments, and the European Social Fund (ESF) more particularly. For de la Rosa it is clear that the relationship between the two instruments works both ways: if the ESF strengthens the OMC, the latter may in turn influence cohesion policy.[60] Hervey and Vanhercke highlight the interlinking between the OMC and the ESF.[61] For these authors, the fact that the ESF Regulation for the 2007–13 programming period explicitly refers to the Open Method of Coordination on Social Protection and Social Inclusion[62] represents a case in point of 'instrument hybridity'. Indeed, for these authors 'there is no reason why in the near future certain elements of the health care OMC would not be taken into account by the Commission, de jure or de facto, to determine whether expenditure is eligible for assistance under the Fund'.[63] The recent appeal from the Council of the EU[64] to make more effective use of EU financial programmes with a view to health system innovation *and reducing health inequalities* seems to confirm this claim.

The link between the OMC and the Community method has also received considerable academic attention. De la Rosa explains how the Social OMC ensures

---

59 B. Vanhercke, 'Is "The Social Dimension of Europe 2020" an Oxymoron?' in C. Degryse and D. Natali (eds.), *Social Developments in the European Union 2010*, ETUI, OSE, Brussels 2011.

60 S. de la Rosa, *La méthode ouverte de coordination dans le système juridique communautaire*, Bruylant, Brussels 2007.

61 T.K. Hervey and B. Vanhercke, n.7.

62 Article 4.3 of Regulation (EC) No. 1081/2006 of the European Parliament and Council of 5 July on the European Social Fund and repealing Regulation (EC) No. 1784/1999 [2006] OJ L210/12.

63 T.K. Hervey and B. Vanhercke, n. 7.

64 European Council, 'Council Conclusions: Towards Modern, Responsive and Sustainable Health Systems' (3095th Employment, Social Policy, Health and Consumer Affairs Council Meeting – Health issues) 6 June 2011 <www.consilium.europa.eu/uedocs/cms_data/docs/pressdata/en/lsa/122395.pdf> accessed 4 November 2011.

a regular follow-up of certain non-discrimination directives.[65] An example in the area of health that can highlight the interlinking of the OMC and the Community method is the Directive on the application of patient's rights in cross-border health care which contains an entire chapter on 'Cooperation in Healthcare'.[66] Within chapter four of this Directive, five types of cooperation can be identified which are clearly inspired by the OMC. Examples include:

- Mutual assistance and cooperation: Member States shall engage in 'cooperation on standards and guidelines on quality and safety and the exchange of information (…)' (Article 10);
- European reference networks, which could 'encourage the development of quality and safety benchmarks and help to develop and spread best practice within and outside the network' (Article 12);
- Concerning rare diseases: 'The Commission shall support Member States in cooperating in the development of diagnosis and treatment capacity (…)' (Article 13);
- With regard to eHealth, 'The Union shall support and facilitate cooperation and the exchange of information among Member States working within a voluntary network (…)', while one of the objectives of the eHealth network shall be to 'draw up guidelines' (Article 14).

According to Sauter (in this volume) these elements are not key in the harmonization setting of the Directive but 'nevertheless important to the continued collaboration between the Member States in this field, and by creating cross-border policy communities they may contribute towards providing support for further integration of health care markets – possibly by spill-over, and including further harmonization'.[67] One possible example of such spill-over effects could be that Member States engage in deliberation about key notions such as 'good quality care' (which may have different interpretations and expectations across, and within, the Member States). Such deliberations could take place in the context of any directive that includes 'soft pockets' such as the ones found in the Directive on the application of patient's rights in cross-border health care.[68] According to Hervey, the latter Directive's chapter IV on 'Cooperation in Healthcare' has the potential to lead to changes in national practices, not through the 'classic Community method' of granting legal rights to individuals within the

65 S. de la Rosa, n. 60.

66 Directive 2011/24/EU of the European Parliament and of the Council on the application of patients' rights in cross-border healthcare [2011] OJ L88/45.

67 W.Sauter, 'Harmonization in Health Care: The EU Patients' Rights Directive' in this volume.

68 See E. Szyszczak, 'Patients' Rights: A Lost Cause or a Missed Opportunity?' in J.W. Van De Gronden, E. Szyszczak, U. Neergaard and M. Krajewski (eds.), *Health Care and EU Law*, T.M.C. Asser Press, The Hague 2011.

EU, 'but by promoting convergence of approaches through mandatory transparent sharing of practices and consequent recognition of practices that are successful, and their development into benchmarks of best practice'.[69]

In this context it seems worthwhile to have a closer look at the EU's Health Technology Assessment (HTA), created as a European-wide coordination framework with a view to a better coordination of national HTA actions. The HTA seems to be a case in point to illustrate the formalization (and thereby further institutionalization) of OMC-based cooperation, which is moving closer to a rule of law framework of good governance practice. Indeed, in spite of the fact that HTA collaboration takes place outside the OMC framework (in fact there is not even a single cross-reference made between both instruments), the instruments used within this collaboration are strikingly similar to the OMC toolbox (even if the HTA has a clearly narrower focus in terms of substance). The (simplified) step-by-step development of HTA[70] (see Box 3) – which started off as a political process and was ultimately inserted in the EU Patients' Rights Directive – not only illustrates how 'soft' governance is consequently translated into 'hard' EU law. It also illustrates how 'hard' law ultimately reverts to 'soft' governance for its actual implementation. This 'soft-to-hard-to-soft' development clearly shows that the 'interaction' between law and policy in the European health care arena is developing into a 'hybridization' of instruments.

Box 3: Health Technology Assessment as an example of EU's 'soft-to-hard-to-soft' governance

The term Health Technology Assessment describes a 'multidisciplinary process that summarizes information about the medical, social, economic, and ethical issues related to the use of health technology'. Its aim is to inform and thereby contribute to the formulation of safe, effective and patient focused health policies.[71] Potential subjects of these assessments are for instance diagnostic and treatment methods, medical equipment, pharmaceuticals, rehabilitation and prevention methods or organizational and supportive systems within which health care is provided.

---

69 T.K. Hervey, 'Cooperation between Health Care Authorities in the Proposed Directive on Patients' Rights in Cross-Border Health Care' in *Ibid.*

70 For a further discussion, see R. Baeten and W. Palm, 'Preserving General Interest in Healthcare through Secondary and Soft EU Law: The Case of the Patients' Rights Directive' in U. Neergaard, E. Szyszczak, J.van de Gronden and M. Krajewski (eds.), *The Role of Social Services of General Interest in EU Law: New Challenges and Tensions*, Springer *forthcoming 2012.*

71 <http://ec.europa.eu/health/technology_assessment/policy/index_en.htm> accessed 4 November 2011.

In 2004, as a result of the work of the High Level Group on Health Services and Medical Care, HTA was identified as a 'a political priority' by the Council and the Commission, who recognized 'an urgent need for establishing a sustainable European network on HTA'.[72] Thus, the European network for Health Technology Assessment (EUnetHTA) Project was set up under Danish leadership to create an effective and sustainable network for HTA across Europe that could contribute to HTAs in Member States by providing necessary information.

In the follow-up, the EUnetHTA Project[73] became the EUnetHTA Collaboration in November 2008 – thereby deepening the degree of its formalization. Since 2010, activities are organized in the framework of the EUnetHTA Joint Action 2010–2012. The EUnetHTA now brings together government-appointed organizations from EU Member States, the European Economic Area (EEA) and the European Free Trade Association (EFTA) countries as well as regional agencies and non-profit organizations that are involved in the field of HTA with the overall aim to, 'facilitate efficient use of resources available for HTA, to create a sustainable system of HTA knowledge sharing, and to promote good practise in HTA methods and processes'.[74] To achieve these aims, the EUnetHTA uses many instruments that can also regularly be found in other new governance mechanisms as for instance the creation of a database on HTA, the guarantee of common standards and the involvement of all relevant stakeholders.

Most recently, Article 15 of the Directive on the application of patients' rights in cross-border health care identifies HTA as an area where '[T]he Union shall support and facilitate cooperation and the exchange of scientific information among Member States within a voluntary network connecting national authorities or bodies responsible for health technology assessment designated by the Member States'. Note the striking similarity between the language used to describe the aims, activities and tools of HTA coordination and OMC jargon.

72 High Level Group on Health Services and Medical Care, 'Report from the High Level Group to the Employment, Social Affairs, Health and Consumer Protection Council on 6–7 December 2004, Executive Summary' HLG/2004/21, p. 11.

73 For more information about EUnetHTA, see the website of the EUnetHTA Joint Action <www.eunethta.net/> accessed 4 November 2011.

74 <www.eunethta.eu/Public/About_EUnetHTA/> accessed 4 November 2011.

4.3. SOFT GOVERNANCE AND THE EUROPEAN COURT OF JUSTICE

A final illustration of the OMC's significance at the EU level is more cautious. Hervey (provocatively) examines adjudicating by the European Court of Justice 'in the shadow of the informal settlement',[75] thereby inverting the idea of 'bargaining in the shadow of the law'.[76] In her analysis, Hervey shows how new governance can cast a shadow over adjudication processes and influences the ECJ's way to frame and solve problems as well as its reasoning by taking account of and learn from the ideas and concepts that are developed and spread within the informal settings. Even though the concrete case studies do not directly deal with the Social OMC (they relate to the European Employment Strategy (EES) and the Bologna Process on Higher Education) the findings are highly relevant for our study. Indeed, they do not only indicate the mere *possibility* that the ECJ would take elements of new governance into consideration, but take this one step further by illustrating that this kind of spill-over is happening *already*.

Furthermore, Hervey argues that the soft norms that develop within the new governance frameworks form part of the interpretation of the Treaties, which the Court in turn has to apply in its ruling. In the field of health services, positions that are developed within the framework of informal settings that deal with possible reasons to justify a restriction of the right of free movement of services have to be taken into account by the ECJ when it interprets Article 56 Treaty on the Functioning of the European Union (TFEU).[77] In any case, it seems that the Court is no more blind to governance measures than it is to legislation or proposed legislation: it will increasingly be inspired by the outcomes of the governance process in its judgements. More particularly when it comes to the question of proportionality, as well as when the Court has to interpret difficult notions such as 'undue delays', 'solidarity' or a definition of 'public interest' in the context of cross-border health care services. Unsurprisingly then, legal

75 See T.K. Hervey, 'Adjudicating in the Shadow of the Informal Settlement? The Court of Justice of the European Union, "New Governance" and Social Welfare' (2010) 63 *Current Legal Problems*.

76 The concept of a 'shadow of hierarchy' (see R. Mayntz and W. Scharpf (eds.), *Gesellschaftliche Selbstregulierung und politische Steuerung*, Campus Verlag, Frankfurt am Main 1995) is used to describe governance settings where the threat of a direct state intervention (understood as the introduction of binding rules) leads to the adoption of voluntary agreements. The main idea is that informal settings are most likely to be effective when a strong hierarchy is looming in the background. Such a 'shadow of hierarchy' provides a crucial incentive for both governments and non-state actors to take non-hierarchical rulemaking and/or service provision seriously. Since self-regulation allows for greater flexibility, the involved actors can influence the policy outcomes. For a more detailed account on the impact of the 'shadow of hierarchy' in governance settings without government, see for example T.A. Börzel and T. Risse, 'Governance without a State: Can It Work?' (2010) 4 *Regulation & Governance*.

77 See T.K. Hervey, n. 75.

scholars like Dawson conclude that 'the political nature of processes such as the OMC – which allow governments to *multilaterally* defend and review important social policy objectives – may offer the European Courts a useful source of information and legitimacy in determining where the boundaries between the internal market and national welfare states really lie.'[78]

This said, the potential influence of the Social OMC through the *erga omnes* effect of ECJ rulings should not be overstated: even if it is true that all Member States would be indirectly influenced by (preliminary or non-compliance) rulings taking into account elements of the OMC, scholars like Obermaier who assess the impact of the ECJ rulings on domestic social policy, conclude that the impact of these rulings is far less potent than previously thought.[79]

In sum, when compared to the somehow disappointing results regarding the (lack of) impact of the health care OMC at the domestic level, this section provided some arguments as to why the health care OMC should not be discarded too easily: at the EU level, this process has some significance, first, as a template for EU soft law mechanisms in health, and second as the centre of various interactions between policy and law. Note that both at the domestic and EU level the impact of the health care OMC is largely of a procedural nature, while so far (almost) no firm evidence of substantial impact (influence on policy contents) could be provided. The next section addresses the question why this is so.

5. EXPLAINING LIMITED SUBSTANTIVE IMPACT: LACK OF OWNERSHIP AND ACTOR RIVALRY?

Section three made it crystal clear that OMC in health care is by no means shaking domestic social policy-making and there is no convincing evidence that actors in health care policy consider the OMC as an important, or even useful, tool in domestic policy-making, as opposed to the Social Inclusion or Pensions strands of the Social OMC.[80] Therefore this section tries to find some explanations for the limited impact of the OMC in this policy field.

---

78 M. Dawson, 'Three Waves of New Governance in the European Union' (2011) 37 *EL Rev*, p. 216. And see R. Baeten, B. Vanhercke and M. Couchier, 'The Europeanisation of National Health Care Systems: Creative Adaptation in the Shadow of Patient Mobility Case Law' (2010) 3 OSE Paper Series, for a discussion of how Member States creatively adapt their domestic legislation in the shadow of patient mobility case law.

79 A.J. Obermaier, *The End of Territoriality? The Impact of ECJ Rulings on British, German and French Social Policy*, Ashgate, Surrey 2009.

80 See for example M.P. Hamel and B. Vanhercke, n. 3, for a discussion of the different usages of the Social Inclusion OMC. B. Vanhercke explains how, against the odds, the Pensions OMC

5.1. OWNERSHIP OF A CLOSED SHOP

Earlier research on the effectiveness of the OMC has clearly highlighted 'leverage' as an important mechanism for *any* OMC to have an impact (or in other words to produce effects on the ground).[81] Indeed, only when an OMC instrument is being 'creatively used' by actors to pursue their goals, one can expect it to have an effect. This section therefore examines stakeholder participation within the health care strand of the Social OMC focusing, again on Belgium as our main case study. It is clear from the stylized description in section three that the Belgian NSR-process in health care is by and large a 'closed shop' which only involves administrations of the different levels of government. Political actors come in only at a very late stage, when the NSR is formally adopted at an 'Inter-Ministerial Conference' (IMC). Some of the most important actors in health care policy-making, such as the mutual funds and health professionals, are not involved. Writing about the health care OMC, Dawson equally finds that the method generally relies on those *already within* the 'inner circle' of 'Europeanized' participants; pointing again to the finding that there is little evidence of the multiplication or 'broadening' of accountable actors.[82] This low level of stakeholder involvement in the health care strand clearly contrasts with the writing of the Social Inclusion section of the NSR (sometimes referred to as NAP/Inclusion), which has been opened up, step by step, to a wide range of actors in many Member States.[83]

Note that one can find two (tiny) 'holes' in this 'closed shop' image of the health care OMC in Belgium. First, several drafts of the NSRs (*including* the health care chapter) are being proposed – by the representatives of the FPS Social Security – to the social partners in the context of the National Labour Council. But even though this procedure was confirmed by the representatives of both sides of industry during our interviews, both employer and employee representatives explained that these sessions involved nothing more than 'information', and

became a selective amplifier for reforming Belgian pension policies (see B. Vanhercke, 'Against the Odds. The OMC as a Selective Amplifier for Reforming Belgian Pension Policies' in S. Kröger (ed.), n. 2 <http://eiop.or.at/eiop/index.php/eiop/article/view/2009_017a/102> accessed 4 November 2011.

81 For a detailed account on the importance of leverage as a mechanism to explain the OMC's impact as well as for an argument to distinguish between the 'impact' versus the 'adequacy' of the OMC, see B. Vanhercke, 'Delivering the Goods for Europe 2020? The Social OMC's Adequacy and Impact Re-Assessed' in E. Marlier and D. Natali (eds.) with R. Van Dam, n. 2.

82 See M. Dawson, 'EU Law "Transformed"? Evaluating Accountability and Subsidiarity in the "Streamlined" OMC for Social Inclusion and Social Protection' in S. Kröger (ed.), n.2, <http://eiop.or.at/eiop/texte/EIoP_2009_SpecIssue_1.pdf> accessed 4 November 2011.

83 See INBAS GmbH and ENGENDER asbl, 'Study on Stakeholders' Involvement in the Implementation of the Open Method of Coordination (OMC) in Social Protection and Social Inclusion' (2010) (Report for the European Commission).

could certainly not be seen as 'participation'.[84] Secondly, the main author of the health care chapter of the NSR explained that he presented a draft of this chapter to the 'Actions' Task Force[85] in charge of the preparation of the National Action Plan on Social Inclusion,[86] thereby 'opening up' the process, a (little) bit. Clearly, these nuances do not change the overall picture of the health care OMC as a well-kept secret. This gloomy picture is further confirmed by more specific questions in the aforementioned on-line survey: while Belgian policy-makers and stakeholders are in general rather familiar with the OMC features, our health care respondents seem to agree that most social policy-makers have not read the national strategic reports or the joint reports. The same is true for the aforementioned country profiles (which are part of the joint reports) and the supporting documents (*Commission* staff working paper) produced by the European Commission, which are even less known. This raises obvious questions with regard to the 'ownership' of the health care strand of the Social OMC. The aforementioned Social OMC assessment confirms that the visibility and ownership of the health care strand is problematic in several (not to say all) Member States, including in France, the UK, Germany and Denmark.

It can thus be safely concluded that the potential of the health care OMC to produce widespread learning effects, or to lead to creative use of the OMC tools at the domestic level, is very weak. Furthermore, it became clear that actors within the field of the health care OMC were only partly informed about the process as such.

5.2. ACTOR RIVALRY

A second explanation for the limited impact of the OMC in health care is the very nature of health and health policies. Health is a horizontal issue that plays a role in many different aspects of daily life (nutrition and food safety, transport, working conditions, housing etc.). The European Commission has recognized that health is determined to a large extent by factors outside the health area (for example agriculture, education, and environment) and that effective health policy must thus involve all relevant policy areas. This can be seen in the EU's

84 Interview with Senior Advisor, Federation of Belgian Enterprises (Brussels, Belgium, 30 November 2010); Interview with Advisor, Studies Department, Belgian General Federation of Labour (Brussels, Belgium, 9 December 2010).

85 This Task Force is presided by the federal 'Social Integration' administration. The Regional administrations are equal members of the Task Forces, together with a variety of stakeholders (service providers, NGOs, experts).

86 Interview with former Advisor in the Federal Public Service for Social Security (Brussels, Belgium, 2 December 2010).

Health in All Policies (HiAP)[87] approach which is also identified as one of the four key principles in the EU Health Strategy 2008–2013.[88] This complexity makes health policy hard to influence *in any case* (including through EU soft law). But there is more: the multifaceted nature of health policy makes this a governance territory where different actors from different policy fields try to influence decision-making through a variety of channels. The resulting actor rivalry exists simultaneously at different levels of governance.

At the *broader EU level* different actors want to have a say when it comes to health care decisions. As Hervey and Vanhercke show, no less than five different sets of actors try to expand their influence on the EU health care debate: the 'social affairs', 'internal market', 'public health', 'economic' and 'enterprise' players. Together, they create a very crowded law and policy-making space to which actors bring their conflicting agendas and different understandings of health policies.[89] According to Greer and Vanhercke the variety of actors, concepts and agendas reduces the 'effectiveness' of this OMC strand, since it entails huge competition for time and political attention with other health policy issues and processes. An additional element is the European Commission's internal divisions (including cleavages between DG Employment, Social Affairs and Inclusion on the one hand and DG Health and Consumers on the other), which allows the Council and national governments to reassert control.[90] In other words: there is a clear lack of leadership in the European health care debate. De Ruijter and Hervey point out that even though health care policies

---

87 The *Health in all Policy* (HiAP) approach has been given a lot of attention while it figured as a major topic on the agenda of the Finish Presidency of the EU in 2005. The core of HiAP is to examine determinants of health that can be altered to improve health but are mainly controlled by the policies of sectors other than health. The core ideas and values of the HiAP approach of the EU is similar to *The Health for All policy framework of the WHO* (see, for example: 'The Health for All policy framework for the WHO European Region: 2005 update' <www.euro.who.int/en/what-we-publish/abstracts/health-for-all-policy-framework-for-the-who-european-region-the-2005-update> accessed 4 November 2011).

88 <http://ec.europa.eu/health-eu/doc/whitepaper_en.pdf> accessed 4 November 2011.

89 Take for instance the ECOFIN Council Conclusion on health systems in the EU that was adopted in December 2010 and that is clearly driven by an economic approach towards health care: in its conclusion, the ECOFIN Council stresses the necessity to further enhance effectiveness within the health care systems of the Member States in view of the need to ensure long-term sustainability in public finances. European Council (ECOFIN), 'Draft Council Conclusions on the EPC-Commission Joint Report on Health Systems in the EU' (2010) 16939/10, ECOFIN 767.

90 Note that an inter-service group on public health was set up with the purpose to improve coordination on health within the different Commission departments. More than 20 departments are represented within this group that also has several thematic sub-groups, dealing with dynamic health systems, global health, health and environment and HIV/AIDS. For more information, see the website of DG SANCO: <http://ec.europa.eu/health/health_policies/coordination/index_en.htm> accessed 4 November 2011.

remain on the EU agenda, it is due to this institutional fragmentation that health care is 'side-lined from the OMC'.[91]

Actor rivalry does not only take place between actors from different policy fields (e.g. the EPSCO and ECOFIN Council formations), but can equally be found *among the EU's health care initiatives.* Apart from the OMC, there are several other fora (such as the recently revamped Working Party on Public Health at Senior Level[92] and the European Health Care Policy Forum[93]), which pursue their own interests and agendas. As a result, the health care OMC is merely 'one of many' instruments that are available (compare this to the area of Social Inclusion, where the OMC is clearly the leading governance tool at the EU level.[94]

Thirdly, actor rivalry also exists *between the EU and other, international organizations* that deal with health care, notably the World Health Organisation (WHO) and the OECD. While the WHO seeks to achieve 'the attainment by all people of the highest possible level of health' within the UN framework,[95] the Organization for Economic Cooperation and Development (OECD) mainly provides comparative analyses on health care systems in industrialized countries. The latter has thereby acquired specific experience in the field of statistics and policy recommendations. Note that several of our interviewees in the health care strand referred to OECD data (instead of data obtained in the OMC framework), since these data have a longstanding tradition and are often more developed and detailed.

Apart from this longstanding OECD expertise (that somehow competes with the EU statistics in the field of health), the 2008 WHO's declaration of the '*Tallinn Charter: Health Systems for Health and Wealth*' provides another example for actor rivalry at international level. The Charter identifies common values and

---

91 See A. de Ruijter and T.K. Hervey, n. 16.

92 In June 2011 the Council of the EU decided to 'initiate a reflection process under the auspices of the Working Party on Public Health at Senior Level aiming to identify effective ways of investing in health, so as to pursue modern, responsive and sustainable health systems'. This sounds quite familiar to the mandate of the OMC in this policy field. The first report from the Working Party is expected by the end of 2012 (European Council, 'Council Conclusions: Towards modern, responsive and sustainable health systems', 3095th Employment, Social Policy, Health and Consumer Affairs Council Meeting – Health issues [2011] OJ C146/1).

93 The European Union Health Care Policy Forum is a stakeholder organization that hosts a diverse range of pan-European health NGOs as well as industry associations. Its stated aim is 'to contribute to and advise on the development, implementation and evaluation of EU health-related policies and actions and to empower European citizens in health for life'. See 'The EU Health Policy Forum Strategic Priorities, Including Specific Priorities for 2009–2010' (Mission Statement), p. 3 <http://ec.europa.eu/health/archive/ph_overview/health_forum/docs/euhpf_priorities_en.pdf> accessed 4 November 2011.

94 S. Greer and B. Vanhercke, n. 8.

95 Constitution of the World Health Organization, Article 1.

common health challenges in the European region in the context of demographic and epidemiological change, increasing socio-economic disparities and limited resources.[96] States thus declare their commitment to act on seven different priorities (including to invest in health systems and related sectors, promote transparency, and make health systems more responsive to people's needs). Note that 'foster cross-country learning and cooperation on the design and implementation of health system reforms at national and sub-national level' and 'engage stakeholders in policy development and implementation' are equally part of the commitment to act.[97] The WHO will therefore provide cross-county coordination 'including the measurement of performance and the exchange of experiences' on these commitments.[98] Furthermore, the Charter foresees the *identification of objectives*, which in turn should be specified in a *measurable way* to allow for *explicit monitoring of progress*.[99] The Programme of the Tallinn Charter thus seems to almost reinvent the core features of the OMC, including common objectives, monitoring, learning and stakeholder involvement. The Tallinn Charter thereby represents another striking example of the density of actors and initiatives that seek to influence policies in this field.

6. WRAPPING THINGS UP: 'SOFT-TO-HARD-TO-SOFT' GOVERNANCE IN THE EU

Health is and will continue to be an area within which the competence of the EU institutions is highly constrained. This has been reconfirmed by the Treaty of Lisbon.[100] At the same time, however, health is no longer a 'non-topic' for the EU, and neither the EU institutions, nor the governments of the Member States, can now retreat from that position. Indeed, (a) the longstanding political incapacity to adopt 'positive' legislation in health (with the key exception of the recent Patients' Rights Directive); (b) an increasing impact of EU law on national health care systems; and (c) a divided policy space (with different sets of actors claiming a say in health care issues), have spurred consecutive rounds of EU policy initiatives (pressed for by domestic policy-makers), to deal with the unintended consequences. One of those initiatives has been the Open Method of Coordination.

---

96 See World Health Organization, *The Tallinn Charter: Health Systems for Health and Wealth*, Recitals 2 and 3 of the Preamble.

97 *Ibid.*, p.2. (Commitment to act (6)).

98 *Ibid.*, p.2, (Commitment to act (7)).

99 *Ibid.*, p.3 (Strengthening health systems: From values to action (12)).

100 See Article 168.7 TFEU: '*Union action shall respect the responsibilities of the Member States for the definition of their health policy and for the organisation and delivery of health services and medical care. The responsibilities of the Member States shall include the management of health services and medical care and the allocation of the resources assigned to them.*'

In section three we saw that the health care OMC is by no means shaking domestic social policy-making. Even if many Belgian actors working in the areas of social inclusion and pensions do perceive the OMC as an increasingly important, and useful, tool in domestic policy-making (features of both, the social inclusion and pensions strand, are being picked up by a variety of actors and used to pursue their policy goals), there is no convincing evidence that this would be the case in the area of health care. Here the OMC remains a largely hidden process, only known to a very small circle of – mostly federal – civil servants. These findings were corroborated for a variety of other Member States. And yet we provided a few examples of needles in the haystack: we described *prudent mirror effects* (Belgium and Germany), discussed the added value of peer reviews, the contribution of the Social OMC to national steering capacity (e.g. use of data and indicators) and the plausibility of OMC influence on substantive issues such as quality in health care.

This relatively gloomy picture can, to a large extent, be explained by two (related) factors: weak ownership by stakeholders, and the fact that the health care policy arena is characterized by extensive actor rivalry. We described such rivalry, first, between different actors emanating from different policy fields (related to health policy); second, between actors and instruments *within* the health care arena; and third, at the international level, between the EU and other international organizations with a longstanding tradition in health care policy coordination. Nevertheless, one should not forget that this institutional fragmentation can at the same time also represent an opportunity. As de Ruijter and Hervey point out correctly, the diverging concepts and responsible actors in the field of health care also make different institutional routes available in case one becomes politically blocked.[101]

In spite of its general uncomfortable institutional position (competing as it is with a variety of EU initiatives in this particular policy area) and the small substantive impact that it has exerted so far on national health policy, section four of this chapter shows that the OMC is increasingly seen as a template for EU health care governance. At the same time, there are indications that law and soft modes of health governance are increasingly interacting, as it is the case between the OMC and different financial instruments, especially the ESF. The influence of soft governance on the adjudicating of the ECJ and the finding that the ECJ is sometimes inspired by the outcomes of soft governance processes, are further examples of the interaction between law and policy in health. The 'soft pockets' in the new Patients' Rights Directive as well as the 'soft-to-hard-to-soft' development of the HTA framework, point to the increasing hybridity of EU instruments in the field of health care. In turn this finding suggests a more

101 See A. de Ruijter and T.K. Hervey, n. 16.

nuanced discussion about 'hard' and 'soft' law in the EU, and more generally speaking also about 'Social Europe'. In view of its multiple functions (supporting domestic reform, strengthening networks, shaping political consensus, influencing hard(er) modes of governance), it seems that the health care OMC is there to stay.[102] More important than whether it will 'survive' is the question as to who will engage.

In other words, the crux of the matter is the following: it is not the 'hardness' or the 'softness' of the OMC that matters, but its capacity (or, as is the case in health, its failure) to stimulate creative appropriation and action by European, national and sub-national actors. This confirms Scott Greer's observation that EU governance mechanisms, including those in the health care field, will continue to flourish only if they promote some kind of tangible benefit for participants, either involving learning or governance or both.[103] Now that the contours of the reinvigorated Social OMC are becoming increasingly clear, it will be up to policy-makers and experts alike to make that happen in the Europe 2020 Strategy.[104]

102 The Lisbon Treaty amends Article 152 EC, to further enhance (or possibly constrain) the Commission's competence to encourage cooperation between the Member States in the public health field. This Commission-sponsored cooperation includes, '*initiatives aiming at the establishment of guidelines and indicators, the organisation of exchange of best practice, and the preparation of the necessary elements for periodic monitoring and evaluation*'. See Article 168.2 TFEU.

103 See S. Greer, 'The Weakness of Strong Policies and the Strength of Weak Policies: Law, Experimentalist Governance, and Supporting Coalitions in European Union Health Care Policy' (2011) 5 *Regulation & Governance.*

104 Social Protection Committee, 'Draft background paper to the SPC from the ad hoc group on reinvigorating the Social OMC in the context of the Europe 2020 Strategy' SPC/2011.09/1.

Annex 1. Integrated Guideline 10 – Promoting social inclusion and combating poverty

'The extension of employment opportunities is an essential aspect of Member States' integrated strategies to prevent and reduce poverty and to promote full participation in society and economy. Appropriate use of the European Social Fund and other EU funds should be made to that end. Efforts should concentrate on ensuring equal opportunities, including thorough access for all to high quality, affordable, and sustainable services, in particular in the social field. Public services (including online services, in line with Guideline 4) play an important role in this respect. Member States should put in place effective anti-discrimination measures. Empowering people and promoting labour market participation for those furthest away from the labour market while preventing in-work poverty will help fight social exclusion. This would require enhancing social protection systems, lifelong learning and comprehensive active inclusion policies to create opportunities at different stages of people's lives and shield them from the risk of exclusion, with special attention to women. **Social protection systems, including pensions and access to healthcare, should be modernised and fully deployed to ensure adequate income support and services – thus providing social cohesion – whilst remaining financially sustainable and encouraging participation in society and in the labour market.** Benefit systems should focus on ensuring income security during transitions and reducing poverty, in particular among groups most at risk from social exclusion, such as one-parent families, minorities including the Roma, people with disabilities, children and young people, elderly women and men, legal migrants and the homeless. Member States should also actively promote the social economy and social innovation in support of the most vulnerable. All measures should also aim at promoting gender equality. The EU headline target, on the basis of which Member States will set their national targets, taking into account their relative starting conditions and national circumstances, will aim at promoting social inclusion, in particular through the reduction of poverty by aiming to lift at least 20 million people out of the risk of poverty and exclusion'

Source: European Council, 'Council decision on guidelines for the employment policies of the Member States' (2010) 14338/10 SOC 599 (emphasis added).

HARMONIZATION IN HEALTH CARE: THE EU PATIENTS' RIGHTS DIRECTIVE

Wolf SAUTER*

1. INTRODUCTION

This chapter seeks to set out the background to and examine the content of the recent Patients' Rights harmonization Directive (the Directive) that arguably forms a watershed in the context of EU involvement in health care.

Apart from the role of harmonization several more specific questions will be addressed:

- Does the Directive codify the patient mobility case law of the Court of Justice?
- What are the scope and the role of patients' rights in the proposal?
- Will the Patients' Rights Directive act as a catalyst for change?

In this context a further question is how politics and law interact and whether these developments are explained by theories of EU integration.

The discussion is structured in three parts:

- First the background to the Directive, its legal basis and scope, as well as the relationship to social security regulation and the criterion of undue delay will be discussed.
- Next the main two topics of the Directive are discussed: prior authorization and the 'old' patients' rights, related to treatment and reimbursement; and then common principles and 'new' patients' rights, related to transparency and accountability.
- Finally we will briefly address the provisions concerning cooperation which constitute flanking measures in the framework set by the Commission, and

* This paper updates and extends W. SAUTER, 'The Proposed Patients' Rights Directive and the Reform of (Cross-Border) Healthcare in the European Union' (2009) 109 *Legal Issues of European Integration*. All views expressed here are personal.

were previously the subject of intergovernmental soft law efforts as examples of the Open Method of Coordination (OMC).

2. BACKGROUND

The EU Member States have a variety of health care systems that are generally classified in broad terms as either insurance based Bismarck systems (with a further distinction between benefits in kind and restitution systems) and publicly funded Beveridge systems (also known as national health services, or NHS). In all cases the Member States are deeply involved both in regulating the market structure and in setting individual entitlements.[1] They also share common funding problems as a result of spiralling costs due to the combination of aging populations, technological developments, and rising expectations. This in turn has triggered cost controls involving various forms of rationing, such as waiting lists. At the same time vested interests frustrate changes, such as moving from centralized supply-driven systems to decentralized demand-led provision, and promoting efficiency by means of market incentives and/or new entry. The resistance to planned reform often leads to de facto emergence of parallel systems that fall outside the scope of social security and are based on ability to pay. Hence rejecting change erodes solidarity.

Given this socially and politically sensitive context it should come as no surprise that the competencies of the European Union in the health care sector are limited. The Court of Justice has time and again recognized the right of the Member States to determine unilaterally (i.e. at national level) the scope of and eligibility for social security benefits.[2] Moreover, to bolster their control over health care provision, the Member States have limited the competence of the EU to take the initiative on health care issues further by adding an explicit Treaty provision to this effect, Article 168 TFEU.

In 2009 the Lisbon Treaty moved 'the protection and improvement of human health' to Article 6 (a) of the TFEU. This concerns those activities of the Member States that the Union is competent to support, coordinate or supplement with

---

1 Cf. E. Mossialos, G. Permanand, R. Baeten and T. K. Hervey (eds.), *Health Systems Governance in Europe: The Role of European Law and Policy*, Cambridge University Press, Cambridge 2010.

2 Cf. e.g. Case 238/82 *Duphar BV et al. v. The Netherlands* [1984] ECR 523, para. 16; Joined cases C-159/91 and C-160/91 *Christian Poucet v. Assurances Générales de France and Caisse Mutuelle Régionale du Languedoc-Roussillon and Daniel Pistre v. Caisse Autonome Nationale de Compensation de l'Assurance Vieillesse des Artisans* [1993] ECR I-637, para. 6; Case C-70/95 *Sodemare SA, Anni Azzurri Holding SpA and Anni Azzurri Rezzato Srl v. Regione Lombardia* [1997] ECR I-3395, para. 27 and Case C-158/96 *Raymond Kohll v. Union des caisses de maladie* [1998] ECR I-1931 (hereinafter *Kohll*), para. 17.

regard to their European dimension. This replaces the earlier explicit connection with the objectives of the Union. The present provision fits better in the context of the emphasis on subsidiarity, or the exercise of public powers at the lowest effective level, which also characterizes Article 168 TFEU on public health. Finally in relation to Article 6 (a) TFEU, it is Article 2.5 TFEU which explicitly makes it clear that the harmonization of laws in this area is excluded.[3]

It is against this unpromising backdrop that over the past decade, from *Kohll* to *Watts*,[4] the European Court of Justice has developed a remarkable line of case law in which it applied the freedom to provide services to health care (alongside, in a number of cases, Regulation 1408/71,[5] the applicable social security legislation based on the free movement of workers of Article 48 TFEU). These cases were driven by patients seeking what they considered to be better (including earlier) medical treatment in other Member States ('Member State of treatment') while claiming reimbursement of such treatment in accordance with the social security rules applicable in their home Member State ('Member State of affiliation').[6] Adopting a 'patient centred, needs based approach',[7] the European Court of Justice has consistently supported such patient mobility. Because most Member States failed to implement this case law properly the resulting need for codification formed the Commission's primary justification for the Patients' Rights Directive.

---

3 *'In certain areas and under the conditions laid down in the Treaties, the Union shall have competence to carry out actions to support, coordinate or supplement the actions of the Member States, without thereby superseding their competence in these areas. Legally binding acts of the Union adopted on the basis of the provisions of the Treaties relating to these areas shall not entail harmonisation of Member States' laws or regulations.'* This makes it all the more remarkable that the European Parliament and the Council agreed to base the Directive on patients' rights inter alia on Article 168 TFEU.

4 *Kohll*; Case C-120/95 *Nicolas Decker v. Caisse de maladie des employés privés* [1998] ECR I-1831 (hereinafter *Decker*); Case C-372/04 *The Queen, ex parte Yvonne Watts v. Bedford Primary Care Trust and Secretary of State for Health* [2006] ECR I-4325 (hereinafter *Watts*). For a detailed discussion of these cases and further references see W. Sauter, 'The Proposed Patient Mobility Directive and the Reform of Cross-Border Healthcare in the EU' (2008) *TILEC Discussion Paper No. 2008–034* <http://ssrn.com/abstract=1277110> accessed September 27, 2011.

5 Regulation (EEC) No. 1408/71 of the Council of 14 June 1971 on the application of social security schemes to employed persons and their families moving within the Community [1971] OJ L149/2, last amended by Regulation (EC) No. 1992/2006 of the European Parliament and of the Council of 18 December 2006 [2006] OJ L392/1 (Regulation 1408/71). It replaced Council Regulation No. 3 on social security for migrant workers [1958] OJ 597. On 1 May 2010 Regulation 1408/71 was replaced by Regulation (EC) 883/2004 of the European Parliament and of the Council of 29 April 2004 on the coordination of social security systems [2004] OJ L166/1. Cf. F. Pennings, *European Social Security Law*, 5th ed. Intersentia, Antwerp 2010.

6 This is the usage in the Patients' Rights Directive, which will be employed here.

7 G. Davies, 'The Effect of Mrs Watts Trip to France on the National Health Service' (2007) 18 *King's Law Journal*.

In July 2008 the Commission proposed a draft Directive on the application of patients' rights in cross-border health care ('the Proposal') in the context of the renewed social agenda of the EU.[8] After considerable debate and a significant number of amendments in first and second reading, the text of the Directive was adopted on 9 March 2011, entered into effect on 24 April 2011 and must be effectively transposed into national law by the Member States before 25 October 2013.[9] The Commission's proposal was daring because, as mentioned above, so far the Member States generally regard health care reform not just as one of the most intractable political problems but also as an issue that should remain the preserve of national politics. Moreover, an attempt by the Commission in 2004 to codify the patient mobility case law in the context of the Services Directive had backfired. It ended up having to withdraw the relevant provisions and adding an explicit exception for health care in order to save the Services Directive itself.[10]

The process summarized above suggests the occurrence of a familiar pattern in EU law where disparities between national markets lead to private litigation based on directly effective rights under the Treaty which trigger Court intervention striking down national barriers – resulting in deregulation (or 'negative integration') – which is then duly followed by legislative proposals to fill the remaining and/or resulting regulatory gaps by new rules at EU level – concluding by re-regulation (or 'positive integration').[11] This process of interaction between case law and legislation tends to involve both harmonization and liberalization of the applicable rules as well as a reassessment of the scope of legitimate public interest requirements. Apart from providing an analysis of the contents of the Directive, this chapter will examine whether the proposed Directive on patients' rights fits this mould of interaction between positive and negative integration. A move beyond negative integration into harmonization in

---

8 European Commission, 'Proposal for a Directive of the European Parliament and of the Council on the application of patients' rights in cross-border healthcare presented by the Commission' (Communication) COM (2008) 414 final.

9 Directive 2011/24/EU of the European Parliament and of the Council on the application of patients' rights in cross-border healthcare [2011] OJ L88/45.

10 European Commission, 'Proposal for a Directive of the European Parliament and of the Council on services in the internal market 2004/0001' (COD) [SEC (2004) 21] COM (2004) 2 final/3, especially Article 23 thereof. Cf. Directive 2006/123/EC of the European Parliament and of the Council of 12 December 2006 on services in the internal market [2006] OJ L376/36 (Services Directive), Article 2.2 (f), and the Preamble, recital 23.

11 Cf. G. Davies, 'The Community's Internal Market-Based Competence to Regulate Healthcare: Scope, Strategies and Consequences' (2007) 14 *Maastricht Journal of European and Comparative Law*; F.W. Scharpf, 'Negative and Positive Integration in the Political Economy of European Welfare States' in G. Marks, F. W. Scharpf, Ph. C. Schmitter and W. Streeck (eds.), *Governance in the European Union*, Sage, London 1996, p. 15; and F.W. Scharpf, 'The European Social Model: Coping With the Challenges of Diversity' (2002) 40 *JCMS*.

this field would be all the more remarkable given the sector-specific subsidiarity clause for health care in Article 168.7 TFEU already mentioned above.

3. SUMMARY OF THE CASE LAW

In the course of its case law over the past decade the Court of Justice has developed a parallel regime for patient mobility based on the freedom to provide services of Article 56 TFEU, alongside the pre-existing rules based on Article 48 TFEU on the coordination of social security rights necessary to implement the free movement of workers elaborated in Regulation 883/2004 (the Regulation, formerly Regulation 1408/71). It successively determined that restitution based insurance systems,[12] benefits in kind based insurance systems,[13] and national health services[14] were obliged to enable the reimbursement of cross-border health care.

Greatly simplified, this case law can be summed up as follows.[15] The scope of social security coverage as such is determined by the Member State of affiliation alone and therefore not at issue. Nor is the right of individual patients to seek treatment abroad and pay for it themselves at stake: they are free to do so. Instead the focus of both the Article 56 TFEU regime and that of Regulation 883/2004 is on *the conditions for the reimbursement of treatment abroad*, when a patient is in principle entitled to the treatment involved in his Member State of affiliation.

- When Article 56 TFEU is relied on, reimbursement is at the level of domestic treatment in the Member State of affiliation; based on Regulation 883/2004 reimbursement is at the level of the Member State of treatment (if the Member State of treatment has a national health service there is just free access to care, at the expense of the Member State of affiliation).[16] This means that only consumers who can pay the up-front costs of treatment themselves (pending *ex post* reimbursement) can avail themselves of the Article 56 TFEU route – raising inequality issues.

---

12 *Kohll*; *Decker*.

13 Case C-157/99 *B.S.M. Geraets-Smits v. Stichting Ziekenfonds VGZ and H.T.M. Peerbooms v. Stichting CZ Groep Zorgverzekeringen* [2001] ECR I-5473 (hereinafter *Smits and Peerbooms*); Case C-385/99 *V.G. Müller-Fauré v. Onderlinge Waarborgmaatschappij OZ Zorgverzekeringen UA and E.E.M. van Riet v. Onderlinge Waarborgmaatschappij ZAO Zorgverzekeringen* [2003] ECR I-4509 (hereinafter *Müller-Fauré*).

14 *Watts*.

15 Cf. T.K. Hervey, 'The Current Legal Framework on the Right to Seek Healthcare Abroad in the European Union' (2007) 9 *Cambridge Yearbook of European Legal Studies*.

16 Where the latter is lower than the former, the difference may be claimed based on Article 56 TFEU. Cf. Case C-368/98, *Abdon Vanbraekel et al. v. Alliance nationale des mutualités chrétiennes* [2001] ECR I-5363 (hereinafter *Vanbraekel*).

- More complicated is the question whether prior authorization may be required. Based on Regulation 883/2004 prior authorization of treatment abroad is always required as a condition for reimbursement. Based on Article 56 TFEU, prior authorization (which is in principle a barrier to the freedom to provide services) may be required for hospital services. This is considered justified to safeguard the financial balance of the national social security systems of the Member States and planning in the hospital sector.
- So far the Court has never required evidence before allowing this justification. Over time it has come to accept that prior authorization may be justified provided that material and procedural due process guarantees are respected concerning the objective and proportionate nature of the authorization process, notably fleshing out the concept of 'undue delay' by requiring due regard to the individual circumstances of each patient. These requirements are similar if not identical for the Article 56 TFEU setting and that of Regulation 883/2004.

In this manner the Court has balanced the public interest justifications invoked by the Member States with the rights of individual patients based on free movement. Against this background, the Patients' Rights Directive will be discussed.

4. THE LEGISLATIVE CONTEXT

4.1. RENEWING THE SOCIAL AGENDA

The Proposal for a Directive 'on the application of patients' rights in cross-border healthcare' as presented in July 2008 formed part of a raft of some twenty documents and proposals jointly billed as a renewed social agenda for 21st century Europe.[17] In stark contrast to the earlier attempt to embed patient mobility in the undiluted economic logic of the Services Directive, the connecting theme behind the July 2008 package was to complement the Lisbon growth strategy of the EU from a social perspective.

Another difference between the proposed patients' rights Directive and the failed earlier attempt to include a single article on health care in the Services Directive is that the Proposal was a fully-fledged legal instrument purporting to provide a complete and coherent legal regime for all the issues involved.

17 Cf. European Commission, 'Renewed Social Agenda: Opportunities, Access and Solidarity in 21st Century Europe' (Communication) COM (2008) 412 final; European Commission, 'Commission proposes renewed social agenda to empower and help people in 21st Century Europe' (Press release) IP/08/1070; European Commission, 'Renewed Social Agenda: The Elements of the Package' (Memo) MEMO/08/471.

4.1.1. *Impact assessment: quantifying the case for codification*

The Proposal was published with an Impact Assessment which the Commission used to motivate its choice between different policy options.[18] The Impact Assessment stated that over 12 months 4% of the EU population had received medical treatment in another Member State, that 70% of the EU population believes such treatment would be reimbursed and that just over half the EU population was open to travelling to another EU Member State to receive treatment.[19]

The Impact Assessment further states that cross-border health care accounts for 1% of public health care expenditure.[20] Hence, the overall impact of patient mobility in the EU is small, although its local impact may be much greater e.g. in border regions, smaller Member States, in tourist areas, and in systems or for treatments involving high co-payments (out of pocket expenses for patients).

Overall, the Impact Assessment identifies 'a rising trend for cross-border health care and significant potential demand from citizens to explore cross-border health care where it is quicker, better, cheaper or more convenient for them'.[21] The Impact Assessment shows that a Directive covering both hospital and non-hospital care provides net benefits in relation to the costs involved, more specifically a positive balance of € 179,6 million, with 780,000 extra patients receiving treatment for the EU as a whole.

These gains appear rather small as a basis for making the case for EU action. There is a contradiction at play here. The Commission struggled with the need to argue on the one hand, that something meaningful is at hand requiring EU legislation and, on the other hand, that the impact of this legislation on national social security regimes will be small enough so that prior authorization requirements are unlikely to be justified.

The Commission has not been successful in doing the latter: one of the main differences between the Proposal and the Directive as adopted is that the latter leaves considerable room for appeals to overriding reasons of general interest based on an exception for planning that the Court had earlier recognized in this

18 N. 8 (with an Explanatory Memorandum); EUROPEAN COMMISSION, 'Staff working document of 2 July 2008, accompanying document to the proposed patients' rights Directive: Impact Assessment' SEC (2008) 2163.

19 *Ibid.*, pp. 6–7 citing Flash Eurobarometer series #210, 'Cross-border health services in the EU', Analytical report for DG Sanco, 2007.

20 I.e. approximately € 9.7 billion. EU GDP is € 12,149 billion of which some 7.6% (€ 967 billion) is spent on public health care. *Ibid.*, p. 9 (Eurostat figures 2006/2007).

21 *Ibid.*, p. 11.

context. This planning exception can even be invoked by the Member State of treatment to justify safeguard measures that had not been foreseen in the Proposal. It is still an open question to what extent quantification will be required in terms of demonstrating the necessity and proportionality requirements with respect to the planning exception. So far however, the Court has not required quantification.

4.2. THE DYNAMICS OF 'OLD' AND 'NEW' PATIENT'S RIGHTS

'Patients' rights', the key to the title chosen by the Commission for the Proposal, refers to a concept that is much broader in scope than the reimbursement of cross-border medical treatment (the 'old' patients' rights that the Court had developed in its case law).[22] This broader concept is primarily linked to the common principles that are framed as obligations of the Member State of treatment. These include quality and safety standards, access to the information necessary for (or 'relevant to') informed choice (i.e. transparency), the means to complain and obtain remedies (i.e. accountability), compensation for harm and privacy rights. These can in effect easily be rephrased as a set of 'new' and potentially highly significant rights to cover all patients, not merely mobile ones. In this way 'old' patients' rights may be generating 'new' ones: both categories will be examined further below.

5. LEGAL BASIS AND SCOPE

5.1. LEGAL BASIS

In line with the Proposal, the Directive as it was ultimately adopted is based on the harmonization provision of Article 114 TFEU. The European Parliament and the Council have added Article 168 TFEU to this so the Directive also has a sector-specific basis in the Treaty. The use of Article 114 TFEU shows the Directive aims to secure the establishment and functioning of the internal market.[23] This is justified by the fact that although the Court judgments clarified patients' rights they have not proven sufficient in, and of themselves to enable

---

22 Cf. the World Health Organization <www.who.int/genomics/public/patientrights/en/> accessed 10 October 2010.

23 On the relevant legal basis cf. D. Wyatt, 'Community Competence to Regulate Medical Services' in M. Dougan and E. Spaventa (eds.), *Social Welfare and EU Law*, Oxford, Hart 2005.

patients to avail themselves of these rights widely or in an effective manner. (Or: they have so far been frustrated by the Member States.)

At the same time the Directive is required to respect not just the general subsidiarity provision in Article 5 TEU but also the provisions of Article 6 (a), Article 2.5 TFEU and Article 168.7 TFEU, which provides a special subsidiarity clause with respect to the responsibility of the Member States for the organization and delivery of health care. As was already clarified by the Court in *Müller-Fauré* and *Watts* however, this provision does not mean that adjustments to national systems may not be required by other Treaty obligations, such as Article 56 TFEU on the freedom to provide and receive services.[24]

In this context, the Directive aims to form a framework that provides clarity about the rights to reimbursement for health care provided in other Member States and assures that such cross-border health care is of high quality, safe and efficient, which could not be done effectively by individual Member States.

The basic assumption however, is that, in line with Article 168 TEFU, the Member States retain full responsibility for determining what medical services are covered by their national social security regimes and for the actual provision of health care.[25] Article 6 (a) TFEU itself is reflected in Article 168.1 TFEU which states: 'A high level of human health protection shall be ensured in the definition and implementation of all Union policies and activities.' This means that the effects on public health must be assessed for every legislative proposal (even when the latter deals with an entirely different subject), a process called 'mainstreaming'.[26] The Directive is the first piece of harmonization legislation in the area of health care: we may now expect any future such legislation to be based on Article 168 TFEU as well.

Finally, Article 168 TFEU is also relevant for the cooperation efforts of the Member States with relation to health care and/or public health, some of which are covered by the Directive (such as E-health and the other cooperation topics that will be addressed below).

---

24 *Müller-Fauré*, para. 102 (without specific reference to Article 152.5 EC); *Watts*, para 147.

25 Cf. Preamble of the Directive, recitals 3 (a) and 5 (a), as well as Article 7.3 of the Directive which reads: *'It is for the Member State of affiliation to determine, whether at a local, regional or national level, the healthcare for which an insured person is entitled to the assumption of costs and the level of assumption of those costs, regardless of where the healthcare is provided.'*

26 Cf T.K. Hervey and J.V. McHale, *Health Law and the European Union*, Cambridge University Press, Cambridge 2004, pp. 76–81.

5.2. SCOPE

The scope of the Directive appears to cover all types of curative care without distinction in relation to their funding regime, hence it is not limited to health care in the sense of Article 168.7 TFEU, but also health care that is provided privately outside the public health setting.[27] The Proposal had made this explicit in its definition of health care. Article 3 (a) of the Directive now defines health care as follows:

> *'"Healthcare" means health services provided by health professionals to patients to assess, maintain or restore their state of health, including the prescription, dispensation and provision of medicinal products and medical devices.'*

The Directive thus appears to cover 'private care' that is not covered by Regulation 883/2004, the scope of which is limited to health care delivered within public insurance schemes, and excluding private doctors or hospitals not affiliated to these schemes. However, the right to reimbursement – which is actually the core of the Directive – is linked to the position of the patient as an insured person covered by a social security system in line with Regulation 883/2004. Long-term care and the donation or medical use of organs and blood, and public immunization schemes are not covered.

6. PARALLEL REGIMES BASED ON ARTICLES 56 AND 48 TFEU CONTINUED

6.1. THE RIGHT TO TREATMENT

The EU will continue to have two parallel regimes for the authorization and/or reimbursement of cross-border health care: one, the existing regime based on Regulation 883/2004 (and thereby on Article 48 TFEU on free movement of workers); and the other, the new regime of the Directive, replacing the one directly based on Article 56 TFEU (never implemented in most Member States).

---

[27] I.e.: *'Union action shall respect the responsibilities of the Member States for the definition of their health policy and for the organisation and delivery of health services and medical care. The responsibilities of the Member States shall include the management of health services and medical care and the allocation of the resources assigned to them. The measures referred to in paragraph 4 (a) shall not affect national provisions on the donation or medical use of organs and blood.'*

The Court had effectively merged the two regimes as far as the right to treatment was concerned, based on the 'undue delay' criterion, first effectively in the *Inizan* case,[28] and then explicitly in *Watts*:[29]

> *'(...) there is no reason which seriously justifies different interpretations depending on whether the context is Art. 22 of Regulation No. 1408/71 or Art. 49 EC, since in both cases the question is (...) whether the hospital treatment required by the patient's medical condition can be provided on the territory of his Member State of residence within an acceptable time which ensures its usefulness and efficacy.'*

Under the terms of the Directive its relationship with the Regulation will henceforth be determined by a clear priority rule and an exception to this rule, while responsibility for both of those is clearly assigned as well. This is because Article 8.3 of the Directive provides that in case of a request for prior authorization the Member State of affiliation will determine whether the conditions for the application of Regulation 883/2004 are met. If this is the case the prior authorization is granted in accordance with the Regulation unless the patient himself requests otherwise – i.e. requests to obtain a prior authorization in accordance with the Directive instead. This appears to be a relatively straightforward system that leaves little room for misunderstandings and is a distinct improvement over the Proposal which left too many responsibilities on this count with the patient – especially as regards determining whether 'undue delay' might be involved. Hence the risk inherent in the Proposal, i.e. that the interpretation of the concept of 'undue delay' would diverge between the Directive and the Regulation, has now been addressed. As a result, the question arises which regime is more favourable. Given the differences in reimbursement at the level of the Member State of treatment and of affiliation, multiplied by the number of 27 Member States at both ends and the fact there may be differences per type of treatment, it is difficult to generalize. From the perspective of the administrative and financial arrangements already in place the Regulation may be more favourable.

28 Determining undue delay requires '*to have regard to all the circumstances of each specific case and to take due account not only of the patient's medical condition at the time when authorisation is sought and, where appropriate, of the degree of pain or the nature of the patient's disability which might, for example, make it impossible or extremely difficult for him to carry out a professional activity, but also of his medical history*'. Case C-56/01, *Patricia Inizan v. Caisse primaire d'assurance maladie des Hauts-de-Seine* [2003] ECR I-12403, para. 46 with reference to *Smits and Peerbooms*, para. 104, and *Müller-Fauré*, para. 90.

29 *Watts*, para. 60.

6.2. UNDUE DELAY: A TIME-LIMIT WHICH IS MEDICALLY JUSTIFIABLE

The right to treatment without undue delay had not been properly addressed by the Proposal because it only came up in relation to the procedure for the treatment of prior authorization requests, but not as a material norm for assessing these requests themselves. On this issue therefore the Directive also provides a clear improvement over the Proposal.

The right to treatment without undue delay features twice in the Directive:

- Article 8 paragraph 5 concerning health care that can be subject to a prior authorization requirement provides that such authorization may not be refused if the health care in question is among the benefits to which the insured person is entitled in the Member State of affiliation, and when this health care cannot be provided on its territory within a time-limit which is medically justifiable, based on an objective medical assessment of the patient's medical condition, the history and probable course of his illness, the degree of pain he is in and/or the nature of his disability at the time when the request for authorization was made or renewed. This means the central role for this important material norm developed in the case law is maintained by the Directive.
- Article 9 paragraph 3 of the Directive provides that requests for prior authorization must be treated within reasonable time limits (as did the Proposal, although it did no more), made public in advance, and that when considering a request for cross-border health care, Member States shall take into account the specific medical condition, urgency and individual circumstances. In addition to this material norm, Article 9 paragraph 4 sets out the procedural requirements developed in the case law, such as the right to a reasoned decision on a case-by-case basis and subject to judicial review.

In this manner undue delay was given an appropriate role, preventing divergence on this criterion with the case law as well as in relation to Regulation 883/2004. As a result, the consistency between the case law and the two parallel pieces of legislation (the Regulation and the Directive) was increased, while reducing the room to invoke the freedom to provide (or enjoy) services directly without reference to the Directive – at least under the presumption that the undue delay rule is respected by the Member State of affiliation. In fact, it is questionable whether there is still scope for a direct appeal to the freedom to enjoy services in this area, aside from incorrect or incomplete implementation of the Directive.

6.3. THE RIGHT TO REIMBURSEMENT

The basis for reimbursement (at the level prevailing in the Member State of treatment for Regulation 883/2004 and at that of the Member State of affiliation for Article 56 TFEU, or now the Patients' Rights Directive) will continue to differ under the two regimes. Whereas under Regulation 883/2004 the general rule is that patients do not have to meet the costs of treatment directly, under the regime of the Patients' Rights Directive, payment by the patient subject to subsequent reimbursement is the rule. The rights under the Regulation depend fully upon the interaction between the scope of reimbursable treatments in the Member State of affiliation and the regime for the particular treatment in the Member State of treatment. The former determines the principle whether reimbursement is possible, the latter at what level. In many cases, benefits in kind (with or without co-payments) are involved, and the accounts are settled directly between the two Member States involved. Finally, where the reimbursement in the Member State of treatment is lower than in the Member State of affiliation, the difference may be claimed based on Article 56 TFEU, under the rule established in *Vanbraekel*.[30]

6.4. WOULD AN AMENDMENT OF THE SOCIAL SECURITY RULES HAVE SUFFICED?

These observations on the similarities and the differences between the two systems raise the question whether a separate Directive was in fact necessary, or whether amending Regulation 1408/71 (read: its successor Regulation 883/04) would have sufficed instead. This could have been done, for example, by simply providing that the more favourable of the two funding regimes applies, and by codification of key elements of the case law. Would this not have been logically consistent with the aim of strengthening the renewed social agenda?

It is striking that this arguably most obvious solution did not even feature as an option in the Impact Assessment. Perhaps it is partly explained by the fact that two competing Directorates General of the Commission are involved here (SANCO for the Directive, and EMPLOY for the Regulation). Another explanation is that given the much broader scope of the Regulation – and given the negative experience with the attempt to include cross-border health care in the Services Directive – the Commission preferred not to open a Pandora's box by reopening the negotiations on the Regulation on this point. In this context, it is important what type of dynamics the Directive is likely to entail: in large

30 Case C-368/98 *Abdon Vanbraekel and Others v. Alliance nationale des mutualités chrétiennes* [2001] ECR I-5363.

measure this is likely to be determined by the new patients' rights and to a lesser extent by the cooperation provisions. However, the increasing need to provide comparable data on prices and quality, and even costs (when required to motivate a reimbursement granted or requested) triggered by the 'old' patients' rights may yet help shake up national health care markets.

7. FRAMING CROSS-BORDER HEALTH CARE: THE 'OLD' PATIENTS' RIGHTS

We now move on to the codification of the Court's patient mobility case law.

7.1. REIMBURSEMENT OF ACTUAL COSTS

The core of the codification of the obligations for the Member State of affiliation is formed by Article 7 on general principles for reimbursement of costs, Article 8 regarding prior authorization requirements, and Article 9 on the procedures concerned.[31]

As a counterpoint to the obligations of the Member State of treatment set out in Article 4 of the Patients' Rights Directive, its Article 7 sets out a number of obligations on the Member States of affiliation in relation to patients ('insured persons') travelling to other Member States for treatment that is covered by the benefits to which they are entitled in their Member State of affiliation. The most important of these obligations is that the Member States of affiliation must reimburse the actual costs for such treatment up to the level applicable to the same or similar treatment in the Member State of affiliation. However, Member States are not blocked from going beyond their obligations under the Directive to provide supplementary reimbursement of treatments in other Member States.[32]

Member States of affiliation will also be required to have a transparent mechanism for the calculation of such costs, which must be based on objective, non-discriminatory criteria that are known in advance.[33] This seemingly self-evident requirement is likely to have far-reaching consequences especially for benefits in kind and NHS systems that in most cases are likely to lack useful pre-

31 Article 5 on the responsibilities of the Member State of affiliation provides an anchor for the various obligations, such as ensuring that the cost for cross-border health care is reimbursed in accordance with the Directive.

32 Case C-208/07 *Petra von Chamier-Glisczinski v. Deutsche Angestellten-Krankenkasse* [2009] ECR I-6095.

33 Cf. *Müller-Fauré*, para. 107; *Watts*, para. 143. Cf. G. Davies, n. 7, pp. 164–165.

existing cost information on which reimbursement can be based. Given the difficulties associated with the introduction of sound cost accounting principles where such practices were not already in place, a common EU understanding of the relevant costing principles may be required before long.

7.2. SUPPLEMENTARY CONDITIONS

Article 7 paragraph 7 of the Directive also provides for the possibility for the Member State of affiliation to impose additional conditions at national, regional or local level upon insured persons who are requesting reimbursement of costs for cross-border health care, such as selection criteria and conditions of an administrative or regulatory nature, as it would impose if this health care were provided in its territory. However, these conditions cannot be discriminatory or go beyond what can be justified based on the planning exception with respect to ensuring access to health care and/or controlling health care expenditure which is repeated at this point of the Directive (and which will be more fully addressed below).

7.3. NON-HOSPITAL CARE: FULL LIBERALIZATION

What the Proposal had made explicit is regulated by omission in the Directive: patients are entitled to seek non-hospital care which is covered by their national social security regime in other Member States without prior authorization, and are entitled to reimbursement at the same level as if the care had been provided in the Member State of affiliation. It is assumed therefore that this will by definition not undermine the financial equilibrium of social security systems.

Although the categories 'intramural' and 'extramural' care do not appear in the Directive – the distinction is now between health care that may or may not be subjected to a prior authorization requirement – the distinction between these two types of care remains sensitive. Apart from the question whether an overnight stay is involved which is easily answered (although it may be answered differently by different jurisdictions or different health care providers within these), health care that can be subject to prior authorization requirements also concerns health care involving the use of highly specialized and cost-intensive infrastructure or medical equipment.[34] The Proposal intended to regulate this based on a list to be set up and regularly updated by the Commission. In the Directive the Member States themselves determine which types of care are involved and communicate these to the Commission.

[34] Case C-512/08 *Commission v. France* (extramural treatment) [2010] ECR I-*not yet reported.*

7.4. HOSPITAL CARE AND SPECIALIZED CARE: THE END OF PRIOR AUTHORIZATION REGIMES?

For the most contested type of cross-border care, that which requires at least one overnight stay as well as specialized and cost-intensive care, the Directive allows the Member State of affiliation to introduce a prior authorization system.[35] Article 8.2 reads as follows:

> *'Healthcare that may be subject to prior authorisation shall be limited to healthcare which:*
> *(a) is made subject to planning requirements relating to the object of ensuring sufficient and permanent access to a balanced range of high-quality treatment in the Member State concerned or to the wish to control costs and avoid, so far as possible, any waste of financial, technical and human resources and:*
> *(i) involves overnight hospital accommodation of the patient in question for at least one night; or*
> *(ii) requires use of highly specialised and cost-intensive medical infrastructure or medical equipment;*
> *(b) involves treatments presenting a particular risk for the patient or the population, or*
> *(c) is provided by a healthcare provider which, on a case-by-case basis, could raise serious and specific concerns relating to the quality or safety of the care with the exception of healthcare which is subject to Union legislation ensuring a minimum level of safety and quality throughout the Union.*
>
> *Member States shall notify the categories of healthcare referred to in point (a) to the Commission.'*

Moreover, a prior authorization system must be limited to what is necessary and proportionate, and may not constitute a means of arbitrary discrimination.

The Proposal had set up something very different: the Member States would have had to provide actual evidence that the outflow of patients due to cross-border hospital care *seriously* undermines their social security system or planning in the hospital sector. However, the Commission clearly believed these data did not exist and even proposed that the Directive should state so explicitly.[36]

---

35 Hospital services and specialized care concern health care that requires an overnight stay (for one or more nights) or that is included on a limited list that is established according to comitology procedures and involves the use of highly specialized and costly medical infrastructure or equipment, or involves treatments that present a particular risk to the patient or the population at large.

36 Recital 31 of the Preamble to the Proposal reads: '*The evidence available indicates that the application of free movement principles regarding use of healthcare in another Member State within the limits of the cover guaranteed by the statutory sickness insurance scheme of the Member State of affiliation will not undermine the health systems of the Member States or*

The Directive itself requires only that prior authorization systems are not just based on planning requirements related to access and/or costs (the financial balance of the social security system is no longer cited as a separate overriding reason of general interest but is also subsumed by the planning exception), but also meet the requirement of necessity and proportionality. It seems that this is a much lighter burden of proof which also approximates more closely the approach that the Court itself has followed so far. A secondary but not unimportant aspect is that in this manner evidence of the underlying cost structure is also less likely to be required. The chance that Member States will prefer to forfeit the opportunity of introducing a prior authorization system in order to avoid having to justify their costs is likewise reduced: hence there is more room to introduce or maintain prior authorization systems under the Directive than there was under the Proposal. Nevertheless, in principle, a least restrictive means test should now be applied to proportionality because of the harmonization of the justification now in place, which may eventually allow for reading across national systems and imposing best practice.

Apart from Article 8.2 (a) about prior authorization requirements for 'intramural care' and Article 7.7 on conditions, criteria of eligibility and regulatory and administrative formalities (such as the requirement to consult a general practitioner in order to obtain a referral for specialized care), Article 7.9 opens the possibility to subject the rules on reimbursement themselves to limitations based on the planning exception. In all three cases the planning exception is invoked, i.e. planning requirements relating to the object of ensuring sufficient and permanent access to a balanced range of high-quality treatment in the Member State concerned or to the wish to control costs and avoid, as far as possible, any waste of financial, technical and human resources.

More remarkable is the fact that based on Article 4.3 of the Directive the same planning exception applies for the Member States of treatment to justify safeguard measures (see further section 8.3. below). In this respect the Directive is both more detailed and more coherent than the original Proposal, although it also means significantly increasing the scope of the overriding reason of general interest as formulated in the case law. A final important difference is that whereas

financial sustainability of their social security systems.' Likewise in its Explanatory Memorandum (n. 18, p. 16) the Commission clearly states that based on its Impact Assessment, 'there is no evidence to suggest that such care [hospital care] will undermine the financial sustainability of health and social security systems overall or the organization, planning and delivery of health services.' *Ibid.*, p 14: '*The evidence available as set out in the impact assessment indicates that the application of free movement principles regarding use of healthcare in another Member State within the limits of the cover or the sickness insurance scheme of the Member State of affiliation will not undermine the health systems of the Member States or financial sustainability of their social security systems.*' I.e. not undermine at all, let alone seriously.

the Proposal required cross-border health care to 'seriously undermine' the financial balance and/or planning of health care in the Member State of affiliation before the exception could be invoked, the Directive itself only mentions the existence of an 'objective justification'. This means the requirements for a successful reference to the overriding reason of general interest have been relaxed considerably in relation to the Proposal and, in some respects, the case law. This concerns the safeguard measures as well as eligibility criteria and the reimbursement rules themselves. These are changes with respect to the Proposal which provide the Member States additional possibilities to fence off their national health care markets. Hence, apart from the fact that the norm for the exception was relaxed, it can now also be applied more widely.

7.5. REASONS TO REFUSE PRIOR AUTHORIZATION

Before discussing the new patients' rights as well as cooperation, I will briefly cover another innovation in the Directive: the reasons for refusal.

Paragraph 6 of Article 8 of the Directive now encapsulates the possible grounds for a refusal of a request for prior authorization. The alleged availability of treatment within the Member State of affiliation, without 'undue delay' has so far been one of the main grounds for refusal in the case law. In addition the new provision lists an unacceptable patient (health) risk; a risk that the general public will be exposed with reasonable certainty to a substantial safety hazard; and health care to be provided by a health care provider that raises serious and specific concerns relating to the respect of standards and guidelines on quality of care and patient safety. This limitation of the grounds for refusal is appropriate given the broadened scope for requiring prior authorization respectively throwing up barriers to cross-border health care based on planning exceptions.

8. COMMON PRINCIPLES FOR HEALTH CARE: THE 'NEW' PATIENTS' RIGHTS

8.1. THE SOCIAL POLICY AGENDA

The new patients' rights, that is the additions to the rights to treatment and to reimbursement that were discussed above, are the main elements of the Directive that should be seen in the light of the European social policy agenda. After all, this was the context in which the Directive was proposed, and these are the elements that are truly new by comparison to the existing mobility case law of the ECJ. As will be seen, this context is reflected in the common principles of universality, access to high-quality care, equity and solidarity embraced by the Directive. At the same time, in terms of substance, the Directive, by primarily setting out individual rights to accountability and transparency, does not reflect these broader values as clearly as might have been expected. It remains to be seen whether they will come to play a more significant role in future. Another relevant aspect here may be the progression from a number of OMC topics from soft law and intergovernmentalism to hard law and harmonized forms of cooperation. This is discussed in the next section under cooperation.

8.2. RIGHTS TO ACCOUNTABILITY AND TRANSPARENCY

Consistent with Article 168.7 TFEU, the Directive starts by setting out the key principle that the Member State of treatment bears responsibility for the organization and delivery of health care. The main innovation in this respect is that its Article 4 sets out common principles for health care that can be seen as a new set of patients' rights. These correspond with the responsibilities of the Member States of treatment and are not based on the free movement case law of the Court. Instead, the principles are based on Council Conclusions of 2006 to the same effect,[37] which drew on the existing systems (or at least ambitions) of the Member States.[38] As was mentioned above, universality, access to high-quality care, equity and solidarity are asserted as the guiding principles for Member States of treatment.

In substance the Directive mainly requires the Member States of treatment to provide quality and safety standards for health care based on dynamic international best practice standards (the application of which is monitored and enforced), and to ensure the right to the information necessary for an informed choice, the right to make complaints and guarantees of redress and remedies, to privacy, equal treatment and non-discrimination. The right to an informed choice involves in particular information about availability, prices and outcomes of health care. The Member State of treatment is obliged to provide for adequate systems of liability insurance. Finally, the Member States of treatment must also create national contact points where patients can access the information concerned.

---

37 European Council, 'Council Conclusions on common values and principles in European Union health systems' [2006] OJ C146/1 (Statement in Annex).

38 This corresponds with the overarching values identified, *Ibid.*, para. 6. The Council had resisted earlier proposals to define patients' rights at EU level. Cf. T.K. Hervey, 'The Legal Basis of European Community Public Health Policy' in M. McKee, E. Mossialos and R. Baeten (eds.), *The Impact of EU Law on Healthcare Systems*, P.I.E. Peter Lang, Brussels 2002, pp. 46–47.

Especially the duty to provide information appears to be of greater significance. It is worth noting that the relevant information to enable patient choice is hardly available at national level, let alone information relevant to patient choice that is comparable to information derived from other Member States.[39] Article 4 does include the proviso that Member States of treatment that already provide 'relevant information' to their inhabitants do not need to provide more extensive information for the benefit of patients from other Member States. In this context the meaning of the term 'relevant information' is significant: the Proposal had required 'all relevant information'. Should the information concerned facilitate making choices between treatments in different Member States or just between treatment options? At least the latter appears probable. The references to information concerning 'outcomes of the healthcare provided' have been purged from the Directive. The toughest category, however, – that of quality – has been retained. This limited obligation to provide information may yet provide the thin end of the wedge towards transparency-based reform.

8.3. UNIVERSAL APPLICABILITY FOR THE NEW PATIENTS' RIGHTS?

In the Proposal the scope of this important provision was not clearly defined:

- The Council Conclusions on which the text is based are clearly of general application.
- The heading ('Member State of treatment') suggested norms that apply for patients from other Member States.
- The wording (referring to health care in general, and not to cross-border health care) of the provision itself implied a general application.

This has now been changed: the responsibilities concerned are clearly marked as regarding cross-border health care. This does not change the general applicability of the underlying Council Conclusions. Moreover it is difficult to see how such fundamental norms of accountability and transparency could possibly be implemented solely for the benefit of patients from other Member States. Although as a matter of EU law this would be possible (reverse discrimination, i.e. of own nationals, is allowed), it seems politically unsustainable. Hence it is assumed here that they are universal rights that will come to apply to all patients, not just those moving across borders. This would involve a major step in terms of accountability of health care providers (and indeed of the authorities responsible for health care systems) to patients.

---

39 Cf. O. Damman, *Public Reporting about Healthcare Users' Experiences: The Consumer Quality Index*, PhD thesis Tilburg University, April 2010.

8.3.1. *Safeguards measures for Member States of treatment*

Although the Proposal enabled a derogation from free movement to the Member State of affiliation in the shape of prior authorization requirements, it foresaw none for the Member State of treatment. In this regard the Directive has introduced an important change: according to Article 4.3 of the Directive the same planning exception (concerning access to health care and/or cost control) that can be invoked by the Member State of affiliation will become available to the Member State of treatment as well. The measures introduced in this respect must be made public in advance. This is an exception to the principle of non-discrimination with regard to nationality that applies to patients from other Member States more generally, including with respect to the prices charged for the health care provided.

This is significant as in the absence of tariff rebalancing it may clearly happen that charges for treatment of patients from other Member States are out of line with actual costs but attractive to the health care provider in question (e.g. to 'fill empty beds'). In such cases payment is likely to cover only marginal costs rather than a share of fixed costs – putting pressure on public funding. Meanwhile competition between health care providers to attract mobile patients is likely to trigger new dynamics with an impact on the national market. On the one hand such developments could well contribute to undermining the financial sustainability and coherence of the existing national social security systems – while on the other hand adding pressure toward much needed rationalization and rebalancing. Hence the impetus toward change as a result of the Directive is likely to involve Member States in their role as Member States of treatment, not just as Member States of affiliation.

9. COOPERATION

The Directive envelops five types of cooperation that were so far the subject of the intergovernmental OMC.[40] This concerns:

- Mutual assistance and cooperation: this regards all kinds of (including bilateral) cooperation including the information exchange between the national contact points that are to be established according to Article 4 of the Directive.
- Recognition of prescriptions issued in another Member State: if a medicinal product is authorized to be marketed on their territory prescriptions issued

[40] Cf. S.L. Greer and B. Vanhercke, 'The Hard Politics of Soft Law: The Case of Health' in E. Mossialos, G. Permanand, R. Baeten and T. K. Hervey (eds.), n. 1.

for such a product in another Member State must be recognized and dispensed (this provision enables delegated rule making by the Commission).
- European reference networks: these are voluntary networks that aim to combat in particular rare diseases requiring highly specialized health care, and promote e.g. the development of new diagnoses and treatments (this provision enables delegated rule making by the Commission as well).
- E-Health: this concerns electronic developments in health care and the work that is being done on developing the interoperability between systems, the necessary minimum data set, with a view to building a high level of trust and security.
- Cooperation on health technology assessment: this aims at avoiding needless duplication of procedures and thereby at contributing to a faster and more effective assessment of the relevant technological developments.

Although not a key element in the harmonization setting of the Directive these elements are nevertheless important to the continued collaboration between the Member States in this field, and by creating cross-border policy communities they may contribute towards providing support for further integration of health care markets – possibly by spill-over, and including further harmonization. This is therefore a noteworthy development from soft law and intergovernmentalism, in areas where the prior consensus had been that harmonization should be excluded, to cooperation through hard law, in the context of a perceived need for increased integration in related fields – in this case patients' mobility and patients' rights under the freedom to provide and receive services.

10. FURTHER ANALYSIS

The development of the law on patient mobility appears to fit the mould of the standard interaction between positive and negative integration: first national measures obstructing the freedom to provide services (in this case) are struck down by the Court, and then the need arises for re-regulation to fill the gap left, providing sufficient consensus for a more liberal Community regime to emerge. This can be illustrated by a more detailed discussion of the following two topics: justifying prior authorization requirements; and the scope for change based on the 'new' patient's rights.

10.1. PRIOR AUTHORISATION REQUIREMENTS: LIBERALISATION

As we have seen the scope for invoking the planning exception has been increased in the Directive. However, the necessity and proportionality of the measures involved – notably prior authorization requirements – remain to be shown by the Member State of affiliation. The practical difficulties of demonstrating the need for a prior authorization system are considerable. The Proposal with its exception based on the financial balance of the social security system raises questions such as how in a sector where the cost of an individual treatment is not known could it be plausibly argued that transferring such treatments abroad would jeopardize the financial balance of the system; and how to demonstrate that the financial balance of a social security system is threatened if basic measures of sound administration and business practice such as proper cost accounting and tariff rebalancing are lacking.

This problem may have been reduced, but did not disappear in as far as the planning exception speaks of the wish to control costs and ways to avoid wasting resources. It may therefore be that, in spite of the Member States' (in Council) best efforts to increase the scope of the planning exception, its application may raise difficulties for them.

10.2. NEW PATIENTS' RIGHTS: HARMONIZATION

Apart from harmonizing the standards for the prior authorization schemes, harmonization is also to be found in the main innovation of the proposal in relation to the case law: the obligations of Member States of treatment, or the 'new' patients' rights. These are likely to ensure the enduring impact of patient mobility on Member States, both when sending patients abroad, and when receiving them. The obligations involved have their origins in the Council Conclusions of 2006,[41] but under the Directive will be made legally binding and justiciable. Moreover, the ensuing rights – especially to accountability, and transparency on availability, prices and outcomes of health care – will accrue not just to mobile patients, but to all patients in each Member State. Arguably, this is the key element of positive integration to be introduced by the Directive. In sum, the addition of the broader 'new' patients' rights (to accountability and transparency) to the codification of the 'old' patients' rights to reimbursement could create momentum for a broader change.

Potentially we are therefore looking at a chain of events leading toward a fundamental change. The links of this chain are the following:

1. The creation of rights to reimbursement for treatment abroad in the patient mobility case law of the Court,
2. The creation of rights to a certain standard of treatment abroad by the Directive,

[41] European Council, n. 37.

3. The extension of these rights to patients treated at home by the Directive,
4. The leveraging of these rights (especially in terms of transparency and accountability) to begin transforming national health care systems.

So far this process appears to have reached step 2 indicated above.

By choosing the legislative route on patient mobility, the Commission has taken the calculated risk that in the course of the legislative process the relatively clear-cut and far-reaching case law of the Court based on Article 56 TFEU itself would be diluted. This may now have paid off because the Directive incorporates a number of elements designed to set in motion further changes in health care systems at national level – to a significant degree precisely based on 'patients' rights', which will in the longer term promote both greater efficiency and accountability.

At the same time, the fact that the focus both of the recent case law and of the proposed Directive has been centred on the patient fits in well with a consumer (and/or citizen) oriented approach to European integration and is consistent with the social policy agenda that is being developed as a response to public scepticism about the benefits of the EU – just as it would be in line with a demand based economic view. It is also consistent with most perspectives that accept the potential of a positive role for the EU.

11. CONCLUSION

The Directive sets out a framework for cross-border health care in the EU. In doing so it follows the logic of positive integration following negative integration, combined with a formalization in law of erstwhile OMC based policy cooperation. Old rights to reimbursement of costs are supplemented by new rights to transparency and accountability, and the principles of universality, access to good quality care, equity and solidarity are set out in EU legislation for the first time. Benefits are not harmonized but the conditions for access to cross-border health care to a significant extent are.

The main technical content of the Directive can be divided into three parts

- In the first place, the Directive is based on the planning exception. For the Member State of affiliation this concerns (i) the system of prior authorization in Article 8.2, as well as (ii) the other requirements that can be imposed in Article 7.7, and (iii) the possibility to limit the application of the rules on reimbursement in Article 7.9. For the Member States of treatment the planning exception can be invoked for (iv) safeguard measures. (It is worth noting that options (ii) through (iv) did not appear in the original Proposal.) The norm applied is whether recourse to this exception is objectively justified, necessary and proportional. In line with the case law – but in contrast to the Proposal – it does not appear necessary for the Member States to provide quantitative evidence (a burden of proof that would have been difficult to meet given the likely scale of cost imbalances prevalent in the various health care systems).

- Second, (and again in contrast to the Proposal) the Directive is clearly based on the concept of 'undue delay', which appears in the limited set of grounds on the basis of which prior authorization may be refused in Article 8.5 (a), and in the administrative requirements for this procedure (concerning time limits) in Article 9.2 (a). In this manner the Directive is also more in line with Regulation 883/2004 as well as with the relevant case law than the Proposal was.
- Third, and finally, other due process guarantees are imposed as well, such as the right to a decision on a case-by-case basis that is subject to judicial review in Article 9.3, and the (entirely new) limited list of grounds for refusal in Article 8.5 (a) that was already mentioned. This completes the material and procedural norms that had already been developed in the case law.

Based on these three elements the Directive forms a coherent system that for this reason alone already constitutes an improvement on the Proposal concerning the aspects just discussed. However, apart from leaving less room for uncertainty it also leaves less room for secondary effects, such as exposing the way in which the costs of treatment are accounted for. In sum, the EU's approach indeed followed the familiar sequence from EU integration theory: the removal of barriers to the market freedoms breeds the need to elaborate rights and obligations in legislation which aims at striking a new balance between private freedoms and legitimate public interests. Actual policy convergence is not required beyond the limitations imposed on the possibility to demand prior authorization requirements, although the effects of the patients' rights to transparency and accountability may well lead in this direction. For health care this development amounts to a watershed given the constitutional barriers that had been erected in the Treaty against harmonization in this field.

EU COORDINATION OF PENSION POLICY: POLICY CONTENT AND INFLUENCE ON NATIONAL REFORMS

David NATALI*

1. INTRODUCTION

While the national level is still the main locus for pension policy (both redistributive and regulatory tasks), the EU level is characterized by expanding competence and influence. The process of European integration has eroded Member States' sovereignty and led to a multi-tiered polity. EU's welfare dimension has emerged as an 'unplanned collage'. Evolving EU pension competence has been mainly centred on two instruments: regulation and post-regulation (consistent with the coordination rather than the harmonization of national policy). Coordination modes of governance are mainly (or exclusively) based on non-legislative instruments (e.g. common guidelines, national action plans, peer reviews, joint evaluation reports, recommendations, and eventually sanctions).

Two main forms of post-regulation are referred to in this chapter. The requirements for budgetary discipline through the Stability and Growth Pact (SGP) – within the broader Economic and Monetary Union (EMU) – represent a source of indirect (and hard) pressure on pension institutions. The coordination of pension reforms through the Open Method of Coordination is a direct (and soft) version of integration.[1] The present contribution has two key aims: to shed light on the evolution of these modes of coordination, and to summarize the main insights for the assessment of the EU influence on national pension reforms.

* I would like to thank Eva Zemantl for the systematic collection of data and information on the most recent evolution of the Stability and Growth Pact (SGP) and the Open Method of Coordination on Social Protection and Social Inclusion.

1 While the chapter by Y. STEVENS does focus on the legal aspects of the EU action in the field of pensions, here the focus is on the policy content of EU coordination processes.

Section two summarizes the key traits of EU direct and indirect forms of coordination of national pensions: the Stability and Growth Pact and OMC on pensions are presented. The main focus is on the policy content of the two pieces of EU socio-economic governance and their changing interaction and (un) balance. Section three provides a schematic framework for assessing the influence of these modes of governance on national pension policy. Section four presents a brief review of some of the contributions for the assessment of the EU coordination in the field of pensions. Section five concludes.

2. EU 'DIRECT' AND 'INDIRECT' COORDINATION OF NATIONAL PENSION POLICY

The process of European integration has been characterized by the rise of the regulatory state. Given the limited financial resources of the EU (consistent with rigid budget constraints), rule making has been the most important instrument of governance at that level.[2] Yet, recently a second set of instruments has been developed. This set consists of post-regulation (aiming at the coordination of national policies) to secure 'structural coupling' between different autonomous social sub-systems (mainly the economy and society).[3] These modes of governance are mainly (or exclusively) based on non-legislative instruments (e.g. common guidelines, national action plans, peer reviews, joint evaluation reports, recommendations, and eventually sanctions).

In the present section, the reference is to two of these new modes of governance: 'hard' and 'soft' forms of coordination. The former imply material (for instance financial) sanctions against a Member State in case of breach of the Treaty's provisions. The latter do not include any sanctions except moral pressure.[4] There are different coordinating modes in different policy areas. On the one hand, EU budgetary policy, via the Stability and Growth Pact – that is part of the Economic and Monetary Union – is a typical example of indirect and hard coordination providing indirect pressure on retirement programmes. It establishes binding and quantitative policy objectives, while governments are free to choose their own paths for convergence. Coordination is thus established through benchmarking, peer pressure and the structured process of multi-level

---

2 S. Leibfried, 'Social Policy Left to the Judges and the Market?' in H. Wallace, W. Wallace and M. Pollack (eds.), *Policy-Making in the European Union*, Oxford University Press, Oxford 2005.

3 D. Natali, 'The Open Method of Coordination: Does it De-Politicise Pensions Policy?' (2009) 4 *West European Politics (WEP)*.

4 W. Wessels and I. Linsenmann, 'EMU's Impact on National Institutions: Fusion Towards a "Gouvernance Économique" or Fragmentation?' in K. Dyson (ed.), *European States and the Euro: Europeanisation, Variation and Convergence*, Oxford University Press, Oxford 2002.

surveillance. In case of non-compliance, sanctions are (or should be) activated. On the other hand, the Open Method of Coordination on pensions is a direct and soft mode of coordination. Qualitative common objectives are set and Member States freely decide to pursue them. In other words, while providing policy players with a relatively clear agenda, it leaves ample room for national contextualization. Benchmarking is aimed at measuring national performance and progress. Peer review and political monitoring are part of an iterative process for joint evaluation. Compared to the SGP, it is a much weaker form of governance.[5]

2.1. STABILITY AND GROWTH PACT: PROCEDURES AND CONTENT

The European fiscal framework was designed in 1991 and then included in the Maastricht Treaty, which entered into force two years later. It was then revised in 1997 with the creation of the Stability and Growth Pact (in force since 1999), and eventually reformed in 2005 and 2010. The Maastricht Treaty consisted of a 'preventive arm' focusing on multilateral surveillance and the avoidance of excessive deficits, and a 'dissuasive arm' tackling excessive deficits once they arise.[6] The Treaty aimed at increasing convergence of the European national economies, eliminating currency fluctuations and unfair competition in monetary policy. Since the beginning of the third stage of EMU, the countries involved have had to comply with the convergence criteria under the Maastricht Treaty of 1991.[7] The Treaty defined automatic procedures for reviewing the qualification for joining the EMU in 1999.

2.1.1. Stability and Growth Pact (I), 1997

To safeguard the sustainability of public finances following the introduction of the euro, the European Council of Amsterdam of 1997 adopted the Stability and Growth Pact (on the basis of Article 99 EC, on coordination and multilateral surveillance of national fiscal policies, and Article 104 EC on corrective measures and sanctions).[8] SGP was adopted by means of Regulation 1466/97 (on the

5 M. Citi and M. Rhodes, 'New Modes of Governance in the EU: Common Objectives versus National Preferences' (2007) European Governance Papers, EUROGOV 2007/01 <www.connex-network.or/eurogov/pdf/egp-newgov-N-07-01.pdf> accessed 10 November 2010.

6 B. Coeuré and J. Pisany-Ferri, 'Fiscal Policy in EMU: Towards a Sustainability and Growth Pact?' (2005) 4 *OREP Oxford review of Economic Policy (OREP).*

7 H. Meyer, 'Restructuring the German Government – Social Policy under Pressure by the Stability and Growth Pact' (2005) Paper presented at the ESPAnet Conference 'Making Social Policy in the Post-Industrial Age' (Fribourg, 22–24 September 2005).

8 L. Diebalek, W. Kohler-Toglhofer and D. Prammer, 'Reform of the Stability and Growth Pact' (2006) 6 *Monetary Policy and Economy (MPE).*

strengthening of the surveillance of budgetary positions and the surveillance and coordination of economic policies)[9] and Regulation 1467/97 (on speeding up and clarifying the implementation of the excessive deficit procedure).[10] As well as the Maastricht criteria, the coordination of fiscal policy thus consisted of two components. The preventive part consisted of requirements for a balanced budget or one that was in surplus in the medium term (Table 1).

Table 1. Stability and Growth Pact and its evolution

SGP 1997	SGP 2005	SGP 2011*
Medium-term objective Cyclically adjusted budget balances: balance of –0.5% of GDP to surplus (applicable to all members)	Medium-term objective Cyclically adjusted budget balances, net of one-off and temporary measures (country-specific range, between –1% of GDP and surplus)	Medium-term objective Cyclically adjusted budget balances as a percentage of GDP in structural terms (i.e. adjusting for the effect of the cycle and excluding one-off and temporary measures) and are differentiated across countries around a close-to-balance position to reflect the level of public debt and liabilities related to ageing
Adjustment path At least 0.5% of GDP	Adjustment path Average 0.5% of GDP depending on the state of the economic cycle	Adjustment path At least 0.5% of GDP structural deficit reduction At least 1/20th debt reduction per year (both focused on the spending rather than the revenue side) 'Prudent fiscal policymaking'
Exceptional circumstances Severe economic downturn	Exceptional circumstances Negative growth or negative output gap for a sustained period of low growth; Extent of government investment relative to deficit, medium-term economic and budgetary position, other factors relevant for the Member State; *Systematic pension reforms*	Exceptional circumstances *e.g. Tax subsidies to promote pension funds*

* proposal from the Commission

The Pact laid down a medium-term objective, which was to reach budgetary positions 'close-to-balance or in surplus'. Each country in the euro area had to

9 [1997] OJ L209/1.
10 [1997] OJ L209/6.

present a stability programme at the end of each year, with macroeconomic medium-term projections and all planned budgetary measures. More importantly, it had to target a budgetary position close to balance or in surplus in the medium-run. These programmes had then to be evaluated by the Commission and the Council for Economic and Financial Affairs. This was the corrective part of the Pact.

While the Pact agreed on at Amsterdam did not concern pensions policy, the Council of Ministers of Economic and Financial Policy (ECOFIN) and related technical committees have explicitly monitored the long-term sustainability of retirement programmes.[11] In 1997 the Ecofin and its technical bodies (the Economic Policy Committee, EPC) addressed pension reforms by a communication.[12] Its guiding philosophy was that pension reform needed to be adapted to the circumstances of an ageing population while at the same time ensuring durable fiscal consolidation and improving the condition of European labour markets. The principal recommendation was to contain benefits, as the main instrument for guaranteeing the solvency of PAYGO schemes.[13] The EPC first recommended delaying the age of retirement. A second recommendation was to move away from a solidarity-based system to a pension system based on individual contributions. A third recommendation was to gradually increase the role of funded schemes.[14]

2.1.2. Stability and Growth Pact (II), 2005

The first version of the SGP was widely criticized.[15] Some of the criticism focused on its implications for the sustainability of welfare programmes. For some, the lack of any reference to structural reforms, especially those related to social policies (those more affected by negative demographic trends), represented a crucial limitation. The focus on public debt did not allow for 'implicit' expenditure, such as future pension payments to be considered. For others, the convergence criteria risked ruling out structural reforms that entailed upfront costs but were desirable for the functioning of the system.[16] That is the case for

---

11 P. Pochet and D. Natali, 'European Networks on Pensions: The Participation of Organised Interests in the EU Policy-making Process' (2005) 5 *RBSS*.

12 Economic Policy Committee, 'The Reform of European Pension Systems' (1997) Opinion addressed to the Council and the Commission.

13 In line with the Pay-as-you-go (PAYGO) method of financing, current contributions paid by both employers and employees (or revenues coming from current taxation) are not accumulated but rather immediately used for financing current benefits.

14 D. Natali, *Pensions in Europe, European Pensions*, P.I.E. Peter Lang, Brussels 2008.

15 I. Begg and W. Shelkle, 'The Pact is Dead: Long Live the Pact' (2004) 1 *National Institute Economic Review (NIER)*.

16 A. Razin and E. Sadka, 'The Stability and Growth Pact as an Impediment to Privatizing Social Security' (2002) 9278 *National Bureau of Economic Research (NBER)* Working Paper <www.nber.org/papers/w9278.pdf> accessed 10 October 2011.

pension privatization, when the government may start to increase both deficit and debt in order to finance the transition (through tax incentives and reduced mandatory contributions) while the consequent fall in implicit liabilities is not recognized in the national accounts.[17]

In 2003, when some countries in the euro-zone (and in particular France and Germany) did not respect the criteria laid down in the Pact, the Commission started to make proposals for revision of the SGP. That debate led to a number of different reform proposals. Some called for the incentives for fiscal discipline to be strengthened, while others stressed the need for greater attention to be paid to economic growth. Some of the proposals concerned pension policy. Scholars proposed the introduction of the 'permanent balance' rule, which allows for higher deficits due to investments in public capital and also demands the reduction of public debt as a consequence of the high permanent level of pension transfers (higher than current pension transfers because of growth in future expenditure).[18] Other commentators called for a more flexible implementation of the Pact so as to open more opportunities for the introduction of structural reforms (such as pension privatization).[19]

In March 2005 the European Council agreed on fundamental changes to the SGP that were consistent with a more flexible approach to sound fiscal policy. European policymakers looked at the main areas for improvement in the working of the Pact and its economic logic.[20] The medium-term objective for the public budget was no longer to be 'close to balance or in surplus' for all countries. Greater account had to be taken of national specificities (especially debt, potential growth and investment expenditure), consistent with differentiated targets for each country (Table 1 above).

The convergence period was extended and softened, and Member States had merely to 'explain' deviations from the recommended adjustment path. Consolidation might be more limited in periods of economic recession, but Member States should act more vigorously in 'good times' (periods in which output exceeds potential). The revised Pact dedicated much attention to

---

17 R. Beetsma and H. Oksanen, 'Pension Systems, Ageing and the Stability and Growth Pact' (2007) 2141 CESifo Working Paper <http://ec.europa.eu/economy_finance/publications/publication9491_en.pdf> accessed 10 October 2011.

18 W. H. Buiter and C. Grafe, 'Patching Up the Pact: Some Suggestions for Enhancing Fiscal Sustainability and Macroeconomic Stability in an Enlarged European Union' (2004) 1 *Economics of Transition (EOT)*.

19 R. Beetsma and X. Debrun, 'Reconciling Stability and Growth: Smart Pacts and Structural Reforms' (2004) 3 *IMF Staff Papers*.

20 A. Watt, 'The On-Going Saga on the Stability and Growth Pact: Is the Spring 2005 Reform Good for Growth and Jobs?' (2005) 5 *European Economic and Employment Policy Brief (EEEPB)* <www.etui-rehs.org/media/files/eeepb/5_2005> accessed 10 October 2011.

structural reforms to be adopted in order to enhance the 'growth-oriented nature of the Pact'.[21] In the second paragraph of the Pact, the respect for the budgetary targets was related to encouragement of reforms improving the long-term sustainability of public finances. Particular attention was thus paid to pension innovations introducing multi-pillar systems that include a mandatory, fully funded pillar. In line with a more flexible understanding of stability, such reforms were favoured because of the consequent improvement in the long-term equilibrium of the public budget and the increase in potential economic growth. The Council agreed that an excessive deficit reflecting the adoption of pension reforms 'should be considered carefully'. In other words, the Commission and the Council were asked to assess the development of budgetary policies while considering the net cost of the pension reform for the initial five years of its implementation.

2.1.3. *Stability and Growth Pact (III), 2010–11*

The Great Recession of 2008–09 and the subsequent debate on the need to reinforce EU economic governance have led to the formulation of proposals that have not left untouched pension schemes. The basic components of the new approach were initially presented in two Commission Communications,[22] while a policy package of legislative proposals was adopted by the Commission in late September 2010. The debate between the Commission, the Council and the Parliament is still in progress, while the reinforcement of the EU economic governance in the new 'Strategy for Smart, Sustainable and Inclusive Growth' (Europe 2020) has started to be implemented.

Proposals cover, in particular, the following three themes: reinforcing Member State compliance with the SGP and deepening fiscal consolidation, broadening economic surveillance and strengthening of enforcement mechanisms.[23]

First, the preventive arm of the SGP is strengthened through the introduction of the new principle of 'prudent fiscal policymaking', aimed at ensuring that prudent fiscal policies in good times allow the building up of a buffer for bad times. This approach is expected to guarantee convergence towards the medium-term objectives. The corrective arm is also amended, so that debt developments

21 See P. Pochet and D. Natali, n. 11.

22 European Commission, 'Reinforcing economic policy coordination' COM (2010) 250 final; European Commission, 'Enhancing economic policy coordination for stability, growth and jobs –Tools for stronger EU economic governance' COM (2010) 37/2.

23 M. Angelaki and D. Natali, 'Pension Policy in Europe since the Crisis: EU Developments and National Reforms' in C. Degryse and D. Natali (eds.), *Social Developments in the EU*, ETUI/OSE, Brussels 2011.

are put on an equal footing with deficit developments. The changes in both the preventive and corrective parts are backed up by a set of gradual financial sanctions. In its assessment of the soundness of national fiscal policies, the Commission will examine the sustainability of pension systems, while giving consideration to the partial or total reversal of previously implemented systemic pension reforms during both the launch and the abrogation of the excessive deficit procedure.

Second, the establishment of the 'European Semester' for economic policy coordination – beginning in January 2011 – should allow Member States to benefit from early coordination at European level, by synchronizing assessment of their fiscal and structural policies. Economic surveillance will be further enhanced by means of a new regulation on the prevention and correction of macroeconomic imbalances. The excessive imbalance procedure will comprise a regular assessment of the risks of imbalances based on a scoreboard of economic indicators, both external (e.g. current accounts, real effective exchange rates) and internal (e.g. private and public sector debt). The first document advanced by the Commission – the Annual Growth Survey – has clearly focused on the need to reform pension programmes in the context of the priorities for enhancing economic growth.[24]

Germany insisted on tougher sanctions, arguing in favour of expelling euro-zone members, as a last resort, in the event of their repeatedly failing to respect the SGP, notwithstanding the fact that such a proposal requires a change in the EU Treaties. In a joint proposal with France on the topic, acknowledging that a mechanism entailing suspension of voting rights would have to be included in a revision of the Treaty, the two Member States argued for a political accord that would enable euro-zone Member States either to bar an offending state from taking part in specific votes or deliberations, or to make a political commitment to neutralize the effect of that member's vote. The joint statement also argues in favour of taking more explicitly into account implicit liabilities such as pension reforms when assessing the fiscal sustainability of a Member State.[25]

Third, new voting procedures have been proposed: proposals have been made to use qualified majority only to block penalties from being applied, while at present a minority of Member States is enough to block sanctions.

---

[24] European Commission, 'Annual Growth Survey: Advancing the EU's comprehensive response to the crisis' COM (2011) 11 final.

[25] C. Barbier, *'Semestre européen ou Pacte de competitivité: bonnet blanc et blanc bonnet?'* (2011) OSE Working Paper Series 4/2011, <www.ose.be/files/publication/OSEPaperSeries/Barbier_2011_OpinionPaper4_Semestre_europ.pdf> accessed 14 May 2011.

But what has been the debate on pension reforms? In parallel to the ongoing debate on the revision of the Pact, the key issue has concerned the cost of pension privatization and their weight on public budgets. In August 2010, the Ministers of Finance of nine Member States (Poland, Bulgaria, the Czech Republic, Hungary, Latvia, Lithuania, Romania, Slovakia and Sweden), in a letter addressed to the Economic Affairs Commissioner and the President of the European Council, stressed that the coordination of national economic policies should take into account pension reforms. They demanded to be allowed to exclude the cost of pension reform from public debt and deficit figures, in order to avoid EU disciplinary actions. Commissioner Olli Rehn, in a letter to these countries, said that while the request was 'justified', it was 'not possible' to accept it under the current accounting system.[26] The Commission, however, offered these countries a five-year leniency period if their budget gaps exceeded the EU's ceiling of 3% of gross domestic product and/or their debt exceeded a cap of 60% of the same. Poland, Slovakia and the other countries considered this proposal inadequate and raised the issue again at the EU summit held on October 2010. The October meeting's conclusions merely invited the EU Council of Ministers to speed up work on ways to integrate pension reform into the EU's revised Stability and Growth Pact. As we will show in Section three below, this then resulted in the progress of reforms in Hungary.[27]

To sum up, the guidelines provided by the SGP (in its different versions) have been that pensions need to be adapted to the circumstances of an ageing population while at the same time ensuring durable fiscal consolidation and improving the condition of European labour markets. If we look at the evolution of the SGP in the last decade, the 2005 revision watered down some of the main constraints on national budgetary policy, whereas the most recent proposals (in 2010–11) contain more stringent limits to the Member States' autonomy and a more strict control on public pension spending.[28]

2.2. OMC ON PENSIONS: PROCEDURES AND CONTENT

In line with the post-regulatory approach, the OMC is not mandatory. Peer pressure represents the means of ensuring that national governments adhere to their European commitments. It is a flexible instrument seeking to harmonize

26 Euractiv, 'Poland Strikes Pension Deal with EU' (2010) <www.euractiv.com/en/euro-finance/poland-strikes-pension-deal-with-eu-news-500531> accessed 5 February 2011.

27 In December, after the Hungarian reform, Poland reached an agreement with the European Union aimed at loosening public finance rules in order to take into account the costs of pension reform. The Polish Prime Minister stressed that the Commission was no longer refusing to allow account to be taken of these costs when calculating public debt and deficit.

28 See M. Angelaki and D. Natali, n. 23.

ideas and knowledge rather than institutions or legislation.[29] And in terms of content, application of the OMC to many different policy issues has been consistent with two complementary sets of goals for the EU: to improve European competitiveness and social cohesion through modernized social protection systems.[30]

The Stockholm Council in 2001 officially launched the 'soft' governance on pensions on a three-year basis. The process involved defining some major policy guidelines (June 2001), then adopting a more precise set of policy objectives (December 2001), adopting national strategy reports by the Member States (September 2002), and the joint report on safe and sustainable pensions by the Commission and the Council (March 2003). After this first cycle of policymaking, a new phase started, and a new round of national reports was implemented in July 2005.[31]

The formulation of common objectives aimed at achieving greater policy convergence between EU Member States in line with both economic and social goals. Eleven objectives for pension reform were agreed around three 'pillars': social adequacy, financial sustainability, and modernization (e.g. responding to changing socio-economic needs).

After the first years of implementation, in May 2003 the Commission proposed 'streamlining' the work on social inclusion and pensions together with the planned work on health and long-term care to form an integrated process. The aim was twofold: creating a stronger process, and integrating better with the Lisbon process, in particular the Broad Economic Policy Guidelines (BEPGs) and the European Employment Strategy.[32] In the words of the Commission, 'streamlining should make the OMC more effective and give it a higher profile'; 'the new framework aimed to make the OMC a stronger and more visible process, better integrated with the Lisbon strategy and with more room for the learning, exchange and policy dissemination which participants value'. The Commission proposed a structure for reporting and evaluation across the three fields and a

29 S. Borras and K. Jacobsson, 'The Open Method of Coordination and New Governance Patters in the EU' (2004) 2 *Journal of European Public Policy (JEPP)*.

30 Z. Simon and M. Rozlal, 'EU Says Pension Accounting Change Sought by Poland, Hungary "Not Possible"' (2010) *Bloomberg*, <www.bloomberg.com/news/2010-10-22/eu-says-pension-accounting-change-sought-by-poland-hungary-not-possible.html> accessed 5 February 2011.

31 In fact, different OMCs deal with the pensions issue. The European Employment Strategy on the one hand addresses active ageing (in other words the need to improve employment rates among the elderly active population), while the OMC on Social Inclusion addresses the problem of poverty in old age.

32 European Commission, 'Working Together, Working Better: A New Framework for the Open Coordination of Social Protection and Inclusion Policies in the European Union' COM (2005) 706 final.

timetable synchronized with the renewed Lisbon Strategy. It was agreed to proceed gradually, with certain elements of the package – the start of work on health and long-term care and the creation of an annual Joint Social Protection and Social Inclusion Report – being addressed during 2004–2005. The final element – the adoption of new common objectives for the three strands was implemented from 2006 onwards. The Council's Conclusions of October 2003 agreed to *streamline* the coordination of social inclusion and social protection.

In 2005, the Commission proposed the following common objectives (subsequently accepted by the Council) for a streamlined OMC on social protection and social inclusion. The primary concern was to promote good policymaking for a high level of social protection and social cohesion, while ensuring good interaction with the revised Lisbon priorities of growth and employment and with the need to bridge the implementation gap identified in the review of Lisbon. The proposal consisted of three 'overarching' objectives, providing a general framework for work across the OMC as a whole:

- promote social cohesion and equal opportunities for all through adequate, accessible, financially sustainable, adaptable and efficient social protection systems and social inclusion policies;
- interact closely with the Lisbon objectives on achieving greater economic growth and more and better jobs and with the EU's Sustainable Development Strategy;
- strengthen governance, transparency and the involvement of stakeholders in the design, implementation and monitoring of policy.

Such broad objectives were then followed by more precise goals referring to each policy area: social inclusion, pensions and health, and long-term care. In the case of pensions, the three key objectives were refined as follows:

- in a spirit of solidarity and fairness between and within generations, to guarantee adequate retirement incomes for all and access to pensions which allow people to maintain, to a reasonable degree, their living standard after retirement;
- in the context of sound public finances, to ensure the financial sustainability of public and private pension schemes, notably by: supporting longer working lives and active ageing; ensuring an appropriate and fair balance of contributions and benefits; and promoting the affordability and ensuring the security of funded and private schemes;
- to ensure that pension systems are transparent, well adapted to the needs and aspirations of women and men and the requirements of modern societies, demographic ageing and structural change; that people receive the

information they need to plan their retirement and that reforms are conducted on the basis of the broadest possible consensus.[33]

Further steps in the actual implementation of the OMC did characterize the period between 2008 and 2010 (with the end of the Lisbon Strategy). First, the toolkit for monitoring and assessing national pensions policy was improved: with the launch of specific peer review sessions on single themes of interest (e.g. the one on the public information on pension systems and their change in Poland in 2008; and the recent one on balancing security and affordability of funded pension schemes in The Hague in 2011). Second, the technical bodies (the EPC and SPC) did work on the assessment of the crisis and its effects on pension systems and pensioners' conditions.[34]

In the context of the new Europe 2020 Strategy, the precise role of the OMC is to be defined.[35] It is not clear how the new governance arrangements under the Europe 2020 Strategy will connect with the broader EU coordination/cooperation and monitoring capacities in the social field developed through the Social OMC over the past decade.[36] It thus remains unclear how the EU's common social objectives – beyond combating poverty and social exclusion – will be monitored, reviewed, evaluated, and followed up within the governance architecture of Europe 2020, what will happen to national reporting of performance against the common indicators developed within the Social OMC,[37] and what will be the mutual interactions between policy fields and the social dimensions of other guidelines of the new encompassing Strategy (see Table 2) (notably Guideline 1 on the sustainability of the public finances, which emphasizes the need for reform of Member State pension and health care systems; and Guideline 7 on increasing labour market participation and reducing structural unemployment, in which active inclusion policies play a crucial part).

---

33 See Euractiv, n. 26.

34 European Commission and European Council, 'Joint Report on Social Protection and Social Inclusion' COM (2010) 10 final.

35 P. Pochet, 'EU 2020: Social Impact of the New Form of European Governance' (2010) 5 *ETUI Policy Brief.*

36 H. Frazer, E. Marlier, with D. Natali, R. Van Dam and B. Vanhercke, 'Europe 2020: Towards a More Social EU?' in E. Marlier and D. Natali (eds.) with R. Van Dam, *Europe 2020. Towards a More Social EU?*, P.I.E. Peter Lang, Brussels 2010.

37 J. Zeitlin, 'Towards a Stronger Social OMC in a More Social Europe 2020: A New Governance Architecture for EU Policy Coordination' in E. Marlier and D. Natali (eds.) with R. Van Dam, *Europe 2020: Towards a More Social EU?*, P.I.E. Peter Lang, Brussels 2010.

Table 2. Ten Integrated Guidelines at the core of the Europe 2020 Strategy[38]

Guideline 1	Ensuring the quality and sustainability of public finances
Guideline 2	Addressing macroeconomic imbalances
Guideline 3	Reducing imbalances in the euro-area
Guideline 4	Optimizing support for R&D and innovation, strengthening the knowledge triangle and unleashing the potential of the digital economy
Guideline 5	Improving resource efficiency and reducing greenhouse gases emissions
Guideline 6	Improving the business and consumer environment, and modernizing and developing the industrial base in order to ensure the full functioning of the internal market
Guideline 7	Increasing labour market participation of women and men, reducing structural unemployment and promoting job quality
Guideline 8	Developing a skilled workforce responding to labour market needs and promoting lifelong learning
Guideline 9	Improving the quality and performance of education and training systems at all levels and increasing participation in tertiary or equivalent education
Guideline 10	Promoting social inclusion and combating poverty

As for the past, the issue at the core of the OMC has not been limited to the adequacy and viability of the first pillar, but to that of the non-public pillars too. A new emphasis has been made on the potential for inter-generational conflict and the need to consider present and future spending in terms of social justice (and not just of financial sustainability). Yet, both scientific contributions and official documents seem to confirm that the evolution of the OMC on pensions (and the broader social area) has not succeeded in counter-balancing the dominant role of macroeconomic (and namely budgetary) coordination in the EU policymaking and political debate.[39]

38 European Council, 'Council Decision on guidelines for the employment policies of the Member States' 14338/10.

39 See S. Borras and C. Radaelli, 'The Politics of Governance Architecture: Creation, Change and Effects of the Lisbon Strategy' (2011) 4 *JEPP*; D. Natali, 'The Lisbon Strategy Ten Years On: A Critical Review of a Multi-disciplinary Literature' (2009) 1 *Transfer: European Review of Labour and Research (TERLR)*; and SPC, 'The Social Dimension of the Europe 2020 Strategy' COM (2011) 11 final.

3. ASSESSING THE INFLUENCE OF EU COORDINATION ON NATIONAL PENSIONS

In line with Dyson,[40] Europeanization – that is the effects of the process of integration on Member States – is a dynamic process consistent with 'the complex interactivity of variables and its diverse, contingent and contradictory effects'. Rather than a simple cause-effect relation, EU action is assumed to lead to the fusion of causes and contingency. And national policymakers filter and may also react to such a 'top-down' influence (through policy reforms, the construction of discourse about EU and its meanings), and the attempt to influence the EU agenda and policymaking ('bottom-up' process).

According to the contemporary literature, the empirical assessment of the coordination methods is extremely challenging. The complexity of these methods and their variety (different institutional features), the typical multi-level nature of the mechanisms implemented to steer policy decisions are all factors that make the assessment of their influence particularly difficult.[41] What is more, there are evident methodological difficulties to assess causal impact of an iterative process based on collaboration between EU institutions and Member States.

Hence, in view of this complexity, the aim here is a non-systematic and 'contextualized' assessment of some of the consequences of the EU project. The following analysis of the implementation of hard and soft forms of coordination refers to policy change, and more precisely to changes in national policy thinking, in policy agendas and in national programmes.

The first dimension has to do with the incorporation of new concepts and ideas in national debates through the challenge of domestic policy assumptions and programmes. The second dimension consists of the innovation of domestic agendas through new ideas and the changing focus on policy issues not covered in earlier periods. The third dimension refers to more explicit substantive changes: new measures introduced to innovate past policy paradigms and packages.

Especially for hard coordination through the SGP (and EMU) a wide literature has already developed instruments for assessing its influence on policy

40 K. Dyson, 'Introduction: EMU as Integration, Europeanization, and Convergence' in K. Dyson (ed.), *European States and the Euro, Europeanization, Variation and Convergence*, Oxford University Press, Oxford 2002.

41 J. Zeitlin, 'The Open Method of Coordination and Reform of National Social and Employment Policies: Influences, Mechanisms, Effects' in M. Heidenreich and J. Zeitlin (eds.), *Changing European Employment and Welfare Regimes*, Routledge, London 2009.

changes.[42] In line with these contributions the following pages will shed some light on the content of pension reforms introduced in the wake of EMU in Belgium, Italy and Slovenia. We will test the two distinct (and complementary) hypotheses proposed by the literature.[43] On the one hand, a strict budgetary policy may lead to cuts in public social spending. On the other hand, macroeconomic and budgetary stability may favour economic growth, add resources to the public budget and then contribute to more opportunities to face endogenous and exogenous challenges (such as ageing) without major welfare retrenchment.

From a second perspective, the modes of coordination under scrutiny are a cognitive instrument. This is especially the case with the OMC. Mutual learning has been signalled in much of the literature as an important feature (even the most important feature) of the generic and issue-specific OMCs. It is argued that the learning process engendered by one or several instruments – benchmarking, indicators, the exchange of best practices, peer review, iterative reporting – could lead to changes adapted to national contexts.[44] European coordination should institutionalize intensive consultation among players at various (European, national and regional) levels, and thus allow for mutual learning from their respective experiences. Learning occurs through processes of deliberation (or reasoning), understood as an epistemic 'struggle' of diverse perspectives in relation to a certain policy.

4. WHAT EFFECT (IF ANY) ON NATIONAL REFORMS?

The evaluation of the influence of non-legislative modes of coordination is particularly difficult. It is a complex process based on the interaction of a number of variables and dynamics. In the case of EU coordination as a source of adaptive pressure for national retirement programmes, its influence may affect policies, political structures, discourse, and identities. The following analysis of the

42 A. Martin and G. Ross (eds.), *Euros and Europeans. Monetary Integration and the European Model of Society*, Cambridge University Press, Cambridge 2004; M. Rhodes and M. Keune, 'EMU and Welfare State Adjustment in Central and Eastern Europe' in K. Dyson (ed.), *Enlarging the Euro Area. External Empowerment and Domestic Transformation in East Central Europe*, Oxford University Press, Oxford 2006; R. Duval and J. Elmeskov, 'The Effects of EMU on Structural Reforms in Labour and Product Markets' (2006) 596 *European Central Bank (ECB)* Working Paper <www.ecb.eu/events/pdf/conferences/emu/sessionIV_Elmeskov_Duval_Paper.pdf> accessed 10 October 2011.

43 I. Begg and F. Nectoux, 'Social Protection and Economic Union' (1995) 5 *JESP*.

44 B. Eberlein and D. Kerwer, 'New Governance in the European Union: A Theoretical Perspective' (2004) 1 *JCMS*.

implementation of hard and soft forms of coordination refers to two main dimensions: policy change and capacity building.

4.1. SGP ASSESSMENT

The influence of the EU criteria for fiscal discipline and sound public finances on national social protection policies has widely attracted the interest of commentators. The present section aims neither to intervene in the theoretical debate about the conceptualization of such a potential impact nor to provide a systematic review of the SGP outcomes on national pensions. We simply try to shed light on some of the dynamics that have been activated in some of the countries under scrutiny. EMU influence is ambivalent. On the one hand, strict budgetary policy may lead to cuts in public spending. On the other hand, macroeconomic and budgetary stability may favour economic growth, add resources to the public budget and then contribute to more opportunities to face endogenous and exogenous challenges (such as ageing).

In particular, the analysis by Natali on Belgium, Italy and Slovenia has shown the wide range of socio-economic reforms triggered by EMU.[45] In Belgium, wage-setting and public debt reduction have been for long at the core of the government's agenda, but pensions have not suffered major cutbacks. Italy, which is a well-documented case of external constraints on national pension policy, has centred its efforts on meeting the Maastricht criteria and, subsequently, the SGP on welfare restructuring. Yet the most recent pension reform of 2007 is expected to increase future pension spending. Slovenia is a much less studied case. Pensions and wages have been reformed in parallel through 'win-win' innovations. Like in Belgium, pensions have been reformed without major retrenchment, but social concertation has contributed to wage freezes combined with support for the development of supplementary pension funds (especially for public sector workers).

More recently, Hungary has re-nationalized funded pension schemes and excluded the cost of the reforms from its public debt figures. Many commentators consider the EU decision to reject the Central Eastern European (CEE) governments' demand for special treatment of pension reform costs to be one of the reasons why the Hungarian government pushed through the new legislation at such speed. In December 2010, Parliament voted to roll back the 1997 pension reform: the pension legislation was adopted with 250 votes in favour, 58 votes against and 43 abstentions. The reform effectively allows the government to seize

---

[45] See P. Pochet and D. Natali, n. 11.

up to 10 billion euros in private pension assets, in order to cut the budget deficit while avoiding austerity measures. The legislation imposes penalties on workers who did not transfer their pension assets back into the state system by the end of January 2011.[46]

Hungary's choice of policies is not unique in the EU. Bulgaria has in fact come up with very similar initiatives. Both countries have chosen to re-nationalize their pre-funded pension schemes, thus reducing public deficit and debt. These policies have surprised the European Commission, as the latter is attempting to provide an EU-wide solution to pension reform in its revised budget rules. The Commission, and especially the Economic and Monetary Affairs Commissioner, expressed its concern regarding the innovations in the pension system announced by the Hungarian authorities. Following the Hungarian vote, moreover, the Commission struck a deal with Poland aimed at loosening public finance rules in order to take into account the costs of pension reform.[47]

EMU seems to have contributed to such a large degree of innovation (at least if we compare EMU countries with OECD countries).[48] At the same time, the long road to 'recalibration' started well before the launch of EMU. In particular in the case of Belgium and Italy, the first steps towards a change of paradigm (from deficit spending and monetary instability to 'sound' monetary and fiscal policy) date back to the 1970s (with the entry of Italy in the European Monetary System) and the 1980s (with further evolution of the deutschmark-zone where Belgium was involved). What is more, recent reforms in CEE countries seem consistent with an 'unintended consequence' of the SGP in some countries. In the context of the huge financial and economic crisis, and the rigid application of the deficit targets, many of the CEE members have decided to reduce costs of pension privatization; some of them through the re-nationalization of pension funds.

4.2. PENSIONS OMC ASSESSMENT

As in the broad analysis of the OMC in the different policies, experts have provided a wide range of assessments. Some analyses have centred on the influence of EU soft governance on pensions reform. One of the first attempts explicitly compared four different countries (Germany, Italy, The Netherlands,

46 C. Bryant and J. Cienski, 'Hungary Reverses Pensions Reform' (2010) *Financial Times* <www.ft.com/cms/s/0/0e01c370-06de-11e0-8c29-00144feabdc0.html#axzz18OEIVgKz> accessed 10 October 2010.

47 See A. Watt, n. 20.

48 See B. Coeuré and J. Pisang-Ferri, n. 6.

and Sweden) and the potential impact of European integration.[49] In this case the study focused on a mix of pressures coming from the EU level: not only from the soft law on pensions, but also from the European Employment Strategy, and EMU. Pressure from the EU, in other words, was expected to depend on the policy distance between the European requirements and the key traits of national systems. Anderson concludes that although 'it is difficult to state with a high degree of certainty' that EU policies have pushed national systems in a certain direction, '(…) the similarity between all four countries' policy reforms and (…) the goals outlined for the application of the OMC to pensions is striking'.

In the same venue, further contributions on the EU impact (via the OMC) on pension reforms in Spain seems to agree with the existence of concrete outcomes. Based on an analysis of the long-term evolution of Spanish pensions policy, these contributions found that the last pension reform in 2001 was a turning point towards more 'active' social protection consistent with the European agenda. New issues such as flexibility of retirement, gender equity, and modernization of pensions to include less favoured groups, were all identified as the result of the EU influence. To sum up, 'the EU with its institutions and policy ideas has had a great deal of influence upon the reform of pensions within Spain'.[50]

The first implementation of the OMC in the area has largely contributed to capacity building through the development of common statistics.[51] Further efforts for mutual learning have also been advanced. As far as the third aspect of the cognitive dimension, 'learning to learn' is concerned, the French case seems to display some influence from the EU. The first was a meeting of trade unions leaders from five European countries at a conference on the issue of pension reform organized by the French Cfdt and Cgt confederations in Paris in January 2003. At the same time, the French Minister of Social Affairs undertook a 'European tour' to meet his colleagues/peers in Germany, Sweden, Finland, and Spain and compare different national experiences. Both of these events happened outside the pensions OMC. What is more, the French government has been active in developing parallel forms of communication. As

---

49 K.M. Anderson, 'The Europeanisation of Pension Arrangements: Convergence or Divergence?' in C. de la Porte and P. Pochet (eds.), *Building Social Europe through the Open Method of Co-ordination*, P.I.E. Peter Lang, Brussels 2002.

50 C.M. Dudek, 'Open Method of Co-Ordination: The EU's Impact Upon Spanish Pension Reform', paper presented at the European Union Studies Association Conference (Nashville, Tennessee, 27 – 29 March 2003).

51 J. Zeitlin, 'The Open Method of Coordination in Action: Theoretical Promise, Empirical Realities, Reform Strategy' in J. Zeitlin and P. Pochet with L. Magnusson (eds.), *The Open Method of Coordination in Action: The European Employment and Social Inclusion Strategies*, P.I.E. Peter Lang, Brussels 2005.

stated during an interview with a civil servant from the EU Commission (DG Employment):

> *'We know that the French members of the Social Protection Committee have developed bilateral exchanges on pensions (but also social inclusion and health care) with their colleagues from Italy, Spain (in these countries at least under right-wing governments) and the UK (a sort of OMC on a bilateral base)'.*[52]

More recently, Vanhercke has proved that the OMC process has shaped Belgium's policymaking. This is the case of the introduction in the Belgian debate of the actuarial fairness issue.[53]

Other contributions have proposed a more pessimistic interpretation of the interaction between supranational policy coordination and national reforms. As argued by Casey, *path dependency* is probably stronger in the pension field than in any other social policy, and consequently it seems unlikely that, countries are likely to make major transformations simply by observing others.[54] For Eckardt, since the effect of pension systems on economic competitiveness is only indirect, and the political market of policymakers remains national, the OMC influence on the reform process at national level seems to be very limited.[55] This more sceptical perspective has been first related to the aim of the Pensions OMC. As stated by Larsen *et al.*, the main ambition of the coordination procedures on national pension systems is to stimulate national and European debate rather than to design optimal practices that should be followed.[56] Thus the National Strategy Reports adopted by different Member States described single systems but did not put forward measures to attain common objectives. The absence of reference to the OMC in national debates (even where the pension issue is high

52 D. Natali, 'The Pensions OMC: Why Did It Emerge and How Has It Evolved?' in U. Diedrichs, W. Reiners and W. Wessels (eds.), *The Dynamics of Change in EU Governance*, Edward Elgar, Cheltenham 2011.

53 B. Vanhercke, 'Against the Odds. The Open Methods of Coordination as a Selective Amplifier for Reforming Belgian Pension Policies' in S. Kroger (ed.), 'What Have We Learnt: Advances, Pitfalls and Remaining Questions in OMC Research' (2009) 13 *EIOP*, Special Issue 1 <http://eiop.or.at/eiop/index.php/eiop/issue/view/21> accessed 25 August 2011.

54 B. Casey, 'Coordinating "Coordination": Beyond Streamlining', VDR/BMGS/MPI, Follow-up Conference on the 'Open Method of Coordination in the Field of Pensions in the European Union - Quo Vadis?' (Berlin, 26 – 27 March 2003).

55 M. Eckardt, 'The Open Method of Coordination on Pensions: An Economic Analysis of its Effects on Pension Reforms' (2004) 3 *JESP*.

56 T.P. Larsen, P. Taylor-Gooby and J. Kananen, 'European Policy Co-ordination and the OMC', Working paper for the WRAMSOC (Welfare Reform and Management of Societal Change) project, Oxford 2004 <www.kent.ac.uk/wramsoc/conferencesandworkshops/conferenceinformation/espanetconference/europeanpolicycoordination.pdf> accessed 10 October 2011.

on the agenda) is proposed as further proof of the lack of concrete outcomes.[57] Some of the limits stressed so far have to do with the intrinsic weakness of structural characteristics of the OMC in the field. Compared to other OMCs (such as the European Employment Strategy), Pensions OMC (at least as for its first years of implementation) has been defined as a 'partial'[58] and 'closed' method of coordination.[59] As Citi and Rhodes put it, the coordination of pension programmes is thus characterized by a low 'convergence capacity' in that it is based on voluntary objectives plus weak forms of benchmarking and peer pressure.[60] In other words, there is little room for learning and no fundamental alteration of the incentive structure of the national policymaking process. A recent review of the OMC influence on pension policy in Italy seems to confirm such limits: no evident impact can be detected while some recent trends – for instance the introduction of different retirement ages for men and women is totally inconsistent with European principles.[61]

As far as the OMC on pensions is concerned, much of the recent literature has thus suggested a very limited impact on national reforms. Yet in terms of mutual learning, recent progress (definition of common indicators and a spread of the exchange of practices and knowledge) represents a promising step forward.[62]

5. CONCLUSION

EU direct (and soft) and indirect (and hard) coordination of retirement programmes represents the most innovative instrument adopted in recent decades (to parallel regulation). The launch and implementation of the Stability and Growth Pact and the Open Method of Coordination have been part of a broad strategy towards the 'sound' money and budget paradigm and, in parallel, the modernization of national social policy. This has been conceived as an attempt to deal with changes in the global economic context and the consequent

57 D. Natali and C. de la Porte, 'OMC Pensions: What Role for Europe in Co-ordinating the Reform of Different Pension Systems? The Cases of France and the Netherlands' in H. Jorgensen, M. Baerenstern and J. Monks (eds.), *European Trade Union Yearbook 2003/2004*, European Trade Union Institute, Brussels 2004.

58 B. Vanhercke, 'Political Spill-Over, Changing Advocacy Coalition, Path-Dependency or Domestic Politics? Theorizing the Emergence of the Social Protection OMC's', paper presented at the Conference on Governing Work and Welfare in an Enlarged Europe, University of Wisconsin (Madison, 19–20 May 2006).

59 M. Lodge, 'Comparing Non-Hierarchical Governance in Action: The Open Method of Co-Ordination in Pensions and Information Society' (2007) 2 *JCMS*.

60 See D. Natali, n. 3.

61 G. Busilacchi, M. Jessoula and M. Reitano ' Il MAC e le politiche pensionistiche, Italia e Europa' (2009) 4 in *Rivista delle politiche sociali (RPS)*.

62 See S. Leibfried, n. 2.

growing tensions between supra-national competencies in the field of economic policy and national prerogatives in social policy.

The present chapter has aimed at addressing two key issues: the analysis of the evolution of the coordination processes, and the review of the main contributions on the assessment of the EU influence on national pension reforms.

First we have analysed the evolution of these modes of coordination. The SGP has progressively addressed pension policy with a reference (explicit since 2005) to the need for reforms to increase the long-term sustainability of public finances. This has become even more evident after the most recent financial, economic and budgetary crises. Since 2001, the OMC on pensions has been implemented to counter-balance the dominance of the EU constraints on pensions. The on-going transformation of this method does not seem to have contributed to enhance its role in the EU policymaking process.

Second, we have summarized the literature on the assessment of the EU influence on national pension reforms. The Pact's influence on national reforms is not assumed to have been consistent with a 'race to the bottom': instead, reforms have led to the recalibration of pension programmes. While the privatization of pension systems has not been explicitly proposed in the first version of the Pact, later on more emphasis has been put on the issue. Its implementation has in any case led to increased tensions between the Commission and those countries facing the short-term costs of the reform. Some analysts have stressed the 'unintended consequence' of these tensions in the recent 'U-turn' of Central Eastern Member States and the re-nationalization of private pension funds.

As for the OMC process, its influence on national pension policy and the institutional capabilities of national Member States has been at the core of a huge scientific debate. Analytical and theoretical problems have shaped such a debate and led to contrasting readings. Some contributions have proved improvements in members' institutional capacities and an impact on the policymaking process (new ideas have influenced reform's agendas). Yet, others have provided a more pessimistic assessment. And the most recent Europe 2020 Strategy raises doubts about the future progress of the OMC method.

A further problem for the assessment of the impact of the EU coordination and the eventual causal link between EU guidelines and national policy change has been represented by the on-going changes the coordination method has seen. Both hard (and indirect) and soft (and direct) coordination have not been immutable. Progressive evolution has taken the form of revisions and refinements (see the revised SGP and the streamlining process of social OMCs). Both processes have led to renewed constraints and opportunities ('adaptational pressures' in the words of Börzel and Risse[63]) on national policymakers and to the reconstruction of norms and ideas about the interaction of welfare policy and economic development. The evidence provided in the previous sections has confirmed the on-going reform dynamics in the countries under scrutiny. But more research is needed to clearly assess the causal impact of hard and soft modes of coordination.

63 T. Börzel and T. Risse, 'Conceptualizing the Domestic Impact of Europe' in K. Featherstone and C. Radaelli (eds.), *The Politics of Europeanization*, Oxford University Press, Oxford 2003.

INTERACTIONS BETWEEN POLICY AND LAW REGARDING PENSIONS

Yves Stevens

1. INTRODUCTION: THE RESEARCH QUESTION

This chapter addresses two questions. How is the substance given to pension protection at the policy level mirrored in the legal domain? And, is the balancing of economic and social considerations consistent in the realms of law and policy?

It would seem that there is a discrepancy at the European level between the legal framework for pensions on the one hand, and the policy level, on the other one. At policy level a lot of the documents only have few legal consequences. Researching this discrepancy between law and policy can provide an answer to the question: What are the legal impediments or opportunities for a European legal pension framework? In other words, when one reads – *ad nauseam* – that the EU wants to develop adequate retirement pensions and ensure long term sustainability of the pensions systems, the question arises: how will or can this be possible from a legal point of view?

The question will be answered in three sections. The first section deals with the overall EU competence concerning pensions: What do the Treaties say on pensions? The second section is about the pension provision under Regulation 883/2004, and the third section deals with occupational, supplementary and individual retirement provisions. At the end of each section a short conclusion is drawn with respect to the research question.

The three sections address the legal impediments or opportunities for a European legal pension framework, but from a different angle. The first section deals with the overall legal structure while the second and third one focus on different types of pension systems. In this regard reference is often made to the so-called three-pillar model. That is because the three-pillar model provides a very easy way of presenting various pension schemes. However, from a legal point of view, it oversimplifies matters to an unacceptable extent. Legally, there is no three-pillar model: the differences between countries are too obvious. The strength of the three-pillar model is of a sociological or economic nature: (nearly) everybody – irrespective of nationality – can recognize his/her own national pension system in the model.[1] However, when modelling pension systems one always risks putting too much emphasis on a certain element of a pension system without taking into account other – equally relevant – elements. As far as legal studies are concerned, I strongly doubt the relevance of modelling pension systems into general types. So, when one looks around in Europe and tries to define – in a legal manner – the different pension systems one cannot but notice that there is a huge variety of elements constituting pension systems. It is this variety of systems that actually complicates the European policy debate.[2]

Since there is such a wide variety of pension types in the European Union, one cannot look at the legal competences concerning pensions as solely bound by social policy. Competences regarding financial markets, consumer protection, prudential measures and solvency also intervene. Furthermore one needs to look at all different aspects of certain pension forms in order to know what kind of rules apply. Due to this huge diversity it is almost impossible for legal scholars to make abstract models of all pension schemes. From a legal perspective such comparisons are far more complicated because of the national competences regarding pensions. However, in my opinion it is possible to make one relevant legal division, namely a division between the pension schemes falling under the field of application of the social security coordination system (Regulation 883/2004) and the other ones, i.e. the occupational, supplementary and individual pension provisions. This justifies the division between the third and fourth sections of this paper.

---

1 G. Amitsis, J. Berghman, A. Hemerijck, T. Sakellaropoulos, A. Stergiou and Y. Stevens, *Connecting Welfare Diversity within the European Social Model,* Intersentia, Antwerp 2004, pp. 103–106. The level of 'recognition' of the model is due to the World Bank. The famous report titled 'Averting the Old Age Crisis: Policies to Protect the Old and Promote Growth' popularized the concept of a pension system supported by three pillars. Ever since that report, there have been many interpretations. World Bank, *Averting the Old Age Crisis: Policies to Protect the Old and Promote Growth*, Oxford University Press, Washington 1994.

2 Apart from the – at least from a legal point of view – absurd notion of the three pillars, sociologists and economists have invented another – legally non existing – model for Europe. Often reference is made to the so-called European Social Model. Legally, this is nonsense. Although it clearly does not exist, many people take it for granted. For example, Alain Euzeby states 'The European Social Model has been developed substantially after the second world war', A. Euzéby, 'European Integration and Disparities in Social Protection Systems' in D. Pieters (ed.), *International Impact upon Social Security,* Kluwer Law International, London 1998; *see also* C. Aubin, 'A la Recherche du Modèle Social Européen' (2008) *Droit Social*, p. 484.

2. THE EU COMPETENCE FOR PENSIONS

2.1. NO TRUE PENSION POLICY, ONLY GENERAL SOCIAL POLICY

The Treaty on European Union (TEU) does not mention the word 'pension' or 'retirement'.[3] The only reference to 'old age' in the European constitutional texts is made in Article 34.1 of the Charter of Fundamental Rights:

> *'The Union recognizes and respects the entitlement to social security benefits and social services providing protection in cases such as (...) old age (...) in accordance with the rules laid down by Union law and national laws and practices.'*

Apart from this general formulation there is no specific competence referring to pensions. So, in order to know the competences of the EU with regard to pensions, retirement and old age, reference needs to be made to the competences of the EU concerning social policy. These competencies are often seen as subsidiaries to the economic objectives of the process of European integration. The various preambles of the European Treaties leave little doubt about this. Nonetheless, some objectives of the Union are 'social' and go further than a pure economic perspective. Recent years have even shown that the EU has been given some genuine (i.e. legal) competences in the field of social policy, including social security. However, it is still obvious that the Treaties consider social policy first and foremost to be a matter of the Member States themselves. This leads to the preliminary conclusion that the EU has a certain legal role to play, but that it has few competences.

2.2. EU PENSION LAW: A GENERIC TERM

The term 'European pension law' might wrongly suggest that there is a legal corpus of acts concerning pensions at a European scale. This is clearly not the case. 'European pension law' is only a generic term for all legal acts the European Union (as a whole) has taken with regard to pensions. Given the division of competences between the European Union and the Member States there are only a few elements of pensions that can be regulated on a European level. For each of these so-called European pension elements there needs to be a defined competence within the European Treaty. On the basis of these competences the European Union has mostly developed directives, which mainly concern the four freedoms of the Union.

---

3 The Treaty on the Functioning of the European Union (TFEU) does. But then it only refers to the pension or retirement of some of the members of the personnel of the EU. This is obviously irrelevant for the research question.

2.2.1. *Freedom of movement of workers*

Articles 45 to 48 TFEU deal with the freedom of movement for workers within the EU. The free movement of persons is an important issue in the TFEU and is intended to assure complete mobility of employees in the internal market.[4] These articles are important in that they state that a Member State is not allowed to discriminate employees from the EU. There can be a link with the transfer of the portability of pensions. Pensions built-up in one Member State that cannot be taken into account when workers move to another Member State lead to the obstruction of their free movement, and some regulations have been enacted to avoid such obstacles.

Regulations 883/2004 and 987/2009 were adopted to bring about freedom of movement for workers; they guarantee that moving within the EU has no detrimental effect on the calculation of the pension in the Member States responsible for paying it (see further part three of this paper).[5]

The directive of 29 June 1998 (98/49/EC) on safeguarding the supplementary pension rights of employed and self-employed persons moving in the Union is also based on the freedom of movement of workers. This directive concerns the equal treatment of foreign and domestic employees with regard to supplementary pension schemes (see further section 4.4 of this paper).

2.2.2. *Freedom of establishment and services*

Articles 49 and 56 TFEU state that all restrictions on free movement of services are forbidden. This prohibition makes an important contribution in organizing the outlines of the internal market for supplementary pensions. To strengthen the internal market for pensions the IORP Directive was introduced in 2003.[6] This directive can be considered as a big step forward, even if it only provides for a regulation of capital-covered pensions.[7] Its merit is that it provides supervision of the activities of the supplementary pension funds. Also, it makes it possible to set up European pension funds, that administer the employees' pensions of different Member States, based on the principle of home-country-control.[8] Home-country-control means that the pension funds may develop

---

4 F. Pennings, *European Social Security Law*, Antwerp, Intersentia 2010, p. 3.

5 European Commission, 'Green paper towards adequate, sustainable and safe European pension systems' COM (2010) 365 final, SEC (2010) 830, p. 13.

6 Council Directive 2003/41/EC of 3 June 2003 on the activities and supervision of institutions for occupational retirement provision [2003] OJ L235/10.

7 European Commission, n. 5, p. 12.

8 European Commission, 'Accompanying document to the Green Paper towards adequate, sustainable and safe European pension systems' COM (2010) 365 final, SEC (2010) 830 final, p. 4.

activities in different Member States under supervision of the country of establishment. This can lead to an internal market for supplementary pensions based on mutual recognition.[9] Pension funds have to respect certain standards, which are discussed in part 4.2.

2.2.3. Free movement of capital and flow of payments

According to Article 63 TFEU, all restrictions concerning traffic of capital and flow of payment between Member States and between Member States and third countries are forbidden. This can be considered as a necessary extension of the above freedoms, because toleration of restrictions of movement of capital might nullify the other freedoms as well. Again the IORP Directive is involved in that it forbids certain demands concerning quantitative investments requirements.[10]

2.2.4. High standards for employees' rights

Article 153 TFEU Treaty determines that the Union shall support and complement the activities of the Member States, for instance when it comes to the improvement of the working environment and the protection of the workers' safety and health. Two important directives are based on this article: Directive 80/987/EEC on the approximation of the laws of the Member States relating to the protection of employees in the event of their employer's insolvency,[11] and Directive 2001/23/EC on the approximation of the laws of the Member States relating to the safeguarding of employees' rights in the event of transfers of undertakings, business or parts of undertakings or businesses.[12] These directives are tantamount to making the high standards as presented in Article 153 TFEU more concrete so that Member States are obliged to take measures to protect employees concerning their supplementary pension rights.

2.2.5. Equality between men and women

According to Article 157 TFEU every Member State must guarantee the application of the principles of equal remuneration for equal work for male and female employees. Equal treatment of men and women is a value of the EU. In fact, it is not just a value, but rather an essential condition so that the EU's objectives with regard to work, economic growth and social cohesion can be

---

9 The directive mentions that pension funds should have at their disposal: enough capital to cover the different pension obligations, good organizational boards and good administrative procedures, adequate internal check procedures and a transparent communication to Member States concerning the level of benefits, risk positions and costs for the management of the investment.

10 N. 6.

11 [1980] OJ L283/23.

12 [2001] OJ L82/16.

reached.[13] Article 157 TFEU led to numerous court cases related to pensions, so that now there is a large jurisprudence concerning this article.[14] This case law has led to a number of directives. Directive 79/7/EEC[15] applies to statutory social security schemes and refers specifically to statutory pensions.[16] Discrimination may not exist for:

- access to the schemes;
- the obligation to contribute and the calculation of contributions;
- the calculation of benefits and the conditions governing the duration and retention of entitlement to benefits.

The following are, however, excluded from the field of application of this directive

- the determination of pensionable age for old-age and retirement pensions;
- advantages granted to persons with children;
- the granting of old-age or invalidity benefit entitlement by virtue of the derived entitlements of a spouse;
- the granting of increases of long-term invalidity, old-age, accidents at work and occupational disease benefits for a dependent spouse.

Directive 2004/113/EC applies the principle of equal treatment of gender for the access and the offer of goods and services, without making distinction between public and private sector, meaning that the directive also relates to private/individual pension products.[17]

2.3. THE RESEARCH QUESTION

The answer to the research question about the legal impediments or opportunities for a European legal pension framework is that there is no real and true exclusive European competence with regard to pensions. Consequently there are no EU-wide solutions for statutory pensions systems. Whether this is wanted or not, is a political question. One could for example plead for some European minimum

---

13 Equal treatment of men and women on <http://ec.europa.eu/social> accessed 10 October 2011.

14 See the website of the European Court of Justice <http://curia.europa.eu/> accessed 10 October 2011.

15 Council Directive 79/7/EEC of 19 December 1978 on the progressive implementation of the principle of equal treatment for men and women in matters of social security [1979] OJ L6/24.

16 European Commission, n. 8, p. 8.

17 Council Directive 2004/113/EC of 13 December 2004 implementing the principle of equal treatment between men and woman in the access to and supply of goods and services [2004] OJ L373/37.

standard guaranteeing all European citizens in old age sufficient financial means. Such a plea can only be interpreted in the light of subsidiarity, and whether a European standard is desired, sought after or necessary is a question of political opportunity as well.

The EU has few legal competences with regard to pensions due to the division of competences and the principle of subsidiarity. This is certainly true when we talk about statutory pensions. However, when it comes to supplementary/occupational pensions or individual retirement provision things might look different. After all these more individual forms of pensions operate in the internal market and thus the market freedoms play a significant role.

3. PENSION PROVISION UNDER THE SOCIAL SECURITY REGULATIONS: LIMITED EU POWER

3.1. COORDINATION OF SOCIAL SECURITY SCHEMES

EU law in the field of social security provides for the coordination but not the harmonization of social security schemes. This means that each Member State is free to determine the details of its own social security system, including which benefits are to be provided, the conditions of eligibility, how these benefits are calculated and what level of contributions should be paid.[18]

EU law provisions, in particular Regulations 883/2004 and 987/2009[19] (replacing Regulations 1408/71[20] and 574/72[21] since 1 May 2010), establish common rules

---

18 F. Pennings, n. 4, p. 21.

19 In 2004 a new coordination instrument was established: Regulation (EC) No. 883/2004 of the European Parliament and of the Council of 29 April 2004 on the coordination of social security systems [2004] OJ L166/1, which initially contributed to a simplification and adaptation of the current system, to the needs of the social security right in the twenty-first century. Regulation (EC) No 987/2009 of the European Parliament and of the Council of 16 September 2009 laying down the procedure for implementing Regulation (EC) No 883/2004 on the coordination of social security systems [2009] OJ L284/1. For a more detailed analysis see: H. Verschueren, 'Regulation 883/2004 and Invalidity and Old-Age Pensions' (2009) 1–2 *EJSS (European Journal of Social Security).*

20 Regulation 1408/71 can be seen as one of the first instruments started on European level to shape the social dimension of the European Union. The aim was not to establish a general European social security right, but to implement a coordination of different systems of the social security that we find in the different Member States of the European Union. Regulation (EEC) No 1408/71 of the Council of 14 June 1971 on the application of social security schemes to employed persons and their families moving within the Community [1971] OJ L149/2.

21 Council Regulation (EEC) No 574/72 of 21 March 1972 fixing the procedure for implementing Regulation (EEC) No 1408/71 on the application of social security schemes to employed persons and their families moving within the Community [1972] OJ L74/1.

and principles which must be observed by all national authorities when applying national law.[22] The regulations ensure that the application of the different national legislations respects the basic principles of equality of treatment, and persons exercising their right to free movement within the EU are not adversely affected by the application of different national legislations. The regulations determine which legislation on migrating persons is applied and see to it that the rights acquired in other Member States are maintained.

With regard to pensions, the EU coordination regulations cover old-age pensions, survivors' pensions and invalidity pensions. In general, only statutory schemes are coordinated. The rules lay down the following principles:

- Aggregation of periods: Entitlements built up in one Member State should be recognized when calculating benefit entitlement in another. Many Member States require a certain time of insurance in order to benefit from a pension.[23] This means that an employee who worked several years in different Member States could end up without having the right to a pension. Of course, this is irreconcilable with the freedom of movement of persons in the EU. To resolve such situations, the periods of insurance in the different Member States are aggregated.
- The 'export' principle: Benefits are payable outside the national territory. This principle states among others that payments for pensions must take place in the same way when the entitled lives or stays in another Member State.
- The non-discrimination principle: This principle says essentially that discrimination based on the nationality of a person is strictly forbidden.
- The 'applicable legislation' principle: At any given moment a person should only be subjected to the legislation of one Member State. This principle is employed to avoid positive or negative conflicts of laws, i.e. situations in which one's social security is neither governed by the legislation of two or more Member States, nor does one's situation remain ungoverned by the legislation of any Member State.

Important to mention is that the regulation principles only apply to the statutory social security schemes, and not to the supplementary, occupational or individual pension provisions. Over the years these coordination regulations of social security schemes have led to an impressive amount of case law by the European Court of Justice. This case law illustrates the every-day importance of this field of law.

---

22 F. Pennings, n. 4, p. 21.
23 *Ibid.*, pp. 180–181.

3.2. THE RESEARCH QUESTION

The vast jurisprudence on the social security coordination regulations indicate how important these regulations are in the every-day lives of European citizens. Each day thousands of cross-border pension files are dealt with by local national pension administrations on the basis of the coordination regulations. Considering the variety of pension schemes this is not all that self-evident. The strength of the coordination is that it combines respect of the 27 various statutory pension systems with a single coordination method. The coordination provisions ensure that EU migrants are treated equally with nationals of the host Member State with regard to social security. They also aim at reducing some of the disadvantages of moving from one state to another, particularly in respect of long-term benefits such as old-age pensions. The objectives of coordination are met, even if some interpretation and implementation problems persist. Above all, the coordination provisions do not oblige states to alter the substance of their social security laws. It is 'only' coordination of existing national legislations, and there is no true European impact in the drafting and developing of the national pension schemes irrespective of coordination.

4. OCCUPATIONAL, SUPPLEMENTARY AND INDIVIDUAL RETIREMENT PROVISION: SOME EU POWER[24]

4.1. GENERAL

The little European impact with regard to statutory pensions is countered in the field of the occupational, supplementary and individual retirement provision. From a legal point of view the EU has more competences for privately funded pension schemes than for statutory pensions. This has mainly to do with the economic nature of funded pension schemes and the presence of private market players in this area. These players are furthermore gaining importance due to the actual demographic situation in which fewer active persons will have to take care of an increasing group of pensioners.[25] Practically every Member State faces this

---

24 This part follows closely European Commission, n. 5.

25 The Indicator Sub-Group of the Social Protection Committee (SPC) has updated calculations on the theoretical replacement rates. These calculations provide the possibility to look at individual case studies and evaluate to what extent current and future pension systems ensure that the elderly have the resources to maintain adequate standards of living. This report has indicated that if career lengths remain unchanged over the next 40 years, the theoretical replacement rate calculations show a decline in many countries across Europe. The drop is more pronounced in statutory pension systems, and in nearly half of the EU Member States a double-digit percentage point decline in replacement rates can be expected from these

aging issue whereby there is a tendency to encourage the supplementary, occupational and individual pensions.[26]

This growing importance of supplementary, occupational and individual pensions has become an item on the agenda of the EU. This way of building-up pensions has not always been spoken of in a positive way, because a lot of people considered it as a possibility for the well-off to enhance their capital.[27] The potential of occupational pensions was not that much taken into account until 2000. Since 2006 there has been growing awareness that these pensions can lead to even more social solidarity in society. In that year the European Commission stated that occupational pensions can be seen as an element of social policy with regard to adequate and sustainable pensions.

Although the role and development of privately funded pension provision is very diverse in the Member States there are some common European features regarding these forms of pension provision. Harmonized European law is to be found in the IORP Directive, the Insolvency Directive, the Quasi-Portability Directive, the Life Assurance Directive, MIFID, UCITS, solvency and tax issues.

4.2. THE IORP DIRECTIVE

In the occupational pensions landscape the adoption of Directive 2003/41/EC on the activities and supervision of institutions for occupational retirement provision (IORP) was a major milestone.[28] The main aim of this directive is to allow businesses to entrust pension funds established in other Member States with their pension plans. The directive enables pension funds to benefit from the internal market principles of free movement of capital and freedom to provide services, and to manage occupational pension schemes for companies that are established in another Member State. At the same time, European-wide companies can thus have only one pension fund for all subsidiaries in Europe. The directive establishes prudential standards to ensure that members and beneficiaries are properly protected, as well as requirements concerning the disclosure of information. The directive is, however, based on minimum harmonization and mutual recognition and it does not cover all forms of occupational pension provision.[29]

---

schemes. See Social Protection Committee, 'Updates of Current and Prospective Theoretical Pension Replacement Rates 2006–2046' <http://ec.europa.eu/social/BlobServlet?docId=4307&langId=en> accessed 25 October 2011.

26 European Commission, n. 8, p. 6.

27 N. Anton, 'The Open Method of Coordination – An Example of "Good Governance"?' (Research Paper) GRIN Verlag, 2008, p. 13.

28 N. 6.

29 European Commission, n. 8, p. 4.

So far there is no uniform internal market concerning pension agreements related to work. The differences between fiscal and labour legislation are still too many. The IORP Directive is meant to create an internal market by abolishing the restrictions for pension funds. By this directive pension funds can propose occupational pension schemes to businesses in other Member States, and European multinationals only have to set up one pension fund for all their subsidiaries in Europe.[30] All this under one name: the European passport.

Furthermore this directive also imposes certain standards on pension funds so that members and beneficiaries are well protected. These standards determine for instance the obligation for the pension funds to:

- have at their disposal sufficient resources to cover the pension obligations;
- have good management, good administrative procedures and adequate internal procedures;
- have clear information for those entitled to payment;
- be under the supervision of an inspector who is empowered to set sanctions;
- have no legal unity with the business for which the pension provision is meant;
- only take care of payment of pensions.

This directive is not only advantageous for the members and beneficiaries who are well protected, but also for European multinationals. These multinationals benefit from:

- reduced administrative costs;
- scaled advantages for capital management;
- avoid complicated international pension fractions;
- advantages in taxes.[31]

To summarize, one can say that the directive harmonizes the legal frame for the activities of the pension funds, and it regulates the supervision of the pension funds.

The European Commission foresees a review of the IORP Directive. It has therefore issued a call for advice seeking to obtain advice from the European Insurance and Occupational Pensions Authority (EIOPA) on how to improve the IORP Directive.[32]

---

30 *Ibid.*

31 *Ibid.*

32 For more details see <http://ec.europa.eu/internal_market/pensions/docs/calls/042011_call_en.pdf> accessed 25 October 2011.

4.3. THE INSOLVENCY DIRECTIVE

This directive, also known as Directive 2008/94 EC, watches over the protection of employees if the employer is financially insolvent, so that they have the guarantee that they will be paid.[33] The most important article of this directive concerning pensions is Article 8. This provision requires that Member States take the necessary measures to protect pensions and to make sure that the claimants of these pensions can really enjoy them. If supplementary pensions become more important it is clear that a stable economy is required if this strategy is to be successful. The directive does not ask that Member States fully guarantee the rights in question.[34] It only calls for adopting the measures required to 'protect the interests' of the persons concerned.[35] So, the directive can be considered as an empty box.

4.4. QUASI-PORTABILITY DIRECTIVE 98/49

Unlike with social security pensions which are aggregated under EU rules, people who have supplementary pension rights may lose out when they change jobs within or between countries. A first step to tackle this issue was Council Directive 98/49/EC, which effectively ensured that people moving across borders were treated no worse than those moving within a Member State. Equality is required concerning the built-up and the maintenance of rights for employees that are mobile within the EU, but also for those who cross its frontiers. Strange as it may sound, equality is not enough here, because if an employee does not meet the conditions of acquisition for a pension fund, he also has no rights – by this directive – to keep his built-up rights.[36] So the directive does not cover what is often called the 'true portability' of supplementary pensions even though this may have a serious effect on worker mobility. The Commission was aware of this and in 2005 it introduced a proposal for a directive to set minimum standards for the acquisition, preservation and transferability of supplementary pensions. So far this has not been approved by the Council.[37]

---

[33] Directive 2008/94/EC of the European Parliament and of the Council of 22 October 2008 on the protection of employees in the event of the insolvency of their employer [2008] OJ L283/36. See also European Commission, n. 8, p. 4.

[34] *Ibid.*

[35] *Ibid.*

[36] Y. Jorens, 'Het Europees sociaalzekerheidsrecht: Quo vadis?' in A. Van Regenmortel, H. Verschueren and V. Vervliet (eds.), *Sociale zekerheid in het Europa van de markt en de burgers: enkele actuele thema's*, die Keure, Brugge 2007, p. 25.

[37] The Commission has recognized that insufficient portability of supplementary pension rights can create large obstacles to workers' mobility, and therefore to the free movement of workers which is one of the basic rights enshrined in the Treaty. The Commission proposed a new Directive in October 2005 to set minimum standards for the acquisition, preservation and

In my opinion, statutory pension rights are far better protected under the various regulations than the occupational pension rights. There is no true coordination of occupational pension rights ensuring their portability.

4.5. THE LIFE ASSURANCE DIRECTIVE

The Life Assurance Directive is intended to give insurance companies the possibility to develop their activities in the entire EU. A first directive was enacted in 1979.[38] This directive was thoroughly modified and adapted in two following directives, namely Directive 2002/83/EC[39] and Directive 2009/138/EC.[40] These directives focus in the first place on the harmonization of the insurance legislation of the Member States, so that the internal market can also benefit the life assurance products. In addition, this directive is meant to increase protection concerning the solvency of underwriter/assurer.[41]

4.6. MARKETS IN FINANCIAL INSTRUMENTS DIRECTIVE (MIFID)

MIFID is a European investment directive that replaces the (old) Investment Services Directive (ISD) and is active in the European Economic Area (the 27 Member States of the European Union plus Iceland, Norway and Liechtenstein) since 1 November 2007. It essentially has three aims:

a) The promotion of honest and transparent financial markets;
b) The harmonization of the European stock trade;

transferability of supplementary pension rights. These standards would apply to people moving both within and between EU countries. Internal mobility was included because it was impractical to separate internal and external mobility. In addition, labour mobility was key to promoting economic dynamism and labour market adjustment, as set out in the Lisbon Strategy. The proposal was revised by the Commission in 2007 to omit the transferability element which had been opposed by some as technically difficult and potentially burdensome or open to abuse. As a result, the emphasis was laid on the timely acquisition of pension rights and their subsequent preservation (indexation). However, it has still not been possible to reach the unanimous agreement needed in Council. European Commission, n. 8, p. 5.

38 First Council Directive 79/267/EEC of 5 March on the coordination of laws, regulations and administrative provisions relating to the taking up and pursuit of the business of direct life assurance [1979] OJ L63/1.

39 Directive 2002/83/EC of the European Parliament and of the Council of 5 November 2002 concerning life assurance [2002] OJ L345/1.

40 Directive 2009/138/EC of the European Parliament and of the Council of 25 November 2009 on the taking-up and pursuit of the business of insurance and reinsurance (Solvency II) [2009] OJ L335/1.

41 European Commission, n. 8, p. 5.

c) The protection of investors.[42]

MIFID retained the principles of the EU 'passport' introduced by the Investment Services Directive (ISD) but also introduced the concept of 'maximum harmonization' which places more emphasis on home state supervision. This is a change from the prior EU financial service legislation which featured a 'minimum harmonization and mutual recognition' concept. The MIFID can be described as a directive that will ensure the freedom of business in financial products, without disadvantaging investors. The MIFID Directive aims at increasing investment opportunities in the EU.

4.7. UNDERTAKINGS FOR COLLECTIVE INVESTMENT IN TRANSFERABLE SECURITIES (UCITS)

The UCITS IV Directive,[43] meant to be implemented in 2011, improves the harmonized European regulation and is the basis for a uniform market of investment funds. The directive aims at increasing competitiveness and at the same time ensuring investors are properly informed.

4.8. SOLVENCY II

Throughout the world there is a movement towards risk based solvency regimes. Examples are Basel II for banks and Solvency II for insurance companies. In the EU Solvency II refers to Directive 2009/138/EC. It is an adaptation of the existing solvability rules. The former rules were not sensitive to risks and gave the Member States a lot of space for national variants. They did not have decent regulations for the group supervision and have since been largely outdated by the developments in this sector, certainly on the international level. The new Directive 2009/138/EC takes into consideration the most recent developments concerning supervision and risk management. The rationale for European Union insurance legislation is to facilitate the development of a single market in

---

42 Directive 2004/39/EC of the European Parliament and of the Council of 21 April 2004 on markets in financial instruments amending Council Directives 85/611/EEC and 93/6/EEC and Directive 2000/12/EC of the European Parliament and of the Council and repealing Council Directive 93/22/EEC [2004] OJ L145/1. See also <www.mifidirective.com> accessed 25 October 2011.

43 Directive 2009/65/EC of the European Parliament and of the Council of 13 July 2009 on the coordination of laws, regulations and administrative provisions relating to undertakings for collective investment in transferable securities (UCITS) [2009] OJ L302/32; European Commission, 'EU legislation, coverage and related initiatives – Accompanying document to the Green Paper towards adequate, sustainable and safe European pension systems' (Staff working document) SEC (2010) 830, p. 5.

insurance services in Europe, whilst at the same time securing an adequate level of consumer protection. The third-generation Insurance Directives established an 'EU passport' (single licence) for insurers based on the concept of minimum harmonization and mutual recognition. Many Member States have concluded that the current EU minimum requirements are not sufficient and have implemented their own reforms, thus leading to a situation where there is a patchwork of regulatory requirements across the EU. This hampers the functioning of the single market. Solvency II is based on economic principles for the measurement of assets and liabilities. It will also be a risk-based system as risk will be measured on the basis of consistent principles and capital requirements will depend directly on this.

An important question is whether rules similar to Solvency II should apply to pension funds. In the Green Paper on pensions question 10 reads:

> *'With the entry into force of the Solvency II Directive in 2012, insurance undertakings will be able to benefit from a three-pillar, risk-based solvency regime and the question is whether this new regime should also apply to IORPs. There is little agreement among stakeholders, partly reflecting the difference in the ways occupational pensions are delivered: book reserve, pension fund or insurance contract.'*[44]

Stakeholders signalled that there needs to be a *sui generis* solvency regime for pension funds and that it is important to avoid pro-cyclical solvency rules. The Solvency II approach could be a good starting point, subject to adjustments to take into account the nature and duration of the pension promise, where appropriate. The suitability of Solvency II for pension funds needs to be considered in a rigorous impact assessment, examining notably the influence on price and availability of pension products.[45]

4.9. TAX ISSUES

In parallel to its proposal of the IORP Directive, the Commission presented a Pension Taxation Communication in April 2001.[46] At the time, many Member States did not grant tax relief for the payment of pension contributions to foreign pension funds, whereas they did so for payments to domestic funds. This would hinder the functioning of the proposed IORP Directive. The Pension Taxation Communication concluded that the Member States cannot discriminate against

---

44 European Commission, n. 5.

45 For more details see <http://ec.europa.eu/internal_market/insurance/solvency/index_en.htm> accessed 25 October 2011.

46 European Commission, 'The elimination of tax obstacles to the cross-border provision of occupational pensions' COM (2001) 214 final.

pension contributions paid to foreign IORPs. After attempts to find common solutions with the Member States in Council discussions, the Commission launched infringement procedures where necessary. Most Member States adapted their legislation. In two cases the Court of Justice of the EU ruled that if domestic pension contributions were tax deductible, contributions paid to IORPs elsewhere in the EEA should also be tax deductible.[47] The concrete result of the Commission's work in this area is that mobile workers can now remain in their home country pension scheme if they take up a job in another Member State and contributions to IORPs in other Member States can now be paid without tax discrimination.

The Pension Taxation Communication also concluded that discriminatory tax rules can be an obstacle to the mobility of pensions. In *Commission v. Belgium*,[48] the Court of Justice of the EU ruled that it is contrary to EU law to tax transfers of pension capital from domestic pension funds to funds established elsewhere in the EEA if transfers of pension capital between domestic pension funds are tax-free. The Commission intends to examine whether there are any other Member States with similar rules.

From a legal perspective tax issues remain the main obstacles towards a true European integrated pension market. This has to do with different possible taxation mechanisms within Europe. There are three possible moments for taxation of funded pension schemes. First, when the premium is paid. Secondly, the investment of the premium can be taxed and thirdly, the pension itself can be taxed. If there is no tax, then there is exemption. Theoretically pension schemes can go from an EEE regime to a TTT regime, meaning from completely untaxed to entirely taxed. Most Member States have various variants of taxation regime depending on the pension type. However, most Member States tax occupational pensions according to the EET system (Exempt contributions, Exempt investment income and capital gains of the pension institution, Taxed benefits) or ETT principle (Exempt contributions, Taxed investment income and capital gains of the pension institution, Taxed benefits). The taxation mechanism is an impediment to free movement. Imagine a Member State that has a regime of EET, then it would be very interesting to move to a Member State that has TEE or TTE at the moment of pension.[49] However, many Member States did and do

47 Case C-522/04 *Commission of the European Communities v. Kingdom of Belgium* [2007] ECR I-5701, and Case C-150/04 *Commission of the European Communities v. Kingdom of Denmark* [2007] ECR I-1163.

48 Case C-522/04 *Commission of the European Communities v. Kingdom of Belgium* [2007] ECR I-5701.

49 Belgians used to refer to the French escape route in this context. Belgian occupational pensions transferred to France were not taxed in Belgium or France. A change in 2011 of the bilateral double tax treaty between France and Belgium has closed this route.

not allow tax deduction for pension contributions paid to pension funds in other Member States. This effectively sealed off their national pension markets from competition from other Member States and created major obstacles to pan-European funds and the free movement of workers. The ECJ has often been asked to judge in these matters (cases *Bachmann*,[50] *Wielockx*,[51] *Safir*,[52] *Danner*,[53] *Skandia*[54] and *Turpeinen*[55]). More recently the Commission launched infringement proceedings against Denmark, Belgium, Spain, France, Ireland, Italy, Portugal and the United Kingdom. In practice, the overwhelming majority of Member States with the EET or ETT system now also allow tax deductibility of cross-border payments. The new focus of the Commission is on any discrimination concerning the cross-border transfer of pension capital. In some Member States domestic transfers are tax-exempt, whereas cross-border transfers are taxed or forbidden.[56]

4.10. SUPERVISION: EIOPA

EIOPA stands for EU Insurance and Occupational Pensions Authority.[57] EIOPA replaced the Committee of European Insurance and Occupational Pensions Supervisors (CEIOPS). The shift from CEIOPS to EIOPA has been triggered by the global financial crisis. Following the report of the High-Level Group on financial supervision in the EU chaired by Jacques de Larosière, the European Commission announced its intention to come forward with a Communication setting out its proposals on the future of the EU supervisory architecture followed by specific legislative measures in autumn 2009. The financial crisis and its spread over the global financial system have revealed the importance of the Commission's initiative to review and reorganize the European supervisory arrangements for all financial sectors. The problems revealed by the financial crisis showed the need for improvement of the existing arrangements of financial regulation and supervision. The European Parliament and the Council of

50 Case C-204/90 *Hanns-Martin Bachmann v. Belgian State* [1992] ECR I-249.
51 Case C-80/94 *G. H. E. J. Wielockx v. Inspecteur der Directe Belastingen* [1995] ECR I-2493.
52 Case C-118/96 *Jessica Safir v. Skattemyndigheten i Dalarnas Län, formerly Skattemyndigheten i Kopparbergs Län* [1998] ECR I-1897.
53 Case C-136/00 *Rolf Dieter Danner* [2002] ECR I-8147.
54 Case C-422/01 *Försäkringsaktiebolaget Skandia (publ) and Ola Ramstedt v. Riksskatteverket* [2003] ECR I-6819.
55 Case C-520/04 *Pirkko Marjatta Turpeinen* [2006] ECR I-685.
56 For more details see <http://ec.europa.eu/taxation_customs/taxation/personal_tax/pensions/index_en.htm> accessed 25 October 2011.
57 Regulation (EU) No. 1094/2010 of the European Parliament and of the Council of 24 November 2010 establishing a European Supervisory Authority (European Insurance and Occupational Pensions Authority), amending Decision No. 716/2009/EC and repealing Commission Decision 2009/79/EC [2010] OJ L331/48.

Ministers reached an agreement in principle in September 2010 on the package of new financial supervision legislation, like the setting up in January 2011 of a European Systemic Risk Board (ESRB) and three EU supervision authorities (ESAs), one for banking, one for insurance and one for securities. The European supervision authorities replaced the committees of national regulators (CESR, CEIOPS and CEBS).

The ESAs have binding powers over national authorities, including where a national authority fails to react directly to a financial institution. These powers over national authorities come into play in the following scenarios: the infringement of EU financial legislation (over banks' capital, for example); in a crisis; and in the event of disagreement among national authorities at the College of Supervisors. In order to take effect, these powers will have to be added to financial industry legislation. In the event of crisis, ESAs will temporarily have the power to ban toxic financial products and/or short selling. Here too, the financial industry rules will have to be adjusted to make this possible. In order to ensure a better application of EU rules, the ESAs will have the power to draw up technical standards. The European Parliament would have the right to scrutinize the standards before the Commission endorses them, a procedure described by a Commission expert as 'cumbersome'.

EIOPA is an European authority which, unlike its predecessor, can develop a EU framework containing binding technical standards in the defined areas. Also, it can act in settlements or in emergency situations, and is conferred the power to address binding individual decisions to insurance institutions.[58]

4.11. THE RESEARCH QUESTION

EU law is far more developed in occupational, supplementary and individual pensions than in statutory pension schemes. We can for example find 'true' EU standards on prudential and solvency level. From a social law point of view it is interesting to note that the social aspects are often seen as elements of consumer protection. In an indirect way the EU uses its competence with regard to consumer protection for the creation of social standards.

One could legitimately ask what is the difference between social protection and consumer protection. Take financial education and information as an example.

58 EU Regulation on insurance and occupational pensions authority <www.cep.eu/fileadmin/user_upload/CEP-Monitor/KOM_2009_501_Aufsichtsbehoerde/PB_EIOPA_EN.pdf> accessed 25 October 2011.

According to the Commission, the best way to increase the financial capability of consumers in the internal market is to develop coordinated strategies in individual Member States. The role of the Commission is to encourage the Member States to tackle the issue of financial education and to facilitate an exchange of best practices.[59] The true issue is whether financial illiteracy should or should not be an element in the debate about social protection. In classical social security the responsibility lies almost solely with the state or government. When financial education is required for social benefits, something is wrong. There is a Matthew effect with regard to unbalanced information: the financial actors will always remain better informed than the individual. Consumer protection in supplementary, occupational or individual pension provision is not the same as social protection.

5. CONCLUSION

Whereas there are many legal impediments when it comes to European actions regarding statutory pensions, the development of European pension law is far easier in the field of supplementary, occupational or individual pensions. However, when looking at the EU pension policy documents to which David Natali refers to elsewhere in this book, the opposite seems to be true. There is a discrepancy at the European level between on the one hand the legal framework for pensions restricting possible EU actions and on the other the policy level wishing to proceed to actions. It is as if there are two separate pension worlds: that of the lawyers and that of the policy-makers, which seem to ignore one another.

What economists and sociologists describe in policy studies are general tendencies, not legal structures, as illustrated by Natali's paper in this book. Notions such as 'indirect' or 'soft' coordination prove to be of little relevance for

59 The Commission has taken initiatives to organize expert meetings, maintain a European database, develop on-line tools for teachers and support events through patronage. Also in the Green Paper on pensions reference is made to financial education (question 12 and 13): '*Shifting choice and responsibility to the individual requires that people understand the information in order to make informed choices, especially as pensions have become more complex. Financial education can help as demonstrated by the work of the OECD and the EU already works with Member States on this. Financial education complements regulation of the industry, both prudential (e.g. the IORP Directive) and market conduct rules, and product disclosure rules. It is important that individuals are properly equipped with economic literacy and planning skills to adequately assess their need for financial and social protection and to avoid behavioural biases. For example, with the growing importance of DC schemes people need to make informed decisions about investments. It is also important that people have a competent body to turn to that can answer their questions relating to pensions, especially in a cross-border mobility context.*' European Commission, n. 8, p. 6; *Ibid.*, n. 5.

lawyers who work on the micro-scale. There are a number of interesting socio-economic reports about pensions, but given the (quasi) legal inactivity, they could be dangerously misleading. Reports and models can create the illusion or even the general perception of European actions while in practice the European Union cannot legally interfere.

BETWEEN DREAM AND REALITY ... ON ANTI-POVERTY POLICY, MINIMUM INCOME PROTECTION AND THE EUROPEAN SOCIAL MODEL

Bea Cantillon and Natascha Van Mechelen

1. INTRODUCTION

Although the Lisbon Strategy boldly envisaged the eradication of poverty in Europe, the number of poor families in Europe (i.e. families with an income below the EU poverty threshold) has not declined in the past ten years. The indications are that this failure is due, at least in part, to downward pressure on social security benefits.[1] While combating poverty presupposes a coherent policy in the fields of employment, education, health care and housing, adequate income protection is equally essential to any effective anti-poverty strategy. Much research therefore concludes with the recommendation to establish binding European minimum income rates defined in terms of the living standard in each Member State.[2]

The prevailing approach to social policymaking in Europe is one of 'soft coordination': common goals are put forward for each Member State to strive for in national and regional policies without concrete policy measures by which

1 B. Cantillon, 'The Paradox of the Social Investment State. Growth, Employment and Poverty in the Lisbon Era' (2011) CSB Working Paper No. 11/03 <www.centrumvoorsociaalbeleid.be/sites/default/files/CSB%20Working%20Paper%2011%2003_March%202011.pdf> accessed 6 October 2011; A.B. Atkinson, 'Poverty and the EU: The New Decade' (2010) Macerata Lectures on European Economic Policy, Working Paper No. 24 <www.unimc.it/sviluppoeconomico/wpaper/wpaper00024/filePaper> accessed 6 October 2011; F. Vandenbroucke and K. Vleminckx, 'Disappointing Poverty Trends: Is the Social Investment State to Blame? An Exercise in Soul-Searching for Policy-Makers' (2011) CSB Working Paper No. 11/01 <www.centrumvoorsociaalbeleid.be/sites/default/files/CSB%20Working%20Paper%2011%2001_January%202011_2_0.pdf> accessed 6 October 2011.

2 For a recent example see A.B. Atkinson, E. Marlier and A. Reinstadler, 'Income Distribution and Financial Poverty: EU-SILC in National and International Context' (2010) Paper Presented at the 2010 EU-SILC, International Conference (Warsaw, 25 and 26 March).

these goals can be obtained being specified.[3] These goals are, moreover, not binding. The model rests merely on a shared belief in the inspirational effect of 'good practices' and 'peer pressure'. As the accelerated process of integration has affected both the sovereignty and the autonomy of the national welfare states, many authors argue that the separation between the supranational sphere of 'the market' and the national sphere of 'the social arena' is untenable.[4] Concern is expressed that the inevitable logic of economic integration is generating growing negative pressure on the Member States' social protection systems.[5]

This gives rise to the question of the possible shape and content of feasible as well as effective European initiatives aimed at achieving a somewhat better balance in the Union's 'highly asymmetrical juristic framework'.[6] What kind of policy tool would allow Europe to introduce the rationale of social cohesion and social justice more forcefully into thinking and discourse, as well as policymaking? Although calls for a more social Europe have been heard for many years, those voices have usually remained rather silent when asked what precisely the objective of such a social policy alignment should be. What should European social policy look like? Considering the great political, economic and institutional differences within the Union, and given that anti-poverty policy cannot and must not be restricted to the financial dimension alone, is there any other option but that of 'soft coordination' towards common goals? Or are there opportunities for enhancing the social dimension by means of concrete policy instruments?

Whichever policy tool is deployed, though, it will undoubtedly have to be modest. In view of the considerable differences in economic development, the divergent design of the various national social protection systems, the multitude of interest groups involved and the lack of any political consensus, the approach taken will need to be incremental and it will have to rely on opportunities that are inherently present: '*one should proceed à petits pas (as Jean Monnet would have put it) and (...), tactically, one should take advantage of emerging "opportunity structures"*'.[7]

In the past, the idea has been put forward of establishing a 'social snake' which, by analogy with the currency snake that preceded the euro, would keep the

3 H. Verschueren, in this volume; M. Dawson and B. de Witte, in this volume.

4 S. Leibfried and P. Pierson, *European Social Policy between Fragmentation and Integration*, Brookings Institution, Washington D.C 1995.

5 See among others F.W. Scharpf, 'The Asymmetry of European Integration or Why the EU Cannot Be a "Social Market Economy"' (2010) 8 *Socio-Economic Review*.

6 *Ibid.*

7 Ph.C. Schmitter and M.W. Bauer, 'A (Modest) Proposal for Expanding Social Citizenship in the European Union' (2001) 11 *JESP*.

national levels of social security expenditures within a given range.[8] This notion has recently been reiterated by Klaus Busch in the context of a European social stability pact.[9] Another proposal was for the establishment of a '13th State' with its own social security system for migrating workers, alongside the existing systems in the then twelve Member States, an idea that has been picked up again in the French policy debate.[10] Others have dreamt of an EU lump-sum benefit to all needy Europeans, funded from, among other sources, the agricultural budgets.[11] But the most commonly heard proposal in academic and policy circles alike concerns the introduction of an obligation for all Member States to guarantee a dignified minimum income to their citizens. This minimum would be defined in terms of the median standardized income in each Member State. In the present article, we examine – from a social policy perspective – the opportunities for and desirability of introducing such binding standards in Europe, as well as the likely obstacles along the way. First we explore the *opportunities*. A realistic interpretation of a European social pact must, after all, inevitably be based on current practices and established ideas: 'for the time being, the best strategy is that of a full exploitation of the existing building blocks'.[12] In part two of this article, we therefore consider the role that the notion of a guaranteed minimum income has played on the slow and tedious road to a European policy framework for social protection and combating poverty. Part three examines prevailing national practices in the EU27. The underlying assumption is that a pan-European regulation only stands a chance of materializing if enough Member States already have in place more or less comparable systems of minimum income protection. Part four of the article deals with the *desirability* of a European minimum income standard. What is the potential of an adequate minimum income guarantee in combating poverty? And how did the notion fare under the system of 'soft coordination'? Are more

8 P. Vandervorst, 'De idee en de "haalbaarheid" van een mechanisme voor de vrijwaring, de consolidering en de ontwikkeling, in de convergentie, van de niveaus van de sociale bescherming binnen sociaal-economische ruimtes op weg naar integratie – de "Europese sociale slang"' (2002) 1 *Belgisch Tijdschrift voor Sociale Zekerheid.*

9 K. Busch, 'Alternatives to the Neoliberal Economic and Social Model of the European Union' (2009) Paper presented at the ZAUBER Symposium (15 January) <www.tascnet.ie/upload/Zauber%20Artikel%20in%20English.doc> accessed 6 October 2011. For an elaboration, see also B. Hacker and T. Van Treeck, 'What Influence for European Governance? The Reformed Stability and Growth Pact, the Europe 2020 Strategy and the "European Semester"' (2010) *International Policy Analysis* <http://library.fes.de/pdf-files/id/ipa/07724.pdf> accessed 6 October 2011.

10 D. Pieters and S. Vansteenkiste, 'Social Security in the European Community: Co-ordination, Harmonization or Thirteenth State?' (1995) 18 *International Journal of Public Administration*; A. Lamassoure, 'Le citoyen et l'application du droit communautaire' (2008) Rapport au Président de la République, Bruxelles.

11 Ph.C. Schmitter and M.W. Bauer, n. 7.

12 M. Ferrera, 'Mapping the Components of Social Europe: A Critical Analysis of the Current Institutional Patchwork' in E. Marlier and D. Natali (eds.) with R. Van Dam, *Europe 2020. Towards a More Social EU?*, P.I.E. Peter Lang, Brussels 2010.

binding initiatives required in order to make meaningful inroads in the struggle against poverty? In part five, attention shifts to the budgetary, policy-related and practical *obstacles* in the implementation of a European minimum income guarantee. Part six concludes the chapter.

2. THE *RITORNELLO* OF THE MINIMUM INCOME GUARANTEE

The European model of social subsidiarity is founded on a shared belief in the dynamic thrust of the market. It was underpinned intellectually in the 1950s by an excellent report by a group of experts of the International Labour Organization, under the chairmanship of Bertil Ohlin, a Swedish economist who made a pioneering contribution to the theory of international trade.[13] The starting point was the law of comparative advantage, according to which social and economic differences between countries stimulate growth and international trade. The reasoning was that this mechanism would easily suffice for an effective improvement in social protection levels. Against the background of the major social pacts that supported the post-war development of the European welfare states, there was a confidence that the spectre of tax competition and social dumping (which the French socialists in particular saw as a threat, prompting them to argue in favour of the inclusion of social clauses in the Treaty of Rome) could be averted through national policies. In essence, this remains the basic philosophy underlying the EU to this day.

Yet the call for a 'more social Europe' has never died completely. Especially since the 1990s, combating poverty and providing income protection have come to the fore more prominently and consistently as specific areas for EU policy cooperation. In this context, a minimum income guarantee is a recurrent theme. Let us briefly consider the main steps in this evolution.[14]

2.1. FROM 'HARMONIZATION' TO 'CONVERGENCE'

The European striving for economic integration has gained momentum since the second half of the 1980s. Initially, social policy remained quietly in the background, despite several not-so-successful attempts to have it included on the EU agenda. After the implementation in the 1970s of three successive 'Poverty

---

13 International Labour Organisation, 'Social Aspects of European Economic Co-operation. Report by a Group of Experts (summary)' (1956) 74 *International Labour Review*.

14 For more extensive overviews, we refer the reader to E. Marlier and D. Natali (eds.) with R. Van Dam, *Europe 2020. Towards a More Social EU?*, P.I.E. Peter Lang, Brussels 2010.

Programmes', with a view to describing and quantifying poverty in the EU, the European Council adopted an inconsequential resolution in 1989 in which it was asserted that '*combating social exclusion may be regarded as an important part of the social dimension of the internal market*'.[15] The European Social Charter of that same year was equally vague. And in the run-up to and actual establishment of the single market in 1993, all preparatory documents remained conspicuously quiet on the issue of social policy. The prevailing view was that a harmonization of social security policy was neither necessary, nor desirable, nor feasible.[16]

Still, with the Council Recommendation of 24 June 1992 on common criteria concerning sufficient resources and social assistance in social protection systems, an attempt was made to add a social dimension to the emerging single market.[17] This recommendation calls on the Member States to 'progressively cover all exclusion situations as broadly as possible' and, to this end, to set a guaranteed minimum income. It also calls on the Member States to recognize the 'basic right of a person to sufficient resources and social assistance to live in a manner compatible with human dignity' and 'to adapt their social protection systems, as necessary'. With this in mind, the recommendation defines a number of principles and guidelines. For those able to work, the right to a minimum income is subject to 'active availability for work or vocational training with a view to obtaining work'. The Member States are called upon to organize vocational training so as to ensure that those 'whose age and condition render them fit to work' would 'receive effective help to enter or re-enter working life'.

This Recommendation subscribed to the spirit of 'harmonization', *in the sense of striving for greater uniformity in the systems of social security.* This had, hitherto, been the prevailing intellectual approach to defining a European social agenda. In that same year, however, a new concept came to the fore, namely 'convergence'. Indeed, another recommendation spoke of the '*convergence* of social protection objectives and policies'. Subsequently, the notion of a harmonization of social protection systems was increasingly abandoned and replaced with that of *convergence towards common objectives.* On the basis of the insight that harmonization was not likely to yield substantial progress (due to its being 'unfeasible, undesirable and unnecessary'),[18] the striving for common policy

---

15 Resolution of the Council and of the Ministers for Social Affairs Meeting within the Council of 29 September 1989 on Combating Social Exclusion [1989] OJ C277/1.

16 See H. Deleeck, *7 lessen over sociale zekerheid*, Acco, Leuven 1991.

17 M. Ferrera, M. Matsaganis and S. Sacchi, 'Open Coordination Against Poverty: The New EU "Social Inclusion Process"' (2002) 12 *JESP*; 92/441/EEC: Council Recommendation of 24 June 1992 on Common Criteria Concerning Sufficient Resources and Social Assistance in Social Protection Systems [1992] OJ L245/46; 92/442/EEC: Council Recommendation of 27 July 1992 on the Convergence of Social Protection Objectives and Policies [1992] OJ L245/49.

18 H. Deleeck, n. 16.

instruments (such as the introduction of minimum income standards) was replaced with a striving for common policy *objectives* (such as poverty reduction). In this new approach, it was left to the Member States themselves to decide in accordance with their own needs, requirements and preferences which policy instruments to deploy (e.g. whether to opt for an employment strategy or to increase social spending). In other words, the social Europe was to be shaped by different national policies towards common European objectives.

2.2. THE LISBON STRATEGY, THE OMC AND THE SOCIAL INDICATORS

With a view to supporting the convergence process, a number of common social objectives were agreed upon at the Lisbon Summit of March 2000, including the eradication of poverty by 2010. To this end, a loose, open policy approach was developed that was supposed to enable the Member States to learn from one another's experiences. The Open Method of Coordination (OMC), which had already been applied previously in the field of employment policy,[19] was extended to the domain of social inclusion at the Nice Summit of 2000. The following year, at the Laeken Summit, a set of social indicators was defined for the purpose of measuring the progress made towards the social objectives.[20]

The present approach may be referred to as one of 'soft coordination', by which we mean that common objectives are put forward for each Member State to strive for individually in accordance with a policy of their own choice. There is no element of obligation, as the model is founded in its entirety on the supposedly inspiring impact of 'best practices' and 'peer pressure'.[21] Insofar as social inclusion is concerned, the objectives are clearly quantitatively defined by means of the so-called 'social indicators'. These indicators measure among other things the number of individuals in a country who must make ends meet on a low income, the extent of income inequality, the number of long-term unemployed, the number of households out of work and the proportion of premature school leavers. The Member States are required to report on these indicators and to draw up a National Action Plan detailing how they intend to improve the domestic social situation.[22]

---

19 Articles 136 and 140 TEC (Amsterdam consolidated version) [1997] OJ C340/1.

20 T. Atkinson, B. Cantillon, E. Marlier and B. Nolan, *Social Indicators. The EU and Social Inclusion*, Oxford University Press, Oxford 2002.

21 J. Zeitlin, 'Towards a Stronger OMC in a More Social Europe 2020: A New Governance Architecture for EU Policy Coordination' in E. Marlier and D. Natali (eds.) with R. Van Dam, n. 14; B. Vanhercke, 'Delivering the Goods for Europe 2020? The Social OMC's Adequacy and Impact Re-assessed' in *Ibid.*

22 J. Zeitlin, in *Ibid.*

In line with the notion of an 'objectives-oriented policy', the indicators were originally intended for measuring social policy *outcomes* (rather than policy *effort*). The authors of the book that laid the intellectual foundation for the social indicators put it as follows:

> *'our concern is with indicators for a particular purpose at a particular stage in the development of the European Union, and it is an important feature of this process that the policies to achieve social inclusion are the responsibility of Member States, under the subsidiarity principle (...) Member States are to agree on the objectives of policy, but they will be free to choose the methods by which these objectives are to be realized'.*[23]

At the Laeken Summit, a political consensus was reached on a portfolio of outcome indicators (on work, health, education, housing, income). Important in the present context is the agreement at the highest policymaking level on the setting of a European poverty line at 60% of median standardized income in any given country. Various other indicators build on this notion, including those relating to poverty in jobless households, and the depth and duration of poverty. These income indicators are prominently present within the portfolio of indicators.

The indicators were subsequently refined and enhanced, not least thanks to the excellent work of the Indicators Sub-Group.[24] In addition to the original outcome indicators, designed to measure progress towards the common objectives, a number of *policy* indicators were introduced. For the purpose of the OMC Social Protection, replacement rates for pensions were included, as was an indicator of the adequacy of social assistance benefits (by comparing them to the relative poverty line), albeit merely as a context variable, not as an indicator for policy evaluation.

Perhaps the introduction of these policy indicators marks the beginning of a new phase in European cooperation in the field of social policy. The fact that the Lisbon targets were not attained and the disappointing results in relation to poverty reduction, combined with the considerable budgetary constraints facing the process of economic integration, have resulted in a growing realization that a set of instruments is required which makes the connection between the 'common social objectives' and policies pursued visible. To this end, a tentative attempt has been made to develop policy indicators besides the original output indicators. The merger of the OMC Social Inclusion and Social Protection has undoubtedly facilitated this process.

---

23 T. Atkinson, B. Cantillon, E. Marlier and B. Nolan, n. 20.

24 J. Zeitlin, n. 21.

2.3. THE LISBON TREATY, THE NEW SOCIAL AGENDA FOR 2005–2010 AND THE EU 2020 TARGETS

With its New Social Agenda 2005–2010, the European Commission put the issue of national minimum income schemes back on the table as part of the striving for 'Active Inclusion'.[25] In the Commission Recommendation of 3 October 2008 on the active inclusion of people excluded from the labour market, the notion of a minimum income guarantee occupies a central place. The recommendation calls on the Member States to 'design and implement an integrated comprehensive strategy' with a view to 'the active inclusion of people excluded from the labour market' by combining three elements: adequate income support, inclusive labour markets and access to quality services. Insofar as income is concerned, explicit reference is made to the criteria set out in the previously mentioned Council Recommendation of 24 June 1992. The European Parliament, in its Resolution of 6 October 2010, goes one step further: it not only stresses that 'minimum income schemes should be embedded in a strategic approach towards social integration' but adds that 'adequate minimum income schemes must set minimum incomes at a level equivalent to at least 60% of median income in the Member State concerned'. Some political factions also argued in favour of a European directive on minimum incomes whereby the Member States would be compelled to introduce adequate social assistance schemes, but this proposal was rejected by the European Parliament Plenary Session. The approved resolution merely states that the Commission should study the impact of the introduction of an adequate minimum income at the European level.

The combined strategy of adequate income support, inclusive labour markets and access to quality services was also incorporated into the Lisbon Treaty.[26] The so-called 'horizontal social clause' (Article 9 TFEU) stipulates that the Union must 'take into account requirements linked to the promotion of a high level of employment, the guarantee of adequate social protection, the fight against social exclusion, and a high level of education, training and protection of human health.'

The EU 2020 targets are the provisional end point in the slow process of defining the European Union's social dimension. A communication from the European Commission of 3 March 2010 outlines the new ten-year plan. EU 2020 is conceived as a strategy for smart, sustainable and inclusive growth towards five headline targets in relation to employment, research and development, climate, the share of school leavers, and – for the first time in European history – poverty. By 2020, the number of people living in poverty should be reduced by twenty

---

25 H. Frazer and E. Marlier, 'Strengthening Social Inclusion in the Europe 2020 Strategy by Learning from the Past' in E. Marlier and D. Natali (eds.) with R. Van Dam, n. 14.

26 *Ibid.*; H. Verschueren, n. 3; M. Dawson and B. de Witte, n. 3.

million.[27] This quantification in a clear and measurable target is both less ambitious and more realistic than the poverty-eradication rhetoric employed in the Lisbon Strategy.

In the initial proposal from the European Commission, the at-risk-of-financial-poverty notion (measured by the 60% threshold) was used to quantify the number of poor and to launch the target of a reduction by twenty million by the year 2020. After some political debate, the European Council of 25 and 26 March 2010 concluded rather vaguely that 'further work is needed on (the) appropriate indicators'.[28] At the following meeting in June, the target was retained, but a number of technical amendments were made. It was specified in a footnote that the extent of poverty should be expressed in terms of 'the number of persons who are at risk-of-poverty and exclusion according to three indicators (at-risk-of poverty; material deprivation; jobless household), leaving Member States free to set their national targets on the basis of the most appropriate indicators, taking into account their national circumstances and priorities'.[29] In other words, henceforth the poverty figure was an aggregate based on three indicators: the financial poverty risk, the extent of material deprivation (i.e. households that were unable to afford four out of nine previously determined items) and the number of households with a low work intensity (i.e. households whose members are either jobless or in work for just a few months per year).

With the new poverty-reduction target – more specifically the objective of reducing the number of households whose income is below the 60% threshold – the notion of minimum income protection came to the fore again. As argued further in this article, history shows that combating poverty requires more than a focus on creating jobs. The degree of poverty is most severe among households that are largely dependent on social security, and precisely these households stand to gain the least from job growth.[30]

However, as demonstrated by the aforementioned political debate on the setting of the EU 2020 poverty targets, the notion of guaranteeing an adequate minimum income as an indispensable element of a coherent anti-poverty policy remains rather ambivalent. Some documents refer quite explicitly to the need for an adequate minimum income, while others do not. The Communication of 16 December 2010 on the 'European Platform against Poverty and Social Exclusion', for example, makes no more than cursory mention of a minimum income guarantee.

---

27 European Commission, 'Europe 2020. A Strategy for Smart, Sustainable and Inclusive Growth' (Communication) COM (2010) 2020.

28 European Council, 'Conclusions', 25 – 26 March 2010, EUCO 7/10.

29 European Council, 'Conclusions', 17 June 2010, EUCO 13/10.

30 B. Cantillon, n. 1; A.B. Atkinson, n. 1.

In sum, the necessity of adequate minimum income protection has been recognized in the European policy agenda for at least twenty years. However, the political majority required for binding agreements on this matter has always been lacking. At the highest decision making level, the Council of Ministers has never shown an interest in taking a legislative initiative with regard to combating poverty. In its conclusions of 17 December 2008, for example, explicit reference is made to the subsidiarity principle and thus to the determination at Member State level of the most optimal policy mix in combating poverty. Still, the accelerated integration that has taken place over the past two decades, and the consistent and repeated presence of the necessity of adequate minimum income protection in the European political discourse, strongly suggest that, if a decisive step is ever made towards binding agreements in the field of social security, then it is quite likely to involve arrangements regarding minimum incomes. This is particularly true in the light of the fact that the budgetary constraints facing economic integration have become very substantial, while outcomes of the fight against poverty have been plainly disappointing and the adequacy of the social OMC is now called into question.[31] We will return to this matter in section four. First, though, let us consider the existing systems of minimum income protection in the various Member States. After all, a realistic implementation of a European social project must inevitably take current practices as its starting point.

3. PRACTICES IN THE EU27

Today, the vast majority of Member States have a general social safety net, implying that all needy citizens enjoy a subjective right to a guaranteed minimum income. The only exceptions are Greece and certain regions in Italy and Hungary (cf. infra). There are however substantial differences between these various national/regional schemes in terms of, among other things, means testing, residence conditions, the level of income protection offered and the extent to which benefit claimants are encouraged to seek work. In the next few paragraphs, we will focus primarily on the latter two divergences, while also pointing out the similarities between the Member States' respective systems.

3.1. GENERAL SOCIAL ASSISTANCE SCHEMES ACROSS EUROPE

Historically speaking, universal (i.e. non-categorical) social assistance schemes are the most recent addition to the range of protection tools in welfare

[31] B. Vanhercke, n. 21.

states.[32] While most other social security branches and categorical social assistance schemes, including those for the elderly and the disabled, already took shape before the Second World War, the first universal social assistance schemes date from the 1960s (Germany, the Netherlands, United Kingdom) and 1970s (Belgium, Denmark and Ireland).[33] In Sweden, Finland, France and Luxembourg, non-categorical social assistance schemes were only introduced in the course of the 1980s. Likewise, Spain's regional social assistance schemes (Basque Country and Catalonia) date from the late 1980s.

These general social assistance schemes introduced a legally binding guaranteed income for all. Unlike the earlier poor laws, which provided discretionary assistance, they imply a subjective right to income protection. Although willingness to work was an entitlement condition, there was hardly any evidence of active policies aimed at labour market integration – or indeed any other form of integration. In most countries, the explicit linkage of an individual's right to social assistance benefits to their job-seeking behaviour or participation in training and employment schemes dates from the 1990s or even later. The primary purpose of the aforementioned social assistance schemes was to provide an ultimate safety net for those not covered by other social protection provisions. In Belgium, this subsistence benefit became known as 'Bestaansminimum' or 'Minimex'. Much more recently, it was superseded by a scheme known as 'Leefloon' (French: 'Revenu Minimum d'Insertion'), which is much more explicit on the efforts claimants must make towards their social reintegration in order not to lose their entitlement.

In other words, the aforementioned 1992 recommendation by the European Council regarding common criteria for social assistance reflected an ongoing trend. At the time, the majority of the fifteen Member States had already introduced a guaranteed minimum income. With the exception of Italy, the countries where an ultimate safety net was still lacking were the youngest EU Member States: Spain, Portugal and Greece. The 1992 recommendation may therefore be seen as a call aimed primarily at those new Member States to implement an encompassing system of income protection.

Some authors feel that the 1992 recommendation effectively contributed to the introduction of universal social assistance schemes in Southern Europe during

32 I. Lødemel and B. Schulte, 'Social Assistance: A Part of Social Security or the Poor Law in New Disguise?' (1992) Paper presented at the 'Social Security Fifty Years after Beveridge' Conference, University of York.

33 B. Cantillon, N. Van Mechelen and B. Schulte, 'Minimum Income Policies in Old and New EU Member States' in J. Alber, T. Fahey and C. Saraceno (eds.), *Handbook of Quality of Life in the Enlarged European Union*, Routledge, London 2008.

the 1990s.[34] Between 1990 and 1995, one Spanish region after another adopted general social assistance programmes. Nonetheless, in some of these regions, social assistance is provided on an ad hoc basis and there is little evidence of a subjective right to assistance.[35] In Portugal, the *Rendimento Mínimo Garantido* was introduced in 1997 during the country's presidency of the EU.[36] Italy, for its part, began experimenting with a universal safety net in 1998, but plans for a national social assistance programme were shelved in 2001 by the Berlusconi government.[37] To this day, Italy is an exception within the European Union because of the inadequacy of social assistance provisions in several of the country's regions. But the most notable exception of all is Greece, where a universal safety net is lacking at the national as well as the regional levels.

The countries of Central and Eastern Europe have also seen the emergence of universal social assistance systems since the 1990s. In the communist era, poverty was hardly an issue: full employment, strong subsidization of basic commodities and services, and adequate social security provisions for those unable or no longer able to work were assumed to prevent poverty effectively.[38] However, the situation changed fundamentally with the fall of communism. Exponential growth of unemployment and soaring inflation caused a steady increase in poverty.[39] In order to meet the new social and economic needs the entire social architecture was redesigned. Existing social provisions were adapted (e.g. pensions) and new schemes were introduced.[40] In many Central European countries, universal social assistance schemes were already implemented in the early 1990s, mostly under the impulse of the World Bank. In the run-up to their accession to the European Union in 2004, the Commission came to play an increasingly influential role, but legislative initiatives focused not so much on

34 A. Arriba and Z. Ibáñez, 'Minimum Income Guarantee and Social Assistance' (2002) Working Paper 02–12 <http://digital.csic.es/bitstream/10261/1526/1/dt-0212e.pdf> accessed 6 October 2011; M. Matsaganis, M. Ferrera, L. Capucha and L. Moreno, 'Mending Nets in the South: Anti-poverty Policies in Greece, Italy, Portugal and Spain' (2003) 37 *Social Policy and Administration*.

35 A. Arriba and L. Moreno, 'Spain – Poverty, Social Exclusion and "Safety Nets" in M. Ferrera (ed.), *Welfare State Reform in Southern Europe: Fighting Poverty and Social Exclusion in Italy, Spain, Portugal and Greece*, Routledge, London 2005; G. Rodríguez Cabrero, 'Assessment of Minimum Income Schemes in Spain' (2009) Peer Review in Social Protection and Social Inclusion and Assessment in Social Inclusion <www.peer-review-social-inclusion.eu/network-of-independent-experts/reports/2009-first-semester/spain-1-2009-en> accessed 6 October 2011.

36 M. Matsaganis, M. Ferrera, L. Capucha and L. Moreno, n. 34.

37 C. Saraceno, 'Social Assistance Policies and Decentralization in the Countries of Southern Europe' (2006) 1 *Revue Francaise des Affaires Sociales*.

38 G. Standing, 'The Folly of Social Safety Nets: Why Basic Income is Needed' (1997) 64 *Eastern Europe Social Research*.

39 Z. Ferge and G. Juhász, 'Accession and Social Policy: The Case of Hungary' (2004) 14 *JESP*.

40 N. Manning, 'Diversity and Change in Pre-accession Central and Eastern Europe since 1989' (2004) 14 *JESP*.

social policy as on economic and monetary policy in the prospective Member States.[41] And to the extent that the social institutions in transition countries were affected, the main focus was on specific aspects of European social policy, such as the labour market participation of specific target groups and the privatization of social services.

3.2. THE COMMON DENOMINATOR OF THE EUROPEAN SOCIAL MODEL?

The similarities between the basic architectures of the various European social assistance systems become very apparent when contrasted with the design of the social safety net in the United States. Although the European and the US social models have undeniably converged in recent decades – particularly with Europe's stronger focus on stimulating transitions from social assistance to work –[42] there continue to be fundamental differences.

In the US, most social assistance benefits are categorical. The principal scheme that provides non-contribution-based benefits to young, healthy citizens – known as TANF or Temporary Aid for Needy Families – is only accessible to households with children. A minority of US States have implemented additional schemes that also provide financial assistance to childless families, but in most States such families qualify only for the Supplemental Nutrition Assistance Program (SNAP). This system involves an electronic debit card that can be recharged on a monthly basis to provide low-income families with a food budget to spend on specified foodstuffs from recognized stores. The budget varies with household composition and it should enable families to purchase what the Department of Agriculture considers to be nutritious foods. Moreover, TANF is usually restricted to a lifetime total of sixty months and the benefit amounts involved are generally very low. Even in the more generous US States, such as Nebraska, net social assistance amounts (SNAP included) as a proportion of the net income of a single earner on an average wage are no higher than benefit

41 Z. Ferge, 'The Perils of the Welfare State's Withdrawal' (1997) 64 *Social Research*; C. de la Porte and B. Deacon, 'Contracting Companies and Consultants: The EU and the Social Policy of Accession Countries' (2002) GASPP Occasional Paper No. 9/2002 <http://gaspp.stakes.fi/NR/rdonlyres/B84DD73B-02E0-4E6B-9471-C3A7D44ADA2A/0/gaspp92002.pdf> accessed 6 October 2011.

42 J. Alber and N. Gilbert, 'The Epistemology of Comparative Analyses: What Do We Know?' in J. Alber and N. Gilbert (eds.), *United in Diversity? Comparing Social Models in Europe and America*, Oxford University Press, Oxford 2009; C. Saraceno, 'Concepts and Practices of Social Citizenship in Europe: The Case of Poverty and Income Support for the Poor' in *Ibid.*, Oxford University Press, Oxford 2009.

amounts in the poorer EU countries, such as Bulgaria, Romania, Estonia and Slovakia.[43]

This brief outline of the US programme underscores the similarity between the various social protection systems in Europe. For one thing, in Europe, the level of welfare enjoyed by social assistance recipients approximates much more closely that of working households. Second, in principle at least, entitlement to social assistance continues for as long as there is a need: unlike in the US, there are no time restrictions in the EU Member States.[44] A third essential trait of minimum income protection in Europe is the existence of general, non-categorical social assistance schemes. Any citizen whose income is below a certain threshold is able to claim benefits. In practice, however, entitlement is restricted through conditions of access and certain obligations (e.g. requirements in relation to age, citizenship, residence, willingness to work etc.).[45] Nonetheless, just about all Member States have a social safety net based on the principle that everyone must have access to a minimum income. The right to financial assistance is usually not restricted to specific population groups, such as families with children, elderly people or persons with a disability. As previously mentioned, the only notable exceptions are Greece and Italy. To an extent, the United Kingdom is also an exception. Here, universal social assistance has been gradually eroded by the introduction of increasingly specific schemes for well-defined target groups. The least fortunate UK citizens are today protected by a range of categorical schemes that together form a quasi-universal system. There are specific social assistance benefits for elderly persons, individuals who are fit for work, sick and disabled persons and other incapacitated individuals. Together, these schemes cover virtually the entire population.[46] A more notable exception is Hungary. It has no universal social assistance system either. Moreover, some population groups are not covered by the various categorical assistance schemes or they are subject to additional entitlement conditions. For example, those who are able to work but have contributed insufficiently to the social security system

---

43 N. Van Mechelen, S. Marchal, T. Goedemé, I. Marx and B. Cantillon, 'The CSB-Minimum Income Protection Indicators dataset (CSB-MIPI)' (2011) CSB Working Paper No. 5/2011 <www.centrumvoorsociaalbeleid.be/sites/default/files/CSB%20Working%20Paper%20 11%2005_April%202011.pdf> accessed 6 October 2011.

44 In this respect, there is a significant degree of convergence to be observed between the Member States. Until recently, the right to social assistance was limited in time in some Eastern European countries. In Latvia, needy households could, until 2009, claim social assistance benefits for up to nine months per year. And in Bulgaria, until 2010, households could receive social assistance benefits for up to twelve successive months. Since the abolition of these rules, such time restrictions apply only in a number of Italian regions.

45 H. Frazer and E. Marlier, 'Minimum Income Schemes across EU Member States. Synthesis Report' (2009) Peer Review on Social Protection and Social Inclusion and Assessment in Social Inclusion <www.ceps.lu/pdf/11/art1464.pdf> accessed 6 October 2011.

46 R. Walker and M. Wiseman, *The Welfare State We Want? The British Challenge for American Reform*, The Policy Press, Bristol 2003.

only become entitled to social assistance after a year of active cooperation with an employment service. Similar restrictions to general social assistance are in place in Bulgaria.[47]

3.3. UNITY IN DIVERSITY

Although the European social assistance schemes are based on common principles, there are considerable differences in terms of generosity, eligibility and implementation.[48] Let us consider two important areas of divergence: benefit levels and the extent to which claimants are encouraged to find work. We rely here on the CSB-MIPI dataset,[49] which is based on a recent survey of experts from twenty-five European Member States and three US States.[50]

Figure 1 compares the net income of social assistance claimants with median standardized household income, taking into account income tax, social security contributions, local property tax and other non-income-related taxes, statutory housing allowances and child benefits. For single persons, only the Irish social assistance benefits are above the European poverty threshold of 60% of median standardized income.[51] In the Netherlands, Denmark and Luxembourg, social assistance benefits for single persons amount to between 50 and 60% of median household income; in Belgium, Austria (Vienna), France and Latvia they amount

47 G. Bogdanov and B. Zahariev, 'Analysis of the Situation in Relation to Minimum Income Schemes in Bulgaria' (2009) Peer Review in Social Protection and Social Inclusion and Assessment in Social Inclusion <www.peer-review-social-inclusion.eu/network-of-independent-experts/reports/2009-first-semester/bulgaria-1-2009-en> accessed 6 October 2011.

48 H. Frazer and E. Marlier, 'Minimum Income Schemes across EU Member States. Synthesis Report', n. 45.

49 The CSB-MIPI dataset provides, among other things, detailed information on the evolution of the net social assistance packages for four household types relative to the net income of single and dual earners on average wage, as well as the net income of single earners on minimum wage. In addition, it contains information on the conditionality of benefits, and on both the formal rules and the actual implementation of activation policy and punitive measures for unwillingness to work. In this sense, the CSB dataset supplements data from, among other sources, the OECD (OECD, *Employment Outlook: Tackling the Jobs Crisis*, OECD, Paris 2009; and H. Immervoll, 'Minimum-Income Benefits in OECD Countries: Policy Design, Effectiveness and Challenges' (2009) IZA Discussion Paper No. 4627 <www.politiquessociales.net/IMG/pdf/dp4627.pdf> accessed 6 October 2011).

50 For a detailed description of the data, see N. Van Mechelen, S. Marchal, T. Goedemé, I. Marx and B. Cantillon, n. 43.

51 The estimations of the net social assistance benefits in the CSB-MIPI dataset are typically lower than those by the OECD (2009). This is due to a lower estimation of housing costs in the CSB-MIPI dataset. Whereas the OECD estimations are based on the assumption that housing costs in all countries and for all households amount to 20% of the national average wage, the CSB-MIPI dataset incorporates an empirical estimation of housing costs based on SILC data See N. Van Mechelen, S. Marchal, T. Goedemé, I. Marx and B. Cantillon, n. 43.

to between 40 and 50%.[52] However, in the majority of countries, including Germany, the UK, Finland and Sweden, benefit amounts are below 40% of median household income. In Portugal, Poland, Slovenia, Slovakia, Lithuania, Estonia, Bulgaria and Romania social assistance benefits for single persons amount to less than 50% of the European poverty threshold.

Figure 1. International comparison of the generosity of net social assistance benefits, 2009[53]

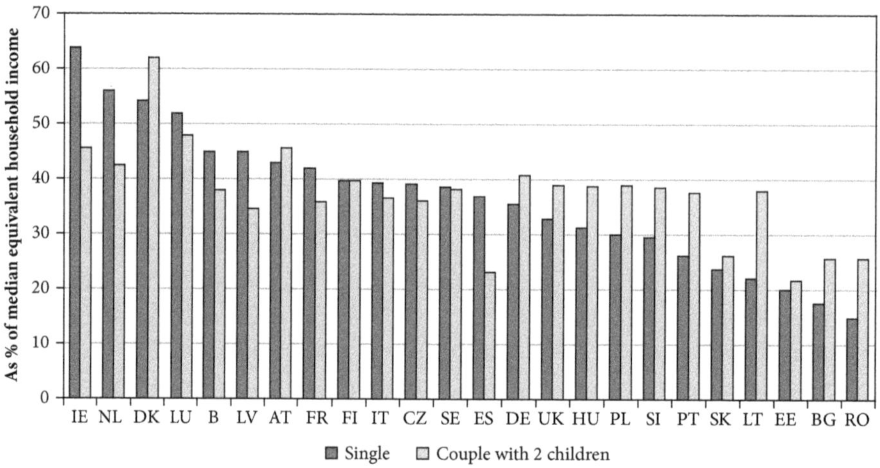

Source: CSB-MIPI data (N. Van Mechelen, S. Marchal, T. Goedemé, I. Marx and B. Cantillon, n. 43.)

The generosity of social assistance benefits varies strongly with household composition. In Ireland, the Netherlands, Spain, Belgium, France and Latvia, benefits for couples with children are deeper below the poverty line than those for single persons. In Romania, Bulgaria, Lithuania, Portugal, Poland, Slovenia, Germany and the UK, the opposite is true: here benefits for couples with two children are considerably more adequate than those for single persons. These countries, in their systems for social assistance claimants (social assistance scheme, rent allowance and/or child benefits), implicitly apply an equivalence scale that is steeper than the adjusted OECD scale on which the poverty line is based. Moreover, in almost all European Member States, benefits for single parents are more adequate than benefits for couples with children. Rarely, though, do they amount to 60% of median standardised income. The degree of

52 In Austria, Italy and Spain, social assistance is a regional competence. Figure 1 shows benefit levels for respectively Vienna, Milan and Catalonia.

53 The median standardized household income is obtained from Eurostat and it is based on SILC 2009 (income data for 2008). Using Eurostat's harmonized indexes of consumer prices, the data for 2008 were adjusted to prices for 2009.

international variation in social assistance benefits for this type of household is however smaller than in the case of either single persons without children or couples with children.

There is also considerable variation across Europe in terms of working conditions and activation. We may distinguish between at least four clusters of countries in this respect (see Table 1 in Appendix). The first group consists of countries where no activation or punitive measures are taken. Estonia and Lithuania are two good examples: the number of activated social assistance recipients is not monitored and sanctions for unwillingness to work are rarely applied. On the other hand, the financial incentive to seek a job is considerable: single benefit recipients can double their income by accepting work, even if at minimum wage. A second group of countries combines strong financial incentives with a strict punitive policy. In the United Kingdom and Romania, for example, social assistance recipients who fail to turn up for training or job mediation meetings risk suspension, implying a loss of benefits for several months. Moreover, sanctions are readily implemented, affecting over 10% of those on social assistance. A third group of countries, including Denmark and the Netherlands, combine a strict punitive policy with a considerable activation focus. In both countries, the share of social assistance claimants reached by activation measures is strikingly large. At the same time, many claimants are affected by sanctions. In the Netherlands, the law provides for rather strict penalties: a reduction in benefits of up to 100% for an unrestricted period. The countries belonging to the fourth group, including Belgium, Austria (Vienna) and Germany, also focus on activation, but the proportion of social assistance claimants undergoing an activation programme in these countries is considerably lower than it is in either the Netherlands or Denmark. Furthermore, activation policy is backed up far less with a strict application of sanctions. The number of persons affected by sanctions in these countries is in any case relatively low.

To conclude, although almost all Member States have a general safety net, there continue to be differences between (and within) countries. In Denmark and the Netherlands, benefits are relatively generous, but they are combined with a strict activation policy. In countries such as Belgium and Austria, benefits are far less generous (though still above average) and there is far less emphasis on activation and sanctions. The United Kingdom and Germany pursue a very selective policy, aimed primarily at the protection of households with children (benefits for single persons amount to less than 40% of median standardized household income). In the UK, low benefits are moreover combined with a high sanctions rate. Differences are also quite considerable among the countries of Eastern and Central Europe. Whereas Romania offers low benefits and applies strict punitive measures for unwillingness to work, sanctions are virtually unheard of in countries such as Lithuania and Estonia.

4. POVERTY TRENDS AND SOCIAL ASSISTANCE GENEROSITY

We have already seen that two important conditions are met for introducing a binding minimum income standard in Europe: the notion has been persistently present in academic and social discourse, and most countries already have (albeit quite diverse) social assistance schemes in place. In the next section, we consider the matter of desirability: would a binding European minimum income standard be effective in combating poverty? First we examine the close relationship between social assistance generosity and the extent of poverty. Subsequently we ask how effective the system of soft coordination has been in the fight against poverty and in guaranteeing a minimum income, and whether more binding initiatives in this field are desirable.

4.1. THE RELATIONSHIP BETWEEN SOCIAL ASSISTANCE AND POVERTY

Social assistance schemes are assumed to play an important role in the fight against poverty, either directly in the shape of income support to society's poor or indirectly as a safety net under the overall structure of the social protection system. In most countries, however, protection for those who find themselves outside the labour market is provided primarily through general social security schemes. The proportion of social assistance claimants in the population is, after all, below 3% in most Member States.[54] Moreover, there is no strong demonstrable connection between the generosity of social assistance schemes and the minimums provided under most social insurance systems.

So Figure 2 shows that, if one applies the 60% poverty threshold, the correlation between benefit generosity and the poverty rate is not particularly strong. This is of course explained in part by the fact that social assistance schemes rarely provide an income equal to 60% of median income. Using the stricter 40% or 50% thresholds, the correlation becomes stronger, but not significantly so. Within the group of the 'old' European Member States, we find a significant, though again not particularly strong correlation. On the one hand, we see that many countries with benefits below 40% of median income indeed have the largest proportions of persons under this income threshold (Spain, Portugal, Poland, Lithuania, Romania, the United Kingdom, Sweden and Estonia). On the other hand, countries such as Slovakia, Czech Republic, Hungary and Slovenia, which are not generous either, report low poverty rates. Finland, despite having comparable benefit levels to Germany, similarly has a higher poverty rate. As

54 N. Van Mechelen, S. Marchal, T. Goedemé, I. Marx and B. Cantillon, n. 43.

previously mentioned, this difference is due in part to the relatively low number of social assistance recipients. Other contributing factors are differences in terms of accessibility, conditionality and take-up of benefits, and – most probably – measurement errors in the samples. In Eastern Europe, such factors are undoubtedly even more relevant than elsewhere. Latvia, for example, combines mediocre, though not extremely low, benefits with a particularly high poverty risk. This is attributable to an extent to the limited duration of entitlement. In addition, the high poverty rates in this and other Eastern European countries are probably also due to a lack of financial and administrative clout, both of which are necessary to implement the right to benefits in practice.[55]

These are very important conclusions, as they suggest that an anti-poverty strategy should not be restricted to setting adequate social assistance amounts, but should also include adequate access criteria and implementation practices. Moreover, one must never lose sight of the fact that social assistance contributes only marginally to reducing poverty. Work and social security are much more potent tools in this respect.

Table 1. The relationship between the adequacy of net social assistance benefits (average for the five household types) and the share of the population (15–64 years) below 60–50–40% of median standardized income, 2009

	EU25 (GR excepted)	EU15 (GR excepted)	EU10
Below 60% of median standardized income			
Pearson's correlation	–.365	–.564	–.238
Significant at	.079	.036	.508
Number of observations	24	14	10
Below 50% of median standardized income			
Pearson's correlation	–.441	–.663	–.229
Significant at	.031	.010	.524
Number of observations	24	14	10
Below 40% of median standardized income			
Pearson's correlation	–.456	–.643	–.254
Significant at	.025	.013	.478
Number of observations	24	14	10

Source: CSB-MIPI data (N. Van Mechelen, S. Marchal, T. Goedemé, I. Marx and B. Cantillon, n. 43.); SILC 2009 (incomes for 2008)

55 H. Frazer and E. Marlier, 'Minimum Income Schemes Across EU Member States. Synthesis Report', n. 45.

Figure 2. The relationship between the adequacy of net social assistance benefits (average for the five household types) and the share of the population (15–64 years) below 40% of median standardized income, 2009

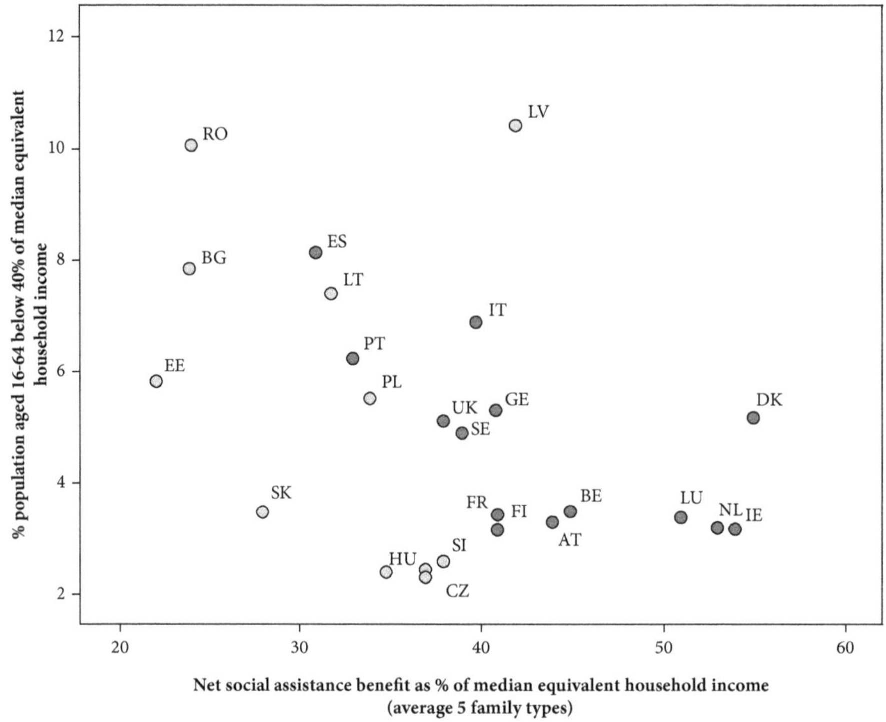

Source: CSB-MIPI data (N. Van Mechelen, S. Marchal, T. Goedemé, I. Marx and B. Cantillon, n. 43.); SILC 2009 (incomes for 2008)

4.2. LISBON AND ITS POVERTY OUTCOMES

During the Lisbon era, the level of welfare and the number of people in work in Europe increased. Yet, despite an ambitious anti-poverty rhetoric and the implementation of the OMC Social Inclusion, most countries failed to transmute these prima facie favourable parameters into a poverty reduction. The strong increase in poverty among social benefit recipients in general and the unemployed in particular[56] points in the direction of the erosion of social protection as an important cause.

---

56 B. Cantillon, n. 1.

Despite renewed attention in European social policy for adequate minimum income protection, this clearly remains the weakest of the three pillars of social inclusion. This is apparent from, among other things, the 2008–2009 National Action Plans for Social Inclusion, where few Member States singled out a guaranteed minimum income as a priority in social policymaking, with visible consequences in terms of the evolution of social assistance benefit levels.

Since 2000, social assistance benefits have eroded in most Member States. Figure 3 shows the evolution of social assistance relative to the poverty threshold between 2001 and 2009. The only significant improvements were recorded in Eastern European countries such as Romania, Hungary, Lithuania and Slovenia. And in Belgium and Ireland, the downward trend of years of gradual erosion of social benefits was broken. However, in all other Member States, social assistance benefits lost ground to varying extents. The greatest relative decline was recorded in the Czech Republic, Estonia, Poland, Denmark and Sweden. In Estonia and Poland, for example, net social assistance benefits for some households declined from between 40% and 50% of median standardized household income in 2001 to just 30% by 2009. In Denmark, benefit generosity declined from over 80% of median household income to 50% and 41% for respectively single persons and single-parent families.

The declining trend was evidently not the same for all household types. Indeed, relative to the 60% poverty line, benefits for single parents became more generous in eleven of the twenty-one countries surveyed. Belgium, Germany, Hungary, the Netherlands, Portugal and Slovenia in particular saw the guaranteed minimum income for single parents increase more rapidly than the general level of welfare.

Considering that the welfare erosion of minimum social benefits occurred in an era when Europe had set itself the goal of eradicating poverty and, to this end, devised an encompassing system of policy coordination, the observed trend is worth more than a mere footnote. The Lisbon Strategy, with its focus on economic growth, more jobs and social inclusion, failed in the latter attempt precisely because of a neglect of those who remained outside the labour market despite employment growth. This suggests that, while the Open Method of Coordination may have had useful policy impacts in some areas,[57] it was largely ineffective when it comes to income protection for the poor. Given the absence of any strong correlation between social assistance generosity on the one hand and poverty rates on the other (see supra), the main culprit is most likely the erosion of unemployment benefits.

---

[57] B. Vanhercke, n. 21.

Figure 3. The evolution of the adequacy of net social assistance benefits for three household types, 2001–2009[58]

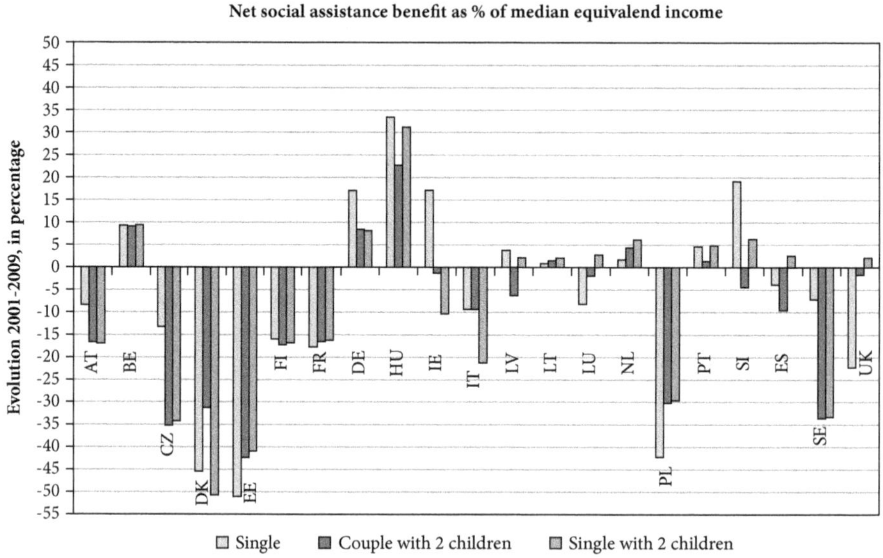

Source: CSB-MIPI data (N. Van Mechelen, S. Marchal, T. Goedemé, I. Marx and B. Cantillon, n. 43.)

5. BETWEEN DREAM AND REALITY STAND CONCEPTS AND PRACTICAL CONSIDERATIONS

The European policy discourse on social inclusion, the fight against poverty and the need for adequacy of resources, as outlined in part two of this chapter, and the existence of general systems of social assistance in most Member States, as described in part three, combined with the necessity of providing adequate income protection in order to effectively combat poverty, as argued in part four, all point at an important opportunity: a guaranteed minimum income would seem to stand a good chance of becoming the first building block in a European social project. As argued in part four, a binding European initiative in this field would moreover be very welcome: the soft approach under the social OMC has, after all, not been able to prevent the erosion of minimum benefits in many Member States. In this respect, a binding system for a guaranteed minimum income would at least establish a 'floor' under the European welfare states, and it

[58] The median standardized household income for 2001 and 2009 are obtained from Eurostat. For 2001, the Eurostat data for most countries are based on ECHP, and on a number of national sources for the Eastern European Member States. All data for 2009 are based on EU-SILC.

would compel the Member States to focus more closely on effective activation and on setting adequate minimum income levels. However, between dream and reality stand laws and practical considerations. Obviously the legal and – even more so – political obstacles are quite daunting. Insofar as a European juristic framework is theoretically attainable,[59] any political consensus on this matter seems a long way off under the given circumstances. A telling example in this respect is the vote on the European Parliament resolution referred to in part two of this chapter. In what follows, though, we focus on the technical and the budgetary bottlenecks that may arise in the implementation of a hypothetical directive on a guaranteed minimum income in the Member States.

5.1. WHAT IS AN ADEQUATE MINIMUM INCOME?

Setting legally enforceable minimum income levels presupposes unequivocal definitions of both the basic amounts and the equivalence scales applied. The European Parliament's resolution of 6 October 2010 stresses that a strategy towards social integration must encompass an income protection scheme with minimum incomes set 'at a level equivalent to at least 60% of median income in the Member State concerned'. The successive steps in the gradual construction of a social Europe as described in part two of this chapter also point at the EU's 60% poverty threshold as a good measure of the adequacy of social protection systems. However, this gives rise to issues of feasibility and legitimacy.

Europe has, since the 1970s, consistently applied a relative poverty concept. The poor are defined as those who are excluded from the minimum acceptable way of life in the Member State where they reside.[60] So unlike in the United States, the EU defines poverty relative to the general level of welfare in a given country at a given moment in time. What is regarded as the 'minimum acceptable way of life' depends on this context, i.e. it is determined by the prevailing level of social and economic development. From this perspective, it is futile to try and formulate an absolute poverty standard that is universally valid, in all countries and at all times. For example, an EU-wide poverty threshold (defined as 60% of median standardized income across Europe) would result in above 95% poor in Romania as compared to below 10% in Belgium.[61] On the other hand, the relative nature of poverty should not be exaggerated either, especially in the context of a binding

59 See also H. Verschueren, n. 3 and A. Van Lancker, 'Working Document on a Framework Directive on Minimum Income' (2010) EAPN (European Anti-Poverty Network) <www.europolitics.info/pdf/gratuit_en/279353-en.pdf> accessed 6 October 2011.

60 See also P. Townsend, *Poverty in the United Kingdom: A Survey of Household Resources and Standards of Living*, Penguin Books, Harmondsworth 1979.

61 T. Goedemé, *European Inequalities: Recent Changes in Social Cohesion and Social Inclusion Compared*, CSB Working Paper (forthcoming).

directive. In order to be feasible and legitimate, a policy-relevant threshold must to an extent be embedded in an absolute notion of destitution and incapacity to satisfy one's basic needs. In a European context, this implies that poverty in the richer Member States should not be overestimated, while that in the poorer ones must not be underestimated. Insofar as the richer countries are concerned, the 60% threshold would appear to be a reasonable measure of the resources required for a minimum acceptable way of life. Indeed, this threshold is since long applied in those Member States and it seems to enjoy wide legitimacy in public discourse. For that matter, as far as Belgium is concerned, the EU poverty threshold corresponds quite closely with alternative measures recently obtained through the budget method (albeit that the cost of children is estimated differently and the equivalence scales applied diverge from the OECD scales used in the calculation of the EU threshold).[62] However, looking at the poorer Member States, it is far less clear to what extent the EU poverty threshold is aligned to what is considered a minimum acceptable way of life. After EU enlargement, the 60% threshold has come under fire, not least because of the counter intuitively low poverty rates obtained for some of the newly acceded countries. It is therefore necessary to confirm the validity of the prevailing threshold through the budget method, particularly in the new Member States.[63]

It is nonetheless our conviction that the notion of relative income poverty that underlies the EU social indicators goes to the heart of the European social model. As the European Commission asserts, the 'key challenge is to make the whole population share the benefits of high average prosperity'.[64] This outlook differs fundamentally from that underlying the American poverty notion, where the official poverty line is determined by the cost of an adequate food basket multiplied by a factor to take account of other spending and merely adjusted for price evolutions.[65] The European concern goes beyond 'severe deprivation of basic human needs, including food, safe drinking water, sanitation facilities, health, shelter, education and information', which the United Nations uses – and justifiably so – as a starting point for defining a global notion of poverty.[66] The

---

62 B. Storms and K. Van den Bosch, *Wat heeft een gezin minimaal nodig? Een budgetstandaard voor Vlaanderen*, Acco, Leuven 2009.

63 See also W. Van Lancker, n. 58 and EAPN, 'Using reference budgets for drawing up the requirements of a minimum income scheme and assessing adequacy. Synthesis Report' (2010) Peer Review in Social Protection and Social Inclusion and Assessment in Social Inclusion <www.peer-review-social-inclusion.eu/peer-reviews/2010/using-reference-budgets-for-drawing-up-the-requirements-of-a-minimum-income-scheme-and-assessing-adequacy> accessed 13 October 2011.

64 European Commission, 'Joint Report on Social Inclusion', Brussels 2004.

65 K. Couch and A. Zaidi, *Measuring Poverty: Lessons from Europe*, Oxford University Press, New York *forthcoming*.

66 United Nations, *The Millennium Development Goals Report 2009*, United Nations, Geneva 2009.

EU's poverty concept is not restricted either to situations of serious dependency that cannot be resolved through macro policy,[67] nor to social exclusion in the sense of a permanent dependency on the State.[68] Instead, it refers much more generally to 'people whose resources are so seriously below those commanded by the average individual or family in their country that they run the risk of being excluded from ordinary living patterns, customs and activities'.[69] The latter part of this definition is particularly relevant to determine a standard for the adequacy of social assistance benefits. Europeans consider social protection not so much as an instrument for lifting individuals out of poverty, but rather as a means of preventing poverty from occurring in the first place. If social inclusion is the overriding objective, then the guaranteed minimum incomes should make it possible to achieve that goal.

Still, as mentioned in part two, there is no country in Europe with a social assistance system in place that guarantees an income anywhere near the 60% threshold. Most countries guarantee an income between 40 and 50% of median income or lower. Consequently, the budgetary burden of introducing guaranteed minimum incomes of 60% of standardized median income would be quite substantial.

5.2. BUDGETARY BURDEN

So what would the budgetary impact be of the introduction of minimum social assistance equal to the EU poverty threshold? Figure 4 provides an overview of calculations based on guaranteed minimums equal to 60%, 50% and 40% of the relevant median national income. In these rough calculations, based on 2008 EU-SILC data (incomes of 2007), household incomes are augmented to the poverty line. It should be emphasized that many practical and technical aspects are ignored in this exercise, so that the result is merely tentative or illustrative. For example, it is implicitly assumed that introducing such a guaranteed minimum income will affect neither taxes paid nor other benefits claimed by the households. It is also assumed that the poverty threshold is fixed.

The tentative calculations show that the total cost of an increase of minimum social benefits to the 60% poverty threshold would amount to over EUR 130 billion, which corresponds to 2.7% of the total disposable income in the EU

67 R. Dahrendorf, *The Modern Social Conflict. An Essay on the Politics of Liberty*, University of California Press, Berkeley 1990.

68 G. Engbersen, 'Moderne armoede' (1991) 37 *Sociologische Gids*.

69 P. Townsend, *A Sociological Approach to the Measurement of Poverty – A Rejoinder to Professor Amartya Sen*, Oxford Economic Papers, Oxford 1985.

(France excluded). Clearly the financial effort required for all countries to attain the 60% level is considerable. Moreover, it is unequally divided between the Member States. In the Czech Republic, Austria and Hungary, the measure would require less than 1.5% of the total disposable income; in Spain, Romania and Latvia, it would require over 4.5%.

As a first step towards a more adequate income protection in Europe, one might consider aligning minimum incomes to the 50% poverty threshold. After all, in many Member States the lowest benefits are far below this line. The budgetary impact of increasing minimum benefits across to the Union to 50% of median standardised income would be EUR 73 billion (1.5% of disposable income, ranging from 0.50% in the Czech Republic to 2.5% in Lithuania).

Figure 4. Gap with the 40%, 50%, 60% poverty lines for households at active age (18–64 years) as a percentage of total income (all households) by Member State

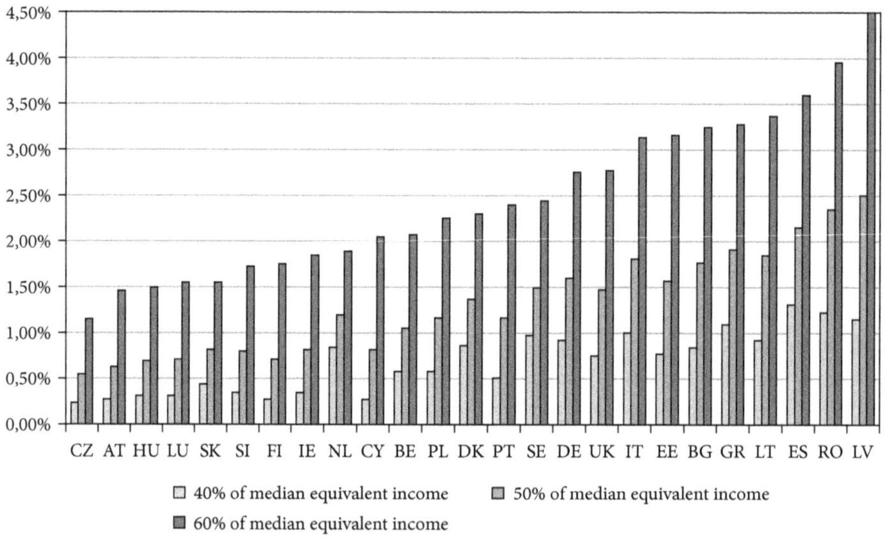

Source: own calculations (based on SILC 2008)[70]

Yet another, less ambitious but perhaps more realistic, alternative is a variant to Atkinson's proposal to guarantee a basic income for every child and defined as a percentage of median income in the Member State concerned.[71] Starting from this notion, Levy, Lietz and Sutherland simulated the consequences of the introduction in the EU of a basic income for each child, using the EUROMOD

70 The authors wish to thank Karel Van den Bosch and Aaron Van den Heede for their help with the calculations.

71 A.B. Atkinson, E. Marlier and A. Reinstadler, n. 2, p.22.

tax-benefit model.[72] They demonstrate that child poverty could be halved with a basic income for children between 18% and 27% of the median national income. However, their analysis is restricted to the old EU 15, while the data applied dates from 2001.

The simulation below deviates from Atkinson's proposal in that it assumes a purely selective supplement granted only to households whose income is below 60% of median standardized income. We use the same method as above and simulate the budgetary impact of increasing benefits to families with children who are below the poverty line so as to elevate their income to the threshold, but no higher. The total cost of such an operation is estimated to amount to 0.94% of the total disposable income in the EU. However, Figure 5 suggests that under this scenario, too, the effort required would be unevenly distributed among the various Member States. The countries of Eastern and Southern Europe would have to deploy over 1% of their total income mass, compared to just 0.5% for several countries of Northern and Central Europe.

Figure 5. Poverty gap for households with children as a percentage of total income (all households) per Member State

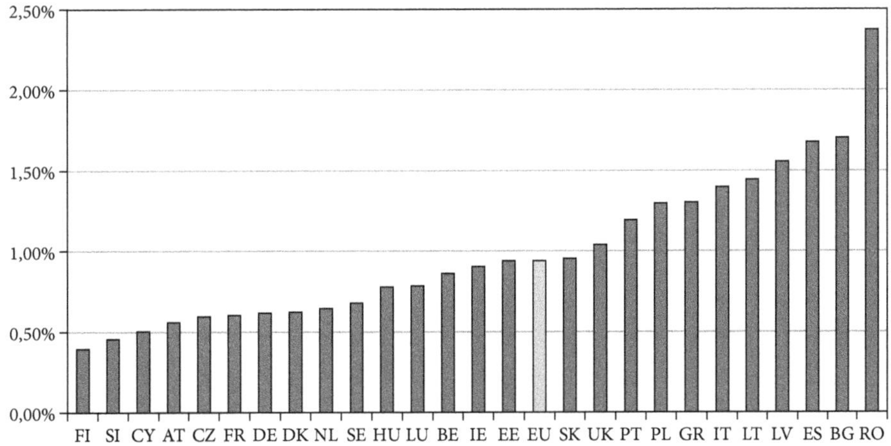

Source: Rijksdienst voor Kinderbijslag voor Werknemers,'Kinderbijslag in de strijd tegen armoede in Europa. Een studie: Sociale toeslagen in de Belgische kinderbijslag' (2010) Paper presented at the European Conference, Marche-en-Famenne, 2 – 3 September 2010 (based on SILC 2008).

72 H. Levy, C. Lietz and H. Sutherland, 'Swapping Policies: Alternative Tax-Benefit Strategies to Support Children in Austria, Spain and the UK' (2007) 36 *Journal of Social Policy*.

5.3. IMPACT ON DEPENDENCY TRAPS

An important political objection to increasing minimum benefits is that it would destroy the necessary tension between minimum wages and benefits. Table 3 illustrates the impact of higher minimum benefits on the difference in household income of social assistance claimants on the one hand and of minimum-wage earners on the other. The Europe-wide introduction of social assistance minimums equal to 60% of median income would create a financial inactivity trap in no fewer than eleven Member States: in Bulgaria, Estonia, Slovenia and Lithuania, the net income of a single benefit recipient would be between 25% and 30% higher than the equivalent income of a single person working at minimum wage; in Spain and the Czech Republic, the relative advantage of the benefit claimant would amount to between 14% and 16%. Less severe dependency traps would appear in Hungary, Luxembourg, Portugal and the United Kingdom. If the minimum benefits were to be raised to 50% of median standardized income, then the hypothetical unemployment traps would obviously be smaller, but they would still be substantial in the case of Lithuania, Slovenia, Estonia and Bulgaria (between 5 and 9%). Only if benefits were augmented to 40% of the median would it pay in all countries to switch from social benefits to minimum wage. These figures demonstrate that, given the great heterogeneity between the Member States, any binding agreement with regard to minimum social assistance incomes would have to be formulated flexibly and introduced gradually.

As mentioned in the third section of this chapter, such large differences in the severity of the dependency trap coincides with a great diversity in activation measures. In some Eastern European countries, a genuine activation policy would appear to be lacking thus far. In countries such as Lithuania and Estonia, the only incentive for social assistance recipients to seek work is the enormous gap between benefits and wages. An increase in benefit amounts would appear to be feasible there only if a new balance is struck between the rights and duties of benefit claimants. A Europe-wide agreement on minimum income protection would only seem possible if convergence is also achieved in the field of activation. Moreover, introducing a reasonable social assistance income inevitably raises the question of minimum wages, which – as the above data demonstrate – are inadequate in many countries.

Table 2. Net social assistance benefits as a percentage of net minimum wage under the assumption that net social assistance benefits are increased to 40–50–60% of median household income, single persons, 2009

	Raise to 40% of median household income	*Raise to 50% of median household income*	*Raise to 60% of median household income*
Austria (Vienna)	61	76	92
Belgium	53	66	79
Bulgaria	85	106	127
Czech Republic	76	96	115
Denmark	44	55	66
Estonia	86	108	129
Finland	54	67	81
France	58	72	87
Germany	50	62	74
Hungary	71	89	107
Ireland	57	71	85
Italy (Milan)	57	71	85
Latvia	51	64	77
Lithuania	85	106	128
Luxembourg	73	92	110
the Netherlands	55	69	83
Poland	66	82	99
Portugal	70	88	105
Romania	61	77	92
Slovakia	75	93	112
Slovenia	88	110	132
Spain (Catalonia)	78	97	116
Sweden	57	71	85
UK	70	87	105

Source: CSB-MIPI data (N. Van Mechelen, S. Marchal, T. Goedemé, I. Marx and B. Cantillon, n. 43.)

6. CONCLUSION

So which policy tools might Europe deploy in an effort to incorporate the rationale of social cohesion and social justice in a more forceful way in policy discourse and policymaking? In this chapter, we have approached this question from a social policy perspective. Assuming that any step towards a more social Europe will inevitably be modest and that it must, moreover, be grounded on established ideas and present opportunities, the introduction of an adequate minimum income guarantee would appear to be a likely candidate for a pioneering European legislative initiative in the sphere of social protection. Indeed, the notion has been persistently present in European policy discourse for many years, and most

Member States already have in place (admittedly quite divergent) systems of minimum income protection. A binding agreement between the Member States in this area is, moreover, desirable. Research has, after all, shown that adequate income protection is an important component in any effective anti-poverty policy, but the present approach of 'soft coordination' has proven unsuccessful in preventing erosion of minimum income protection in many countries. This has no doubt contributed to the failure of anti-poverty policy under the Lisbon Strategy.

As, in the absence of a social adequacy logic in the legal toolset of the European Union, there is justified concern over growing negative pressure on the national systems of social protection, generated by the compelling logic of economic integration, it would seem useful to set common minimum income standards, not only as a guideline for national governments, but also to resolve the juristic asymmetry between economic and social standards.[73] Such a regulation would, for the first time in the history of European unification, explicitly incorporate the social adequacy logic into the legal framework of the EU. In addition to guaranteeing an adequate income to needy households, this might encourage Member States to develop an effective activation policy. It could moreover form a solid foundation under the overall architecture of social protection, including minimum wages.

However, there are considerable politico-legal, conceptual and practical obstacles to be overcome in the implementation of such a strategy. One concerns the questionability of the validity of the EU poverty thresholds (defined as 60% of median income), leading to uncertainty over what is the most appropriate way of defining an adequate minimum income. This holds in particular in relation to the poorer EU Member States. In this sense, a validation of the EU threshold by means of country-specific budget standards may be worthwhile.[74] In many countries, the budgetary burden of raising social assistance benefits would moreover be quite substantial and any such measure would generate significant unemployment traps. Given the great heterogeneity between countries, any binding agreements on minimum incomes will have to be worded flexibly, introduced gradually and implemented in unison with a convergence in activation measures and minimum wages. In this context, priority must be given to measures aimed at covering the cost of child-rearing, restricted in an initial phase to guaranteeing to all families with children an income equal to 40% of median standardized income. This goal may seem to be lacking in ambition, but, like the national social protection systems, the social Europe will need to be established incrementally, step by step.

---

73 See for example F.W. Scharpf, n. 6; S. Leibfried and P. Pierson, n. 5.

74 T. Goedemé, B. Storms and K. Van den Bosch, 'Budget Standards: An Alternative to the Current European Poverty Line' (2011) Paper for the 18th FISS International Research Seminar on 'Issues in Social Security', Sigtuna, Sweden.

Appendix: Table 1. Aspects of activation policy for social assistance recipients, 2009

	Net social assistance as % of net minimum wage for single person	*Share of social assistance recipients at active age participating in activation measures*	*Failure to turn up for a training or job-seeking meeting*		*Share affected by punitive measures*
			Maximum punishment (for first infringement)	Duration	
Austria (Vienna)	66	Approx. 33%	50% cut	2 months	Low
Belgium	59	Approx. 20%	Benefit cut/ suspension[75]	1 month	Low
Bulgaria	37	Approx. 20%	Benefit termination	n.a.	n.a.
Czech Republic	74	n.a.	50% benefit cut	n.a.	n.a.
Germany	No national minimum wage	13% of all benefit recipients (17% of work-able benefit recipients)	30% benefit cut	3 months	2.5% of benefit recipients (June 2009)
Denmark	No national minimum wage	Almost all	Benefit cut	Until end of infringement	49%
Estonia	43	n.a.	Benefit termination (re-offenders only)	n.a.	Low
Spain	71	In principle: all	No standard	No standard	n.a.
Finland	No national minimum wage	n.a.	20% benefit cut	2 months	n.a.
France	62	n.a.	No standard	No standard	n.a.
Ireland	64	n.a.	Suspension	9 months	Low
Italy (Milan)	56[76]	n.a.	No standard	No standard	Low, but increasing
Lithuania	46	n.a.	No standard	No standard	2.4% of those entitled (2009)
Luxembourg	95	9% of all benefit recipients (incl. children and elderly persons)	Benefit termination	3 months	n.a.

75 If participation in training is part of the claimant's so-called Individualised Project for Social Integration.
76 Minimum wage in the fur and leather industry.

	Net social assistance as % of net minimum wage for single person	*Share of social assistance recipients at active age participating in activation measures*	*Failure to turn up for a training or job-seeking meeting*		*Share affected by punitive measures*
			Maximum punishment (for first infringement)	Duration	
Latvia	57	n.a.	Benefit termination	Until end of infringement	n.a.
the Netherlands	77	78%	Benefit cut by between 5 and 100%	No maximum	17% of entitled households (2004)
Poland	49	n.a.	No standard	No standard	n.a.
Portugal	45	n.a.	Benefit termination	24 months	2.8% of those entitled (December 2008)
Romania	23	n.a.	Suspension	3 months	14.07% of those entitled
Sweden (Stockholm)	No national minimum wage	Local initiatives (excl. national programmes): 20–25%	Benefit cut or suspension	Rest of the month	10%[77]
Slovenia	64	Very low	Benefit termination	6 months	17% of the entitled aged between 15–64 (June 2009)
Slovakia	44	n.a.	No standard	No standard	n.a.
United Kingdom	33	Approx. 11%	Suspension	1 to 26 weeks	10% (average since April 2000)

Source: CSB-MIPI data (N. Van Mechelen, S. Marchal, T. Goedemé, I. Marx and B. Cantillon, n. 43.)

77 Over 50% of the social assistance claimants between 18 and 25 have their benefit amounts cut due to non-participation in activation programmes. Approx. 10% of social assistance claimants have their social assistance benefits cut for other reasons.

UNION LAW AND THE FIGHT AGAINST POVERTY: WHICH LEGAL INSTRUMENTS?

Herwig VERSCHUEREN

1. INTRODUCTION

Ever since the launch of the Lisbon Strategy in 2000 the EU has paid full regard to the fight against poverty and social exclusion when formulating policy objectives and instruments. It was a central theme within the context of the Open Method of Coordination in the field of social protection and social inclusion as well as in the employment strategy.[1] This objective has further been confirmed for the coming 10 years by the conclusions of the European Council of 17 June 2010 on the Europe 2020 Strategy. Indeed, the European Council adopted an EU headline target for promoting social inclusion, in particular through the reduction of poverty, by aiming to lift at least 20 million people out of the risk of poverty and exclusion by 2020. It was also taken on board by the Europe 2020 Strategy Integrated Guidelines, including the Broad Guidelines for the Economic Policies adopted by the Council on 8 June 2010 and the Guidelines for the Employment Policies adopted by the Council on 21 October 2010, in particular Guideline 10 'Promoting social inclusion and combating poverty'. Furthermore, on 20 October 2010 the European Parliament adopted a report on the role on minimum income in combating poverty and promoting an inclusive society in Europe.[2] In this document the European Parliament recalls the numerous initiatives taken, both in the past and recently, at the level of the EU and at international level to combat poverty and calls upon the EU institutions and the Member States to take new initiatives and strengthen

1 For recent analysis, see amongst others: K. ARMSTRONG, *Governing Social Inclusion. Europeanization through Policy Coordination*, Oxford University Press, Oxford 2010; H. FRAZER, E. MARLIER and I. NICAISE, *A Social Inclusion Roadmap for Europe 2020*, Garant, Antwerp 2010; M. HEIDENREICH and P. ZEITLIN (eds.), *Changing European Employment and Welfare Regimes: The Influence of the Open Method of Coordination on National Labour and Social Welfare Reforms*, Routledge, London 2009.

2 INI/2010/2039.

their policies in this field. On 16 December 2010 the European Commission adopted a communication on 'The European Platform against Poverty and Social Exclusion'.[3] This communication presents different policies to contribute to the goal of reducing poverty and increasing inclusion and also proposes a number of actions. These policy goals were endorsed by the Council of Ministers in its conclusions on this platform of 7 March 2011.[4]

The main objective of these European policy initiatives is to support the Member States in their national policies to combat poverty. However, they do not have a direct impact on legal claims for financial or other support of persons faced with poverty or social exclusion.

Still, in the meantime these objectives found their way into legal instruments of the EU, and more specifically into the Treaties as amended in the Lisbon Treaty that came into force on 1 December 2009. Article 9 TFEU declares that 'in defining and implementing its policies and activities, the Union shall take into account requirements linked to (…) the fight against social exclusion (…)'.[5] In this context the Council of Ministers in its conclusion of 6 December 2010 on the 'Social dimension in the context of an integrated Europe 2020 Strategy' invited the Commission 'to promote and reinforce the social component of the Commission's Impact Assessment system's integrated approach as a key instrument to ensure full reflection at EU level on Article 9 TFEU and the objective of Europe 2020' (point 19).[6] Furthermore, Article 3.3 TEU declares that the construction of the internal market is to be realized by means of policies based on 'a highly competitive social market economy, aiming at full employment and social progress'. This article moreover confirms that: 'It (i.e. the EU) shall combat social exclusion (…)'. Article 151.1 TFEU also refers to the combating of social exclusion as an objective of the Union and the Member States. These goals are also reflected in the Charter of Fundamental Rights, which in its Article 34.3 states that

> '*in order to combat social exclusion and poverty, the Union recognizes and respects the right to social and housing assistance so as to ensure a decent existence for all those*

---

3 European Commission, 'The European Platform against Poverty and Social Exclusion: A European framework for social and territorial cohesion' (Communication) COM (2010) 758 final.

4 See <http://register.consilium.europa.eu/pdf/en/11/st07/st07434-re01.en11.pdf> accessed 25 August 2011.

5 Advocate General Cruz Villalon qualified the provision of Article 9 TFEU as a 'social obligation': Case C-515/08 *Criminal proceedings against Vítor Manuel dos Santos Palhota and Others* [2010] ECR I-*not yet reported*, Opinion of AG Cruz Villalon, paras. 51–52.

6 See <http://register.consilium.europa.eu/pdf/en/10/st16/st16512.en10.pdf> accessed 25 August 2011.

who lack sufficient resources, in accordance with the rules laid down by Union law and national law and practices'.

Furthermore, Article 1 of the Charter of Fundamental Rights states that human dignity is inviolable and must be protected and respected.

There is no doubt that the fight against poverty and social exclusion is a policy objective that is high on the political agenda of the European institutions. But in this chapter we intend to examine to what degree the EU institutions could take legislative and legally binding initiatives or have already taken with a view to preventing and combating poverty and social exclusion.

First we will examine the question of whether the EU has the power to adopt legally binding instruments with regard to the fight against poverty and social exclusion. This could involve European rules to be complied with by the Member States in the development of their legislation guaranteeing a minimum income to all persons or certain categories of persons or in certain circumstances. However, we shall find that this kind of European legislation is not only lacking but also that it is very doubtful that the European institutions have the power to adopt such legislation at European level.

Yet, in situations concerning the right of Union citizens to reside and move freely within the Union, European legislature and case law have paid a lot of attention to the legal position of the migrating Union citizens when they are confronted with financial problems. We will have a closer look at this legislation and case law and analyse to what extent persons who are not capable of providing for themselves can or cannot exercise the fundamental right of free movement of persons, and whether or not they can invoke EU law to claim financial support in a host Member State. From this it will become clear that Union law regarding free movement of persons offers very strong legal instruments to protect migrating Union citizens who are in danger of getting into financial difficulties when they find themselves in a Member State other than their own. This legislation and case law led to an ample debate on the boundaries, within the EU context, of the national solidarity systems.

There appears to be a big discrepancy between the lack of a clear legal basis for a binding EU legal instrument with regard to minimum income on the one hand, and the extensive EU legal framework, including case law of the Court of Justice to prevent both economically active and economically inactive citizens moving within the Union from ending up in poverty, on the other.

2. EU LEGAL INSTRUMENTS FOR GUARANTEEING A MINIMUM INCOME: LEGAL AND POLITICAL BASIS

2.1. PROVIDING ADEQUATE INCOME SUPPORT AS A PILLAR IN THE ACTIVE INCLUSION STRATEGY

In this part we will examine the question of whether new legally binding initiatives at EU level could be taken to oblige the Member States to guarantee their citizens a minimum income.

As early as 1992 the Commission submitted a proposal for a directive regarding minimum income, but it was downgraded to a mere recommendation, more specifically Council Recommendation 92/441/EEC of 24 June 1992 on common criteria concerning sufficient resources and social assistance in social protection systems.[7] The Council only recommended Member States to recognize the basic right of a person to sufficient resources and social assistance to live in a manner compatible with human dignity as part of a comprehensive and consistent drive to combat social exclusion, and to adapt their social protection systems.

More recently, providing adequate income support has been recognized by the EU institutions as an essential pillar in the so-called active inclusion strategy. In its recommendation of 3 October 2008 the Commission recommends the Member States to recognize '*the individual's <u>basic right to resources and social assistance</u> sufficient to lead a life that is compatible with human dignity as part of a comprehensive consistent drive to combat social exclusion*' (point 4(a)).[8] Moreover, the European Parliament in its resolution of 6 May 2009 specifically pointed out that any active inclusion strategy has to be built on <u>the principles of individual rights</u> and called on the Member States to implement adequate income support so as to fight poverty and social exclusion (points 1 and 4).[9] The European Parliament explicitly stressed again the role of minimum income in combating poverty and promoting an inclusive society in its resolution of 20 October 2010 on this subject (see for instance points 1, 6 and 14).[10]

---

7 [1992] OJ L245/46.

8 See Commission Recommendation 2008/867/EC of 3 October 2008 on the active inclusion of people excluded from the labour market [2008] OJ L307/11 and the related Commission Communication COM (2008) 639 of 3 October 2008.

9 European Parliament Resolution of 6 May 2009 on the active inclusion of people excluded from the labour market [2010] OJ C212E/23.

10 INI/2010/2039.

In its conclusions of 17 December 2008 the Council of Ministers also confirmed adequate income support as being the first pillar of the active inclusion strategy.[11] The Council acknowledged that active inclusion entails a combination of adequate income support, inclusive labour markets and access to quality services. Active inclusion policies are intended for all those excluded from the labour market by supporting them with the resources they need to lead a dignified life and with opportunities for social participation, and promoting access to quality and lasting employment that corresponds to their aptitudes and abilities (point 19). However, the Council also emphasized that active inclusion is not a single-model approach. With due regard for the principle of subsidiarity and on the basis of the common principles, the Member States shall define the level of adequate income support and the policy mix best adapted to the needs identified at local, regional and national level (point 24).[12] For the Council it is clear that the instruments necessary for adequate income support have to be provided for by the Member States themselves.

Ideas on a legally binding instrument kept turning up and have recently been presented once again. Ferrera and Sacchi suggested in 2007 that the issue of a minimum income guarantee would deserve much attention insofar as it may well be a very promising way of securing the social complements of the internal market. Such a guarantee might take the form of EU legal provisions regulating minimum income schemes at national level.[13] In their study of 2009 on the minimum income schemes in the Member States, Frazer and Marlier suggest that in order to reinforce the importance of the minimum income schemes within the active inclusion agenda consideration might be given to adopting an EU framework directive on the adequacy of minimum income schemes which would incorporate agreed common criteria.[14] In addition, a number of organizations, in particular the European Anti Poverty Network (EAPN), made

---

11 See <http://register.consilium.europa.eu/pdf/en/08/st15/st15984.en08.pdf> accessed 25 August 2011.

12 For an extensive study of the implementation of these recent initiatives see, inter alia, H. Frazer and E. Marlier, *Minimum Income Schemes Across EU Member States,* EU Network of National Independent Experts on Social Inclusion, 2009. This study assesses the key strengths and weaknesses of the minimum income schemes across the Union and their impact on reducing poverty and social exclusion. Generally speaking the conclusion of this report is that the current EU instruments have not produced the desired outcome. To be consulted on <www.ceps.lu/pdf/11/art1464.pdf?CFID=451345&CFTOKEN=25257824&jsessionid=84304d3530c875f0d8e84b234493f7535374> accessed 25 August 2011. See also E. Marlier, T. Atkinson, B. Cantillon and B. Nolan, *The EU and Social Inclusion. Facing the Challenges*, The Policy Press, Bristol 2009.

13 M. Ferrera and S. Sacchi, 'A More Social EU? In What Areas? In What Forms?' (2007) 1 *European Governance.*

14 H. Frazer and E. Marlier, n. 12, p. 13.

a number of concrete proposals regarding such a framework directive on minimum income.[15]

Furthermore, during the discussion in the autumn of 2010 in the European Parliament regarding the abovementioned resolution on the role of minimum income in combating poverty and promoting an inclusive society,[16] a number of political groups also suggested asking the European Commission to submit a proposal for a European framework directive on minimum income. Such a framework directive would create a legal obligation for the Member States to introduce effective minimum income schemes. However, on 20 October 2010 these proposals were rejected during the plenary vote. In its resolution the European Parliament only takes the view that the Commission should study the impact which a legislative proposal it might submit concerning the introduction of an adequate minimum income at European level would have in each Member State (point 21).

We will now examine in more detail whether initiatives like these are even legally possible.

2.2. EU LEGISLATIVE COMPETENCES FOR A DIRECTIVE ON MINIMUM INCOME SCHEMES

In the introduction we already mentioned a series of provisions in EU Treaties that refer to the Union's objectives regarding the fight against social exclusion. However, the fact that the objectives are formulated does not suffice to grant the Union power as regards the approval of a legal instrument to oblige the Member States to take initiatives, for instance regarding minimum income schemes.

Indeed, Article 5 TEU explicitly declares that the limits of Union competences are governed by the principle of conferral and that the use of these competences is governed by the principles of subsidiarity and proportionality. Under the principle of conferral, the Union shall act only within the limits of the competences conferred upon it by the Member States in the Treaties. Article 1.1 TFEU refers to this principle by stating that this Treaty organizes the functioning of the Union and determines the areas of, delimitation of, and arrangements for exercising its competences. Article 7 TFEU adds to this that the Union shall ensure consistency between its policies and activities in accordance with the principle of conferral of powers.

---

15 A. Van Lancker, *Working Document on a Framework Directive on Minimum Income*, EAPN, Brussels 2010.

16 INI/2010/2039.

So we have to look for a specific legal basis in the TFEU, on the grounds of which the European legislator could adopt a directive or another compulsory instrument. This could perhaps be found in Title X of the TFEU on 'Social Policy'. Article 153.1 (j) TFEU explicitly mentions 'the combating of social exclusion' as a field in which the Union shall support and complement the activities of the Member States with a view to achieving the objectives of Article 151 TFEU. However, Article 153.2 (a) TFEU limits the measures that the Union <u>may</u> adopt in the field of 'the combating of social exclusion' to measures designed to encourage cooperation between Member States through initiatives aimed at improving knowledge, developing exchanges of information and best practices, promoting innovative approaches and evaluating experiences, excluding any harmonization of the laws and regulations of the Member States.[17] By contrast, Article 153.2 (b) TFEU does not include the field of 'the combating of social exclusion' where it allows the Union to adopt minimum requirements for gradual implementation by means of directives.

However, other fields listed in Article 153.1 TFEU could also be considered to be related to minimum income schemes. First, in the field of 'social security and social protection of workers' (Article 153.1 (c) TFEU) the Union may support and complement the Member States' activities by means of directives laying down minimum requirements because Article 153.2 (b) TFEU applies to this field.[18] It must be said from the outset that so far the Union has never used this specific power in the field of 'social security and social protection of workers'.[19] But we do have to mention the very broad interpretation the Court of Justice gave to the concept of 'social security' in the context of the EU coordination of social security systems for migrating persons. Benefits intended to complement insufficient social security benefits fall, according to this case law, under this coordination of the Member States' social security schemes and therefore under the term 'social security' (see further point 3.6.). However, it would seem that the field covered by Article 153.1 (c) TFEU is limited to social rights for workers and therefore not an appropriate legal basis for EU legislation on generally applicable minimum income schemes.

---

17 See also in this respect the mandate of the Social Protection Committee in Article 160 TFEU.

18 Article 153.2 paragraph 3 TFEU stipulates however that in the field of 'social security and social protection of workers' the Council shall act unanimously, in accordance with a special legislative procedure, after consulting the European Parliament, the Economic and Social Committee and the Committee of the Regions. Furthermore Article 153.4 TFEU states that the provisions adopted pursuant to Article 153 TFEU shall not affect the right of Member States to define the fundamental principles of their social security systems and must not significantly affect the financial equilibrium thereof.

19 The only harmonizing initiatives to have been taken in this field are a number of directives concerning the equal treatment of men and women in matters of social security. However, these measures were taken in the context of the prohibition on discrimination on grounds of sex. See for instance Council Directive 79/7/EEC of 19 December 1978 on the progressive implementation of the principle of equal treatment for men and women in matters of social security [1979] OJ L6/24.

Hence, EU legislation on minimum pay could be considered as coming under the field of 'working conditions' mentioned in Article 153.1 (b) TFEU. Yet, Article 153.5 TFEU explicitly excludes 'pay' from the scope of the Union competences under Article 153 TFEU, which, in principle, makes it impossible for the EU to adopt directives that include provisions on minimum pay for workers.

Another field mentioned in Article 153.1 TFEU that could be used as a basis for an EU legislative instrument would be 'the integration of persons excluded from the labour market' (Article 153.1 (h) TFEU). Indeed, the abovementioned policy initiatives of the Commission, the European Parliament and the Council on the active inclusion strategy, refer in their titles to the active inclusion of people excluded from the labour market.[20] All these initiatives mention adequate income support as an essential pillar in this so-called active inclusion strategy. In its communication of 3 October 2008 (COM (2008) 639) on the active inclusion of people excluded from the labour market the Commission starts by stating that

> *'Combating social exclusion and poverty is among the priorities of the European Union, whose action in this area is based on Article 137 EC (now Article 153 TFEU). With regard to fundamental social rights, the latter also provides that 'the Community shall support and complement the activities of the Member States in (…) the integration of persons excluded from the labour market.'*

So the Commission explicitly referred to the text of Article 153.1 (h) TFEU on the integration of persons excluded from the labour market, as the basis for action on the combating of social exclusion and poverty. Moreover, the Council in its conclusions of 17 December 2008 on common active inclusion principles to combat poverty more effectively, also explicitly refers to Article 137.1 (h) EC (now Article 153.1 (h) TFEU) as a legal basis for its conclusions on adequate income support (point 5).[21]

So, there seems to be a consensus to use the field of 'integration of persons excluded from the labour market' to adopt measures in the field of the combating of social exclusion and poverty as well. The first field allows the EU legislature to adopt minimum requirements by means of a directive under the ordinary legislative procedure pursuant to Article 153.2 (b) TFEU. However, such conclusions could be in contradiction with the provisions of Article 153.1 (j) TFEU combined with Article 153.2 (a) TFEU which does not allow the adoption of minimum requirements in the field of 'the combating of social exclusion'.

---

20 See above the references in n. 7, n. 8 and n. 9.

21 See <http://register.consilium.europa.eu/pdf/en/08/st15/st15984.en08.pdf> accessed 25 August 2011.

Moreover, such a directive could only relate to persons excluded from the labour market, whereas the problem of poverty also exists among workers themselves.

This analysis shows that it is doubtful that Article 153 TFEU offers a sufficient legal basis for the approval of a directive with regard to minimum income schemes.

But, even if it would be accepted that there is a legal basis, the measures adopted should respect the subsidiarity and proportionality principle. The principle of subsidiarity means that the Union shall only act if the objectives of the proposed action cannot be sufficiently achieved by the Member States and can therefore, by reason of the scale or effects of the proposed action, be better achieved at Union level (Article 5.3 TEU). The principle of proportionality means that the content and form of the Union action shall not exceed what is necessary to achieve the objectives of the Treaties (Article 5.4 TEU). In this context it is clear that the Member States themselves have to remain responsible for the structure and content of their minimum income schemes or social security schemes guaranteeing a minimum income. So a directive would only call upon the Member States to guarantee the right to an adequate minimum income and would at the same time allow the Member States to maintain a broad sphere of competence with regard to the choice of instruments to achieve this objective, even if this is legally enforceable. A directive could include a methodology to determine in each of the Member States what would be considered an adequate minimum income, which a citizen would be entitled to pursuant to this directive.[22]

However, the legal and especially the political feasibility of a directive on minimum income that would be legally binding for the Member States remains uncertain. Perhaps Article 153 TFEU could offer a legal basis through the field of 'the integration of persons excluded from the labour market' of Article 153.1 (h) TFEU in which the EU legislature would have the power to adopt a directive with minimum requirements. But this remains disputable. Furthermore, such an instrument could only be realized after an initiative on the part of the European Commission and with the approval of the European Parliament and the Council of Ministers by means of the ordinary legislative procedure. As far as the Commission is concerned we cannot but find that this institution in its most recent initiative, notably in its communication of 16 December 2010 on the 'European Platform against Poverty and Social Exclusion',[23] no longer mentions initiatives regarding the guarantee of minimum income and certainly not any legal instruments. The entire platform hardly announces any legislative initiatives

22 See for a detailed proposal: A. Van Lancker, n. 15.

23 European Commission, n. 3.

that could lead to legally binding texts.[24] And during the vote of 20 October 2010 on the resolution on the role of minimum income in combating poverty and promoting an inclusive society the European Parliament also rejected the proposal of a number of political groups to ask the European Commission for a proposal on a European framework directive on minimum income. The Council of Ministers for its part never showed any interest in a legislative initiative by the EU to combat poverty and social exclusion and always emphasized the Member States' competence in this respect. For instance in its conclusions of 17 December 2008,[25] the Council of Ministers underlined that with due regard for the principle of subsidiarity and on the basis of the common principles, the Member States shall define the level of adequate income support and the policy mix best adapted to the needs identified at local, regional and national level.

So it is highly unlikely that a legally binding EU instrument is politically feasible, even if it had a legal basis in the TFEU.

3. FREE MOVEMENT OF PERSONS AND THE RIGHT TO MINIMUM SUBSISTENCE BENEFITS

3.1. LEGAL FRAMEWORK

In the absence of any harmonization or adoption of minimum requirements at EU level, EU law does not detract from the powers of the Member States to organize their social security and social assistance systems, including minimum income schemes. However, the Court of Justice has always emphasized that the Member States must nevertheless comply with EU law when exercising those powers.[26]

In particular the principles of free movement of persons (now Articles 21, 45, 49 and 56 TFEU) played and continue to play an important role in this field. These principles are laid down in the relevant secondary legislation. Regulation 1612/68 on the free movement for workers[27] and Directive 2004/38 on residence rights

---

24 The only proposal refers to a legislative initiative to ensure access to certain basic banking services: see p. 8.

25 See <http://register.consilium.europa.eu/pdf/en/08/st15/st15984.en08.pdf> accessed 25 August 2011.

26 See for instance Case C-158/96 *Raymond Kohll v. Union des caisses de maladie* [1998] ECR I-1931, paras. 17–19 (hereinafter *Kholl)* and more recent Case C-228/07 *Jörn Petersen v. Landesgeschäftsstelle des Arbeitsmarktservice Niederösterreich* [2008] ECR I-6989, para. 42 (hereinafter *Petersen*).

27 Council Regulation (EEC) 1612/68 of 15 October 1968 on freedom of movement for workers within the Community [1968] OJ L275/2 (hereinafter Regulation 1612/68). It implements (now) Article 45 TFEU. This regulation was recently replaced by the European Parliament

for EU migrants and the members of their family,[28] are the first relevant EU legal instruments in this field. Both contain clauses on the prohibition of discrimination on grounds of nationality to be applied by the host State vis-à-vis workers and citizens of another Member State.[29] The ECJ considered these clauses to be applicable also to minimum subsistence benefit schemes of the Member States. However, for those Union citizens who are regarded as economically inactive, Directive 2004/38 contains a 'self-sufficiency' condition for the right to reside for more than three months in the host State. This condition may have an impact on the entitlement to social assistance benefits in the host State.[30] In addition to the application and interpretation of these secondary legal instruments, the Court of Justice chose for a direct application of the Treaty provisions on the free movement of persons in a number of cases concerning the right to social minimum benefits for migrating Union citizens.

Another important piece of EU legislation in this respect is the EU social security coordination system, which until 1 May 2010 was formalized by Regulation 1408/71[31] and Regulation 574/72[32] and from this date by Regulation 883/2004[33] and Regulation 987/2009.[34] These coordination rules are also applicable to a number of minimum subsistence schemes of the Member States.

---

and Council Regulation (EU) 492/2011 of 5 April 2011 on freedom of movement for workers within the Union [2011] OJ L141/1 (hereinafter Regulation 492/2011). This new regulation only codified the previous provisions of Regulation 1612/68, and did not alter their wording or legal meaning.

28 European Parliament and Council Directive 2004/38/EC of 29 April 2004 on the right of citizens of the Union and their family members to move and reside freely within the territory of the Member States [2004] OJ L158/77; 1st corrigendum [2004] OJ L 228/35; 2nd corrigendum (only for the English version) [2005] OJ L197/ 34 (hereinafter Directive 2004/38).

29 Article 7.2 of Regulation 1612/68 and Article 24 of Directive 2004/38.

30 See further in point 3.5 on possible limitations of the application of the non-discrimination principle on such benefits.

31 Council Regulation (EEC) 1408/71 of 14 June 1971 concerning the application of the social security schemes to employees and self-employed persons, as well as to their family members travelling within the Community [1971] OJ L149/2 (hereinafter Regulation 1408/71).

32 Council Regulation (EEC) 574/72 of 21 March 1972 laying down the procedure for implementing Regulation (EEC) 1408/71 [1972] OJ L74/1.

33 European Parliament and Council Regulation (EC) 883/2004 of 29 April 2004 on the coordination of the social security systems [2004] OJ L200/1, as amended by European Parliament and Council Regulation (EC) 988/2009 of 16 September 2009 [2009] OJ L284/43 (hereinafter Regulation 883/2004). See on this regulation the special issue of (2009) 11 *EJSS* and F. Pennings, *European Social Security Law*, Intersentia, Antwerp 2010. See also the special website of the European Commission on this coordination system, to be consulted on <http://ec.europa.eu/social/main.jsp?catId=26&langId=en> accessed 25 August 2011.

34 European Parliament and Council Regulation (EC) 987/2009 of 16 September 2009 [2009] OJ L294/1.

Further in this part we will examine to what degree and under which conditions these provisions of primary and secondary Union law guarantee the access to minimum subsistence benefits.

3.2. UNION LAW GUARANTEES ACCESS TO MINIMUM SUBSISTENCE BENEFITS IN THE HOST STATE TO POOR MIGRANT WORKERS

Regulation 1612/68 (now Regulation 492/2011) concerns the rights of workers and their family members who have made use of the right of free movement. This regulation does not only regulate the access to the labour market in the host State, but also the legal position of migrant workers and their family members. They can rely on the prohibition of discrimination on grounds of nationality which has also been included in Article 45.2 TFEU. This ban on discrimination does not only refer to working conditions, but also to all social and tax advantages granted by the legislation of the Member State of employment (Article 7.2 Regulation 1612/68, now Regulation 492/2011). The ECJ considers social assistance to be such a social advantage.[35]

The personal scope of these provisions has been interpreted very broadly by the ECJ. Any person who pursues activities which are real and genuine, to the exclusion of activities on such a small scale as to be regarded as purely marginal and ancillary, must be regarded as a 'worker'.[36] The origin of the funds from which the remuneration is paid or the limited amount of that remuneration cannot have any consequence in regard to whether or not the person is a 'worker'.[37] The fact that the income from employment is lower than the minimum required for subsistence does not prevent the person in such employment from being regarded as a 'worker' within the meaning of Article 45 TFEU and Regulation 1612/68 (now Regulation 492/2011),[38] even if the person in question seeks to supplement that remuneration by other means of subsistence such as financial assistance drawn from the public funds of the State in which he resides.[39] Furthermore, with regard to the duration of the activity pursued, the

---

35 Case 249/83 *Vera Hoeckx v. Openbaar Centrum voor Maatschappelijk Welzijn, Kalmthout* [1985] ECR 973 and Case 316/85 *Centre public d'aide sociale de Courcelles v. Marie-Christine Lebon* [1987] ECR 2811.

36 See, inter alia, Case 66/85 *Deborah Lawrie-Blum v. Land Baden-Württemberg* [1986] ECR 2121, paras. 16 and 17 and *Petersen*, para.45.

37 Case 344/87 *I. Bettray v. Staatssecretaris van Justitie* [1989] ECR 1621, para. 15, and Case C-10/05 *Cynthia Mattern and Hajrudin Cikotic v. Ministre du Travail et de l'Emploi* [2006] ECR I-3145, para. 22.

38 Case 53/81 *D.M. Levin v. Staatssecretaris van Justitie* [1982] ECR 1035, paras. 15 and 16, and Case C-317/93 *Inge Nolte v. Landesversicherungsanstalt Hannover* [1995] ECR I-4625, para. 19.

39 Case 139/85 *R. H. Kempf v. Staatssecretaris van Justitie* [1986] ECR 1741, para. 14.

fact that employment is of short duration cannot, in itself, exclude that employment from the scope of Article 45 TFEU.[40] Moreover, for the Court of Justice the income can also consist of an indirect contribution such as board and lodging.[41] Recently the Court explicitly confirmed this case law in a ruling of 4 June 2009.[42] The same case law also applies if EU migrants are self-employed persons.[43]

Apart from that, the provisions of Directive 2004/38 also show that there can be no resource requirement vis-à-vis citizens of other Member States who can prove that they are working as employed or self-employed persons within the meaning of this case law of the Court of Justice. The same applies to their family members.[44]

This case law implicates that poor migrant workers and self-employed persons, in the very broad sense of these terms, can claim social assistance and other minimum benefits in the host country where they are economically active, on an equal footing with the nationals of this host country. This is even the case when these workers only contribute to the economy of the host State to a limited extent. The social integration into the host society is seen by the ECJ as an instrument of promoting participation in the EU internal market and its economic goals of free movement of factors of production, even if their 'productivity' would be rather low. The rationale behind this case law has more to do with the 'internal market' than with the 'combating of social exclusion', even if this actually contributes to the latter.

3.3. UNION LAW GUARANTEES ACCESS TO MINIMUM SUBSISTENCE BENEFITS IN THE HOST STATE TO FORMER MIGRANT WORKERS AND THE MEMBERS OF THEIR FAMILY

Moreover, in some circumstances certain categories of economically inactive persons can invoke the EU provisions with regard to the free movement of

40 Case C-3/90 *M. J. E. Bernini v. Minister van Onderwijs en Wetenschappen* [1992] ECR I-1071, para. 16, and Case C-413/01 *Franca Ninni-Orasche v. Bundesminister für Wissenschaft, Verkehr und Kunst* [2003] ECR I-13187, para. 25 (hereinafter *Ninni-Orache).*

41 Case 196/87 *Udo Steymann v. Staatssecretaris van Justitie* [1988] ECR 6159.

42 Cases C-22/08 and C-23/08 *Athanasios Vatsouras and Josif Koupatantze v. Arbeitsgemeinschaft (ARGE) Nürnberg 900* [2009] ECR I-4585, paras. 26–29 (hereinafter *Vatsouras and Koupatantze*).

43 See Case 63/86 *Commission v. Italy* [1988] ECR 29, and Cases C-4/95 and C-5/95 *Fritz Stöber and José Manuel Piosa Pereira v. Bundesanstalt für Arbeit* [1997] ECR I-511.

44 See Article 7.1 (a) and Article 14.4 (a) Directive 2004/38. See point 3.5 for further analysis of the resources requirement applicable to economically inactive migrant citizens.

workers and the principle of equal treatment included therein. Indeed, the European legislator confirmed in Article 7.3 Directive 2004/38 that an EU citizen can maintain his status as an employee or self-employed person in certain circumstances, i.e. if he/she is temporarily unable to work as a result of illness or accident or is in duly recorded involuntary unemployment or embarks on vocational training.[45] In these circumstances the person concerned does not only retain the right to reside in the host State, but on the basis of Article 24.1 of this directive, he/she can claim the same treatment as the nationals of this host country with regard to all kinds of social benefits, including study finance grants for those on vocational training. In 2009 the ECJ expressly confirmed this in *Vatsouras* and *Koupatantze* concerning a dispute with regard to a German basic benefit in favour of jobseekers.[46] Normally these persons will be entitled to a number of social security benefits such as unemployment benefits or compensation for incapacity for work. But this does not rule out that these persons, because of the low amount of this benefit, find themselves in a state of poverty and have to ask for additional social assistance or other social minimum benefits.

So being economically active does not appear to be an absolute prerequisite for entitlement to equal treatment with workers from the host State. Persons finding themselves in an intermediate situation, because they are (temporarily) unemployed or started vocational training, remain covered by the provisions applicable to migrant workers. Hence the legal position of these economically inactive persons continues to be governed by the EU internal market law on the free movement of workers.

Furthermore, the right to access to social minimum benefits also applies to the worker's or ex-worker's economically inactive family members, even when they are no longer living together with this worker in the host State. This was illustrated by the recent judgments of the Court of Justice in *Ibrahim* and *Teixeira* of 23 February 2010.[47] These cases concerned single mothers, who were economically inactive and had applied for housing assistance in the UK. This was denied to them with the argument that their right of residence, and that of their children, was not based on EU law. To demonstrate that it did rest on EU

---

45 Unless the person involved is involuntarily unemployed, the retention of the status of worker shall require the training to be related to the previous employment. This provision was inspired by the case law of the Court of Justice: see for instance Case 39/86 *Sylvie Lair v. Universität Hannover* [1988] ECR 3161 and *Ninni-Orache*.

46 *Vatsouras and Koupatantze*, paras. 31–32.

47 Case C-310/08 *London Borough of Harrow v. Nimco Hassan Ibrahim and Secretary of State for the Home Department* [2010] ECR I-1065 (hereinafter *Ibrahim*) and Case C-480/08 *Maria Teixeira v. London Borough of Lambeth and Secretary of State for the Home Department* [2010] ECR I-1107 (hereinafter *Teixeira*).

law, both mothers invoked Article 12 of Regulation 1612/68 (now Article 10 of Regulation 492/2011). This provision grants the children of EU migrant workers the right to access to general education, apprenticeship and vocational training. In these judgments the ECJ confirmed its earlier case law that, pursuant to Article 12 of Regulation 1612/68, the children of an EU citizen who settled in a Member State during the exercise by their parent of rights of residence as a migrant worker in that Member State are entitled to reside there in order to attend general educational courses there. The fact that the parents of the children concerned have meanwhile divorced and the fact that the parent who exercised rights of residence as a migrant worker is no longer economically active in the host Member State are irrelevant in this regard. It is sufficient that the child settled in the Member State concerned at the time that one of the parents resided there as a migrant worker.[48] The Court also ruled that, as a consequence of the children's right to reside, the parents who are their carers must be allowed to remain in the host Member State during the period of their children's education.[49]

This means that these economically inactive family members of a person who at one time worked as a migrant worker in the host country can continue to invoke the status of family members of a worker within the meaning of Regulation 1612/68 (now Regulation 492/2011) with a view to maintaining a right of residence while the children pursue an education. As a result of their EU status as family members of a worker they will also be able to claim the social benefits the host Member State grants its own nationals (such as housing assistance in *Ibrahim* and *Texeira*).

From this most recent case law it can be inferred that in quite a number of circumstances migrant persons within the EU, even when they are inactive, can claim rights linked to the status of worker in the host Member State, including the access to social assistance or other social minimum benefits. This also applies to certain family members of such a worker, even when this worker only used to be economically active in this Member State or has meanwhile returned to his Member State of origin. The link with the exercise of one of the economic freedoms of the internal market becomes very remote in these cases. So perhaps the first objective of the Court is perhaps the combating of social exclusion even if it does not mention this objective specifically.

48 *Teixeira*, paras. 72 and 74.

49 *Ibrahim*, para. 50, and *Teixeira*, para. 61. See already in Case C-483/99 *Baumbast and R v. Secretary of State for the Home Department* [2002] ECR I-7091, paras. 63 en 71 (hereinafter *Baumbast*).

3.4. UNION LAW GUARANTEES ACCESS TO MINIMUM SUBSISTENCE BENEFITS IN THE HOST STATE TO FIRST TIME JOBSEEKERS

In a number of cases the ECJ also brought jobseekers within the scope of these EU provisions on the right of free movement for workers. As a result, persons for the first time looking for a job in a Member State other than their own were able to claim the financial support that a Member State granted its own jobseekers. In *Collins* the Court held the view that nationals of a Member State seeking employment in another Member State fall within the scope of Article 39 EC (now Article 45 TFEU) on the right to free movement for workers and jobseekers and, therefore, enjoy the right to equal treatment.[50] This right also applies to financial benefits intended to facilitate access to employment in the labour market of a Member State. The ECJ confirmed this approach in *Ioannidis*[51] and more recently in *Vatsouras* and *Koupatantze*.[52] It referred in this context to the adoption in Article 17 EC (now Article 20 TFEU) of EU citizenship, thus making a bridge with its case law on Union citizenship that will be discussed in point 3.5.[53] However, the Court considered it legitimate for a Member State to grant such an allowance only after it has been possible to establish a real link between the jobseeker and the labour market of that State.[54] The existence of such a link can be more specifically determined by establishing that the person concerned has, for a reasonable period, in fact genuinely sought work in the Member State in question.[55]

But, according to this case law an economically inactive person like a jobseeker coming to a Member State with the intention of looking for a job, may invoke provisions initially aimed at workers with regard to the prohibition of discrimination on grounds of nationality on the part of the Member State where this person seeks employment. This right to equal treatment can also refer to a social minimum benefit as in *Collins,* which concerned the means tested jobseekers allowance in the UK, or in *Vatsouras* and *Koupatantze,* which concerned a dispute with regard to a German basic benefit in favour of jobseekers.

---

50 Case C-138/02 *Brian Francis Collins v. Secretary of State for Work and Pensions* [2004] ECR I-2703, para. 56 (hereinafter *Collins*).

51 Case C-258/04 *Office national de l'emploi v. Ioannis Ioannidis* [2005] ECR I-8275 (hereinafter *Ioannidis*).

52 *Vatsouras and Koupatanze*, paras 36–37.

53 *Collins*, para. 63; *Ioannidis*, para. 22 and *Vatsouras and Koupatantze*, para. 37.

54 Case C-224/98 *Marie-Nathalie D'Hoop v. Office national de l'emploi* [2002] ECR I-6191, para. 38, and *Ioannidis*, para. 30.

55 *Collins*, para. 70, and *Vatsouras and Koupatantze*, paras. 38–39.

3.5. THE RIGHT TO FREE MOVEMENT FOR ECONOMICALLY INACTIVE PERSONS AND EQUAL TREATMENT IN THE HOST STATE FOR MINIMUM SUBSISTENCE BENEFITS

3.5.1. Residence Directive 2004/38 and the self-sufficiency requirement for economically inactive Union citizens

The above analysis shows that a lot of persons migrating within the EU can invoke the prohibition of discrimination on grounds of nationality to exercise rights regarding social minimum benefits in the host country because of their status as workers or self-employed persons. However, if a person does not belong to the category of economically active or post-active persons, then this economically inactive Union citizen is in principle subject to the requirement of self-sufficiency if he wants to have the right to reside in another Member State.

For the first period of residence of up to three months, Directive 2004/38 confirms that Union citizens and their family members have the right of residence without any conditions or any formalities other than the requirement of a valid identity card or passport (Article 6). Yet, these persons will only have the right of residence provided for in Article 6 of Directive 2004/38 as long as they do not become an unreasonable burden on the social assistance system of the host Member State (see Article 14.1 Directive 2004/38).[56]

If economically inactive European citizens want to acquire a right of residence of more than three months the condition is that they have sufficient resources for themselves or their family members so as to prevent them from becoming a burden on the social assistance system of the host country. In addition, they have to have comprehensive sickness insurance cover in the host country (Article 7.1 (b) Directive 2004/38). Yet, the ECJ confirmed that the origin of a person's resources is not relevant to assess the fulfilment of this resources requirement.[57]

As far as the resources are concerned, Article 8.4 Directive 2004/38 states that the Member States may not lay down a fixed amount which they regard as 'sufficient resources', but must take into account the personal situation of the persons concerned. In all cases this amount shall not be higher than the threshold below which nationals of the host Member State become eligible for

56 See further on the concept of 'unreasonable burden' in point 3.5.2. See on the application of this directive: European Commission, 'Guidance for better transposition and application of Directive 2004/38/EC' (Communication) COM (2009) 313 final.

57 Case C-200/02 *Kunqian Catherine Zhu and Man Lavette Chen v. Secretary of State for the Home Department* [2004] ECR I-9925, para. 30–31. See also Case C-408/03 *Commission v. Belgium* [2006] ECR I-2647, para. 40.

social assistance. Furthermore, on the basis of Article 14.3 Directive 2004/38 a Union citizen's or his family members' reliance on social benefits of the host country may not automatically lead to expulsion measures. Recital 16 of Directive 2004/38 provides three sets of criteria for this purpose, linked to the duration of the benefit, the person's situation such as the level of his connection with the host Member State and the amount of benefit.[58] Moreover, first-time jobseekers may not be expelled for as long as they can provide evidence that they are continuing to seek employment and that they have a genuine chance of being engaged (Article 14.4 (b)).[59]

All this does mean that the host country could expulse an economically inactive person who no longer complies with the resources requirement interpreted in such a way. Indeed, the ECJ recognizes the right of the host Member State to terminate the right of residence of the persons concerned, although this should not become the automatic consequence of reliance on the social assistance system.[60] This means that for economically inactive migrant persons poverty could lead to the loss of the right of residence.

3.5.2. Union citizenship and access to social minimum benefits for economically inactive migrant Union citizens

Article 24.1 of Directive 2004/38 guarantees the right to equal treatment with the nationals of the host Member State to all Union citizens residing there on the basis of that directive for all benefits falling within the scope of the EU Treaty. Already in *Martinez Sala*[61] the ECJ confirmed that all benefits covered by Regulation 1612/68 (now Regulation 492/2011) as well as by Regulation 1408/71 (now Regulation 883/2004) fall under the scope of the Treaty. Therefore this right to equal treatment also applies to social minimum benefits.

Yet, in its Article 24.2 this directive provides for a derogation on the principle of equal treatment for social assistance during the first three months of residence of economically inactive persons, as well as for first-time jobseekers referred to in Article 14.4 (b) of this directive. Students do not even have access to maintenance

---

58 As the Court held previously, those limitations and conditions must be applied in compliance with the limits imposed by Union law and in accordance with the general principles of that law, in particular the principle of proportionality (*Baumbast*, para. 91, and Case C-456/02 *Michel Trojani v. Centre public d'aide sociale de Bruxelles (CPAS)* [2004] ECR I-7573, para. 34 (hereinafter *Trojani*)).

59 Case C-292/89 *The Queen v. Immigration Appeal Tribunal, ex parte Gustaff Desiderius Antonissen* [1991] ECR I-745.

60 Case C-184/99 *Rudy Grzelczyk v. Centre public d'aide sociale d'Ottignies-Louvain-la-Neuve* [2001] ECR I-6193, para. 43 (hereinafter *Grzelczyk*), and *Trojani*, para. 36.

61 Case C-85/96 *María Martínez Sala v. Freistaat Bayern* [1998] ECR I-2691 (hereinafter *Martínez Sala*).

aid during the first five years of residence.[62] However, the Court of Justice appears to give a rather narrow interpretation to the concept of 'social assistance' in this provision, as demonstrated in *Vatsouras and Koupatantze*. Indeed, the Court decided that for instance benefits of a financial nature, which are intended to facilitate access to the labour market, cannot be regarded as constituting 'social assistance' within the meaning of Article 24.2 of Directive 2004/38.[63]

Moreover, EU citizens residing in a Member State may also rely on other non-discrimination provisions of EU law, and in particular the Treaty provisions. Indeed, relying on Article 18 and Article 21 TFEU the ECJ confirmed that economically inactive EU citizens may claim equal treatment with the citizens of the host State in order to be granted a social assistance benefit.

In *Martinez Sala* the Court recognized that nationals of a Member State lawfully residing in another Member State come within the scope of EU law and its rights and duties, including the right in Article 12 EC (now Article 18 TFEU) not to suffer discrimination on grounds of nationality in the instant case with regard to a non-contributory child-raising allowance. In *Grzelczyk* the Court acknowledged that having recourse to the host State's social assistance schemes could be a basis for that State to withdraw the student's residence permit, but the Court also stated that such a measure was not allowed to become an automatic consequence of his financial problems. In the Court's view the beneficiaries of the right of residence must not become an unreasonable burden on the public finances, and thus it accepts a certain degree of financial solidarity between nationals of the host Member State and nationals of other Member States, particularly if the financial difficulties of the student are temporary. In *Trojani* the Court recognized that a person who does not have sufficient resources can, in principle, not acquire a residence right under EU law. Nevertheless, if such a person has been lawfully resident in the host Member State for a certain time or possesses a residence permit he may rely on Article 12 EC (now Article 18 TFEU), including with a view to claiming social assistance. In *Bidar*[64] the Court checked Article 12 EC (now Article 18 TFEU) with regard to the refusal to grant migrant students financial assistance to cover their maintenance cost on the basis of the condition of having previously resided for at least three years in the Member State concerned (the UK). The ECJ considered it legitimate for a Member State to grant such assistance only to students who have demonstrated a certain degree of

62 As the ECJ confirmed in Case C-158/07 *Jacqueline Förster v. Hoofddirectie van de Informatie Beheer Groep* [2008] ECR I-8507 (hereinafter *Förster*).

63 *Vatsouras and Koupatantze*, para. 45. For critical comments see: E. Fahey, 'Interpretive Legitimacy and the Distinction between "Social Assistance" and "Work-Seeker's Allowance": Comment on *Vatsouras*' (2009) 34 *EL Rev.*

64 Case C-209/03 *The Queen, on the application of Dany Bidar v. London Borough of Ealing and Secretary of State for Education and Skills* [2005] ECR I-2119 (hereinafter *Bidar*).

integration in the society of the host State. More recently the ECJ found in *Förster* that a condition of five years' uninterrupted residence is appropriate and proportionate for the purpose of guaranteeing that the student applying for a maintenance grant is integrated in the host Member State's society.

In these cases on access to minimum subsistence or basic social benefits in the host State, the ECJ's starting point was the question of how to guarantee the rights of EU citizens, including the economically inactive ones, to move and reside freely within the Union. A central element in this is the possibility for these persons to rely, as migrant persons, on the prohibition of discrimination on grounds of nationality. Even if secondary EU legislation puts some limitations on these rights and national law introduces some requirements that are potentially discriminatory for migrant EU citizens, such limits must stand the proof of proportionality. This follows from the principle of free movement as laid down in Article 21 TFEU (former Article 18 EC) which the ECJ already declared to have direct effect in *Baumbast* (paras. 84–86).[65] In several cases Member States were considered to fall short in complying with these principles of EU law when defining the national boundaries to their tax-funded basic social benefits, identified by the ECJ as unjustified (direct or indirect) discrimination on grounds of nationality or as an unjustified non-discriminatory restriction to the right to free movement,[66] even for economically inactive migrants.

3.5.3. *Unjustified interference by the EU into the national boundaries of minimum subsistence schemes?*

The above described developments in EU law have been very much debated. According to some commentators the Court has been interpreting EU law against its wording and purpose while using the proportionality principle to establish rights which do not yet exist.[67] Scholars have also pointed at the right for Member States to protect themselves against interference from the EU level in the definition of the boundaries of their basic welfare systems or consider this case law as being counterproductive since it threatens to promote abuse and social benefit tourism.[68] National welfare systems would not be based any longer on bona fide ties, loyalties and contributions towards the host society.[69] Some commentators take the view that the Court embarked on a top-down judicially

---

65 See also Case C-408/03 *Commission v. Netherlands* [2006] ECR I-2647, para. 34.

66 Such as in Case C-192/05 *K. Tas-Hagen and R. A. Tas v. Raadskamer WUBO van de Pensioen- en Uitkeringsraad* [2006] ECR I-10451.

67 This view is expressed by O. Golynker, 'Jobseekers' Rights in the European Union: Challenges of Changing the Paradigm of Social Solidarity' (2005) 30 *EL Rev.*, p. 120, and K. Hailbronner, 'Union Citizenship and Access to Social Benefits' (2005) 42 *CML Rev.*

68 As suggested by: Ph. Larkin, 'The Limits to European Social Citizenship in the United Kingdom' (2005) 68 *Modern Law Review (ML Rev.)*, pp. 440–442.

69 O. Golyncker, n. 67, p. 121. This author even talks about 'changing paradigm of social solidarity'.

led process of social engineering which touches upon the underlying moral fabric of national solidarity systems[70] or threatens to compromise the legitimacy of any idea of 'European social citizenship'.[71] Some even feel that this could undermine deep-seated social and political equilibriums with social and political consequences that are not fully predictable.[72] Identifying the subjective and individual rights of EU migrants could interfere with the Member States' political choices of distributive justice.[73]

In response to this criticism we would like to point out that the ECJ is actually taking a traditional 'functional approach' in its interpretation of the Treaty provision on free movement of persons. Indeed, in this case law Union citizenship appears to be an instrument to increase mobility within the EU.[74] In the past this functional approach guaranteed migrant workers equal treatment as regards almost all rights and benefits which are available to workers and residents of the host Member State.[75] In the abovementioned case law the Court extended this functional approach to all EU citizens whether they exercise an economic activity or not, giving full effectiveness to the right to move and reside freely within the Union enshrined in Article 21 TFEU.[76] However, we explained above that the Court did not allow economically inactive migrants unconditional access to welfare benefits of the host State. Legal residence in the host State is the first condition to be fulfilled by the applicant. In addition, and depending on the case,

---

70 M. Dougan, 'The Court Helps Those Who Help Themselves... The Legal Status of Migrant Work-Seekers under Community Law in the Light of the *Collins* Judgment' (2005) 7 *EJSS*, p. 18.

71 M. Dougan, 'The Spatial Restructuring of National Welfare States within the European Union: The contribution of Union Citizenship and the Relevance of the Treaty of Lisbon' in U. Neergaard, R. Nielsen and L. Roseberry, *Integrating Welfare Functions into EU Law. From Rome to Lisbon*, DJØF Publishing, Copenhagen 2009, pp. 162–164.

72 M. Ferrera, 'Towards an "Open" Social Citizenship. The New Boundaries of Welfare in the European Union' in G. de Burca (ed.), *EU Law and the Welfare State. In Search of Solidarity*, Oxford University Press, Oxford 2005, p. 24.

73 A. José Menéndez, 'European Citizenship after *Martinez Sala* and *Baumbast*: Has European Law Become More Human but Less Social?' in M. Poiares Maduro and L. Azoulai (eds.), *The Past and Future of EU Law. The Classics of EU Law Revisited on the 50th Anniversary of the Rome Treaty*, Hart, Oxford 2010, pp. 391–392.

74 E. Spaventa, 'The Constitutional Impact of Union Citizenship' in U. Neergaard, R. Nielsen and L. Roseberry (eds.), *The Role of Courts in Developing a European Social Model. Theoretical and Methodological Perspectives*, DJØF Publishing, Copenhagen 2010, p. 165.

75 See above under points 3.1 to 3.4.

76 See also: N. Ach, 'La citoyenneté européenne au service d'une Europe sociale' (2006) *Journal des tribunaux droit européen* pp. 133–134; K. Lenaerts and K. Heremans, 'Contours of a European Social Union in the Case-Law of the European Court of Justice' (2006) 2 *European Constitutional Law Review*, p. 103; C. Timmermans, '*Martinez Sala* and *Baumbast* Revisited' in M. Poiares Maduro and L. Azoulai (eds.), *The Past and Future of EU Law. The Classics of EU Law Revisited on the 50th Anniversary of the Rome Treaty*, Hart, Oxford 2010, pp. 348–349; A.P. Van der Mei, 'Union Citizenship and the "De-Nationalitsation" of the Territorial Welfare State' (2005) 7 *EJML*, pp. 207–209.

he/she should 'not become an unreasonable burden on the public finances',[77] must 'have a genuine link with the employment market of the State concerned',[78] or 'need to demonstrate a certain degree of integration into the society of the host State'.[79] Traditionally, justifications like these are even outlawed by the classic four economic freedoms' legal regime.[80]

The Court's approach seems to be incremental in the sense that a certain degree of integration in the host Member State is a prerequisite in order for EU citizens to be treated equally with citizens of that State with regard to minimum social benefits. This approach differs from the 'perfect assimilation' approach, which amounts to EU citizens being entitled to full equal treatment as soon as they settle in a host Member State.[81]

3.6. EU SOCIAL SECURITY COORDINATION AND THE ACCESS TO SOCIAL MINIMUM BENEFITS FOR MIGRANT PERSONS

The EU social security coordination in (former) Regulation 1408/71 and now in Regulation 883/2004 also plays an important part in preventing persons using their right to move freely within the EU from landing into poverty.

The coordination system of Regulation 883/2004 applies to the large majority of the persons residing in the territory of a Member State, irrespective of whether they are economically active or not, irrespective even of whether they are citizens of the Member States or citizens of third countries.[82]

---

77 *Grzelczyk*, para. 44.

78 *Collins*, paras. 67–69.

79 *Bidar*, para. 57. See also *Förster*, para. 54.

80 See: S. Besson and A. Utzinger, 'Introduction: Future Challenges of European Citizenship – Facing a Wide-Open Pandora's Box' (2007) 13 *EL Journ. (European Law Journal)*, p. 587, referring to Case C-55/94 *Reinhard Gebhard v. Consiglio dell'Ordine degli Avvocati e Procuratori di Milano* [1995] ECR I-4165 and Case C-442/02 *CaixaBank France v. Ministère de l'Économie, des Finances et de l'Industrie* [2004] ECR I-8961.

81 See also: Ch. O'Brien, 'Real Links, Abstract Rights and False Alarms: The Relationship between the ECJ's "Real Link" Case Law and National Solidarity' (2008) 33 *EL Rev.* pp. 650–656 and F. Wollenschläger, 'A New Fundamental Freedom beyond Market Integration: Union Citizenship and its Dynamics for Shifting the Economic Paradigm of European Integration' (2011) 17 *EL Journ.*, pp. 22–24.

82 See Article 2 Regulation 883/2004 and European Parliament and Council Regulation (EU) 1231/2010 of 24 November 2010 extending the provisions of Regulation (EC) No 883/2004 and Regulation (EC) No 987/2009 to nationals of third countries who are not already covered by those provisions solely on the ground of their nationality [2010] OJ L344/1.

In quite a number of cases this EU social security coordination system guarantees that persons migrating within the EU can keep their social security allowances (export of benefits) or have access to benefits in the new host country through the mechanism of aggregation of periods or the right to equal treatment. Therefore, this coordination is an important instrument in preventing poverty as a result of exercising this right to free movement.

Yet, social assistance is excluded from the scope of this coordination,[83] although the Court of Justice has always interpreted this exclusion quite narrowly. Confronted with claims to export a number of minimum subsistence benefits, the ECJ had to rule on the question whether they fall under the notion of social assistance and are therefore excluded from export on the basis of this regulation. These benefits were called special non-contributory benefits of a mixed kind since they were half way between traditional social security and social assistance. Examples of such benefits are supplements to pensions and special benefits for disabled or invalid persons. In its case law of the 1970s and 80s, the ECJ developed a broad definition of social security within the meaning of Regulation 1408/71. This also included these special non-contributory benefits to which the ECJ applied the export provision.[84] In response to this case law, the EU legislature intervened in 1992 by creating a special coordination system for these benefits.[85] For the benefits listed in the newly created Annex IIa of Regulation 1408/71, Member States could apply a residence condition preventing the export of these benefits. As a consequence beneficiaries of such a benefit would, on the one hand, lose it when transferring their residence to another Member State and would, on the other, be entitled in their new Member State of residence to benefits of that state listed in Annex IIa.[86]

The justification for limiting the export of these benefits was mainly that they were not based on the payment of contributions by the beneficiary and that they were meant to guarantee a level of subsistence taking into account the cost of living and integration in a particular Member State. It was nonetheless clear that

---

83 Former Article 4.4 of Regulation 1408/71 and now Article 3.5 of Regulation 883/2004.

84 See for instance Case 1/72 *Rita Frilli v. Belgian State* [1972] ECR 457 (on the Belgian 'Guaranteed income for old people'); Case 187/73 *Odette Callemeyn v. Belgian State* [1974] ECR 553 (on the Belgian 'Benefits to handicapped persons'); Case 63/76 *Vito Inzirillo v. Caisse d'allocations familiales de l'arrondissement de Lyon* [1976] ECR 2057 (on the French 'Allowance for handicapped adults'); Case 139/82 *Paola Piscitello v. Istituto nazionale della previdenza sociale (INPS)* [1983] ECR 1427 (on the Italian 'Social aid pensions'); Case C-356/89 *Roger Stanton Newton v. Chief Adjudication Officer* [1991] ECR 3017 (on the UK 'Mobility allowance' for the disabled).

85 By Council Regulation (EEC) 1247/92 of 30 April 1992 [1992] OJ L192/1.

86 See for more details on this discussion: A.P. Van der Mei, 'Regulation 1408/71 and Coordination of Social Non-Contributory Benefit Schemes' (2002) 27 *EL Rev.*, and H. Verschueren, 'Special Non-Contributory Benefits in Regulation 1408/71, Regulation 883/2004 and the Case Law of the ECJ' (2009) 11 *EJSS*.

the loss of these benefits would create an evident obstacle to the right of free movement, as there is no guarantee that the person concerned would be entitled to similar benefits in the new host Member State. Comparable benefits may not exist there or not be listed in Annex IIa.

Yet, the ECJ proved to be very critical as to whether the benefits included in the relevant annexes did really respond to the criteria of being 'special' and of a 'mixed kind'.[87] For the Court, derogations from the principle of the exportability of social security benefits must be interpreted strictly. Consequently it annulled some of the inscriptions in Annex IIa but confirmed other ones.[88] Further to this case law the provisions on the special non-contributory benefits were completely redrafted and the list of non-exportable benefits in Annex IIa was reviewed. These provisions were also integrated in the new Regulation 883/2004 and its Annex X.[89]

Article 70.4 of Regulation 883/2004 confirms that the special non-contributory cash benefits listed in Annex X shall be provided exclusively in the Member State in which the persons concerned reside at the expense of this Member State's institutions. This means that on the basis of Regulation 883/2004 persons falling under the (broad) scope of this regulation are entitled to the social minimum benefits included in this list in the Member State where they reside. The only requirement for entitlement to these benefits is being a resident.

87 See Case C-215/99 *Friedrich Jauch v. Pensionsversicherungsanstalt der Arbeiter* [2001] ECR I-1901 and Case C- 286/03 *Silvia Hosse v. Land Salzburg* [2006] ECR I-1771, on the Austrian 'Care Allowance' ('*Pflegegeld*'); Case C-43/99 *Ghislain Leclere and Alina Deaconescu v. Caisse nationale des prestations familiales* [2001] ECR I-4265 on the Luxembourg 'Maternity allowances'; Case C-160/02 *Friedrich Skalka v. Sozialversicherungsanstalt der gewerblichen Wirtschaft* [2004] ECR I-5613, on the Austrian 'Compensatory supplement to pensions'; Case C-154/05 *J. J. Kersbergen-Lap and D. Dams-Schipper v. Raad van Bestuur van het Uitvoeringsinstituut Werknemersverzekeringen* [2006] ECR I-6249 on the Dutch 'Incapacity benefit for disabled young people' ('Wajong') and Case C-265/05 *José Perez Naranjo v. Caisse régionale d'assurance maladie (CRAM) Nord-Picardie* [2007] ECR 347 on the French 'Supplementary allowance from the National Solidarity Fund'.

88 See European Parliament and Council Regulation (EC) 647/2005 of 13 April 2005 [2005] OJ L 117/1. However, following the request of the European Commission the ECJ again annulled the listing by Regulation (EC) 647/2005 of some of these benefits in Annex IIa of Regulation 1408/71 in its ruling of 18 October 2007: Case C-299/05 *Commission v. European Parliament and Council* ECR [2007] ECR I-8695. The listed benefits were: the Finnish 'Child care allowance', the Swedish 'Disability allowance and care allowance for disabled children' and the UK 'Disability Living Allowance', 'Attendance Allowance' and 'Carer's Allowance'.

89 See European Parliament and Council Regulation (EC) 988/2009 of 16 September 2009 [2009] OJ L284/43. The list of Annex X currently contains about 70 benefits, including for instance the Belgian guaranteed income for elderly persons, the German Basic subsistence income for the elderly, the Spanish Cash benefits to assist the elderly and invalids unable to work, the Irish Disability allowance, the Italian Social pensions for persons without means, the Hungarian Non-contributory old age allowance, the Finnish Housing allowance for pensioners and the UK's State Pension Credit. About 2/3 of these benefits are related to old age, invalidity or disablement.

So, this arrangement guarantees that a migrating person can claim a benefit included in the list of Annex X Regulation 883/2004 in the Member State where he/she resides. It goes without saying that considering the nature of the benefits this is an important instrument to prevent a migrating person from ending up in poverty in the host country.

This shows that the European social security coordination is a strong legal instrument to help prevent persons using the Treaty right to free movement from ending up in poverty. First of all this instrument guarantees, through the principle of export of benefits, that migrant persons do not lose their social security benefits as a consequence of their migration. Even though this coordination does not guarantee the export of a number of minimum benefits, it does provide for the right of migrating persons to these benefits as soon as they move to another Member State.

4. CONCLUSION

There is no doubt that more than ever before the fight against poverty and social exclusion is one of the policy priorities of the EU institutions. In 2010 this was explicitly confirmed by a number of important policy declarations and initiatives, such as the Europe 2020 Strategy. This interest reflects the Union's objectives as laid down in the Treaties that became effective on 1 December 2009.

In this chapter we examined whether these policy initiatives at EU level have also been translated into legally imperative provisions that would compel the Member States to introduce certain rights for citizens with regard to minimum subsistence schemes.

What we have seen is that there is a big contradiction in this respect. On the one hand, there is the lack of political will, and perhaps also of a legal basis, to compel the Member States to provide for certain minimum requirements with regard to the citizens' right to minimum subsistence schemes by means of an EU legal instrument. This despite the explicit references in the Treaties, as introduced in 2009 by the Lisbon Treaty, to the EU's objective of combating social exclusion. The recent proposals, both by political groups of the European Parliament and by scholars, have clearly met with the refusal by the EU institutions to take initiatives at this stage. Furthermore, it is uncertain that, considering the limited powers the TFEU granted to the EU institutions regarding the 'combating of social exclusion', there is a legal basis in the Treaties for the EU to take such an initiative.

On the other hand the EU legislature, supported and stimulated by the Court of Justice, created various legal means to guarantee that persons using the right of free movement within the EU have the same rights in their host country as the nationals of this country with regard to a whole range of social benefits, including minimum subsistence benefits. This legislation and case law do not only apply to the traditional beneficiaries of the right to free movement within the internal market, i.e. economically active persons. Recently this right to equal treatment has also been guaranteed to persons who are not, not yet or no longer economically active. Indeed, the legislation and case law applying to economically active persons were also declared applicable by the Court of Justice, albeit under certain conditions, to persons planning to become economically active (first-time jobseekers) or to persons who are no longer economically active (and their family members). In this case law the ECJ carries the scope of the hard-core EU legal provisions on the free movement rights in the internal market to its limits. The ECJ seems to follow an economic integration rationale. But in fact its case law contributes maybe more to the social integration in the society of the host State of the persons involved, even though sometimes they only have a remote link with an economic activity. Moreover, in its citizenship case law the Court of Justice extended this right to equal treatment to migrant persons who are not linked to any economic activity. But this right is subject to a number of conditions, such as sufficient ties with the host Member State, and reliance on social assistance does not rule out that the economically inactive migrant can lose his right of residence in the host Member State.

The role of the EU in guaranteeing sufficient income for migrant persons has furthermore been confirmed by the EU social security coordination system. This guarantees that persons migrating within the EU maintain their social security rights. As far as some minimum subsistence schemes are concerned this system itself creates a right to benefits from such schemes in the Member States where a migrant person settles.

This much is clear: the legislation and case law with regard to the right of migrant persons to social minimum benefits is an important enforceable instrument that contributes to the fight against poverty and social exclusion. Still, some consider this to be unjustifiable interference with the Member States' power to determine the boundaries of their solidarity schemes. On the other hand, there is the fact that these instruments of 'free movement' themselves do not impose any obligation on the Member States with regard to the conditions, extent and amount of their minimum benefit schemes. They only lay down that in principle Member States should offer citizens of other Member States living on their territory the same rights as their own nationals.

However, there is a blatant contrast between the complete lack of political will, and probably even a legal basis, to adopt EU legislation that would impose obligations on the Member States with regard to the content and amount of their minimum benefits schemes, on the one hand and the important number of instruments to give migrating persons access to these schemes in a host Member State on the other. This contrast seems to be a reflection of the fact that within the EU the emphasis is still on free movement in the context of an internal market, even if this is complemented with the right to free movement for economically inactive persons, rather than on the integration of the social policies of the Member States.

Law and Cosmopolitan Values

In this series, the editors envisage monographs and collections of essays that address fundamental topics in law and globalisation, which range over doctrinal as well as normative questions of International and European law, human rights, justice and democracy. A main purpose of the series is to encourage scholarship that explores and transcends the categories and assumptions on which contemporary debates on globalization are conducted, and to stimulate reflection upon questions concerning the interplay between law, policy and principle. Recognizing that there is no occasion to distinguish sharply between theoretical and systematic work in the field from an analysis of law in context, the editors welcome studies from a wide variety of methodological traditions. Contributions to the series, inevitably crossing disciplinary lines, will be of interest to students, researchers and professionals in public law, international law, human rights law, political science, legal and political philosophy. Although the series aims in the first place to reflect the diverse scholarly activity within the Centre for Law and Cosmopolitan Values, University of Antwerp, submissions of manuscripts by anyone who is working in the same field are strongly encouraged.

Instructions to authors

Manuscripts can be forwarded to any member of the editorial board at any time.

If the entire manuscript or a minimum of 2 chapters are available then the author is required to submit a detailed table of contents and brief proposal (up to 3 pages) outlining methodology, likely public, and the contribution the book is or is likely to make. If no manuscript is available, then the proposal should, in addition to the above, contain summaries of all chapters (no longer than 10 pages).

Every contribution should be accompanied by a statement that it is the author's own original work, that it is not being considered for publication elsewhere, and that it does not constitute a substantial repetition of work published or to be published elsewhere.

Manuscripts that are deemed worthy of further consideration will be forwarded by the editors to a member of the advisory board or an external expert for a second review. Peer review reports are signed and should be detailed, describing and commenting on content, methodology, likely public, and the contribution the book makes or is likely to make. In case of disagreement between first and second reviews, the editorial board will ask a third reviewer for a further opinion.

It is expected that the reviewing process will not exceed 2 months in each case.

Related Links:
http://lcv.intersentia.com
Centre for Law and Cosmopolitan Values: www.lcv.ua.ac.be.

www.ingramcontent.com/pod-product-compliance
Ingram Content Group UK Ltd.
Pitfield, Milton Keynes, MK11 3LW, UK
UKHW051847100926
8556IPUK00005B/496

9 781780 680569